TO GIVE DIGNITY TO A MAN IS ABOVE ALL THINGS

Indian Proverb

Why the title "INDIAN GIVER"?

It was a custom among many Indian tribes that when a man was presented with a gift, he in return gave back as a gift, an object of comparable value. This was an act of honor and respect.

The white man distorted this philosophy and degraded it into a selfish act—a person who gives but expects to take back something in return. Hence, the slang term "Indian Giver" came into our language.

If that is the case, then I too am an **Indian Giver** because I want something in return for these monumental gifts I am sculpturing. In return, I ask that honor and understanding be shown toward the Native Americans because of the tragic fate that has befallen these noble people.

— P.W.T.

(Cover photo by Peter Wolf Toth, Valdez, Alaska Statue.)

(Nationwide Associated Press Release on the 'Whispering Giants' June 1978)

Artist Blazing 'Trail of Tears'

Iowa Falls, Iowa (AP) — "The treaties and promises, continuously broken; Trail of Tears, Wounded Knee, in history are never spoken."

That stanza is from a poem by Peter Toth, a traveler who is spending his life alerting the nation to the "Cry of the Red Man."

But the Hungarian-born artist's message is offered not only through poetry and lectures.

Toth is a sculptor blazing his own "Trail of Tears" across the country, creating from logs and stone Indian likenesses to keep watch on America from the Great Lakes to the Gulf of Mexico and from sea to sea.

Iowa Falls is the site of Toth's 28th monument, dedicated on the Fourth of July to the Sac and Fox and other Midwestern tribes that have disappeared in the last 100 years."

The 33-foot Indian head was carved from a cottonwood felled by a lightning bolt.

Toth has been chipping his way across the nation for nearly eight years in artistic protest against the "betrayal" of the American Indian.

"I am protesting against the plight of the Indian," Toth said. "Against the theft and trickery through which we took this land. We left them with barren waste to suffer poverty and prejudice.

"But, my protest is constructive . . . one of giving, not destruction," he said. "I want also to honor the Indian as the proud, brave and dignified people they are."

Toth has studied the American Indian since before he "adopted" the U.S. at age 11, when he moved with his family from Europe to Ohio 20 years ago.

His interest turned to an

—AP Laserphoto

Toth puts finishing touches. . .on Iowa Falls monument.

inspiration that in 1970 coaxed him to leave his college studies for the open road to tell of the Indian's plight in his special way.

Toth supports himself and his wife largely through sale of smaller sculptures and art objects he makes along the way. He refuses payment for the

monuments he considers "gifts" to a people and to posterity.

"My monuments are...my way of saying what I must say," Toth said. "They are made to remind people of the contributions of the Indian to this country and the fate we've left them.

My monuments have been referred to as the TRAIL OF THE WHISPERING GIANTS because they are symbolic to the tragic TRAIL OF TEARS where southeastern Indians were forced to march from their homelands to reservations in Oklahoma. Thousands died on this cruel journey.

Now there is a trail of my Indian sculptures moving across this country as a reminder of the Native American's past and present difficulties. Many of my large monuments are sculptured with parted lips as if whispering of the Indian's fate in our history.

I would like to hear from anyone interested in my work. All letters with an enclosed self-addressed, stamped envelope will be answered. Also, would like information on huge trees (4 and 5 + feet in diameter) for possible future sculptures.

An easy order form can be found at the end of this book to assist you in obtaining additional autographed copies.

Mailing Address: Peter Wolf Toth
                  Rt. 2, Box 599
                  Cable, Wisc. 54821

Indian Giver

By
Peter Wolf Toth

These statues have nothing to do with totems, poles, or Indian art, but rather symbolically represent a composite of the physical images of the Native Americans, indigenous to each state, as seen through the eyes of the artist.

Another book by Peter Wolf Toth:
Indians Too Have Heroes

Published by Tribal Press

Library of Congress Catalog Card Number 81-90250
ISBN 0-9607044-3-4

Manufactured in the United States of America
by Arbor Printing, Lincoln, Nebraska.

"THANKS"
(from the depth of my heart)

This book is published in behalf and upon request of many interested Americans.

To all the good and kind people across this beautiful country who have taken an interest in my crusade and helped to make my dreams and visions of a better, more understanding Nation a possibility. . .

All of you that really care, especially you who gave me food, a cool drink to quench my thirst, or a place to rest from the rigors of the road. . .

All I can say is THANKS!

Though this book is not big enough to mention all your names, you and I will know who you are.

To my loving wife Kathy, who contributed her advice and guidance, deciphered my nearly illegible handwriting, and her many months of typing. . .

THANKS!

To my dear brother Endre, and his wife Peggy, my many American Indian friends, sources of information, and persons who have contributed directly or indirectly to this book. . .

THANKS!

Because of my sometimes faulty memory please forgive any inaccuracies that may have occurred in the following pages.

(The following editorial appeared in the Lincoln Journal in July 1980—Nebraska)

A stranger's legacy

In a perfect world, it wouldn't be particularly noteworthy that a stranger appears on the scene, offers to do something nice and create something impressive, then disappears to perform the same good deed elsewhere.

In the imperfect world we live in, though, this sort of generosity, extended without a request for financial gain, is unusual enough to deserve both attention and high praise.

So it is that the Lincoln community extends its praise and its deep gratitude to a young Hungarian named Peter Toth who came to town specifically to transform a Nebraska cottonwood into a striking figure of an Indian chief gracing the front of the Lincoln Indian Center — asking no compensation for his talents and his efforts.

Only by seeing the tree sculpture, at 1100 Military Road, can one appreciate the artistry and dedication of this 32-year-old immigrant.

There is a special rugged beauty in the "whispering giant" Peter Toth leaves behind in Lincoln — the craggy,

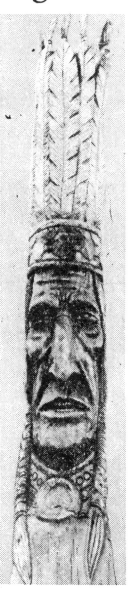

pensive face, not brooding or angry, but, as Toth sees him, with a flicker of a smile.

In Lincoln, Toth says, the chief has something to smile about. He refers to the recently-completed structure housing the Indian Center and the work of its staff to assist the Indian population of the city.

Lincolnites generally can take satisfaction that the progress being made here is viewed favorably by both the sculpted chief and his creator.

Toth says his goal of creating an Indian tree sculpture in each of the 50 states — Lincoln's is his 35th — springs from his deep feeling that "the Indian was the victim of long abuse and injustice."

"Even above and beyond American Indians, this monument stands against racism and prejudice," Toth says. "It stands for all people for all the problems they face."

Surely the whispering giant and the man who gave him form will consider it appropriate thanks if the people of Lincoln now adopt the commitment which Toth has ascribed to his creation.

TABLE OF CONTENTS

California

GRANDMOTHER OF
PYRAMID LAKE

In an enchanted place,
That the Nevada native people
Know simply as Pyramid Lake,

Lives Katie,
The Paiute lady.

She's walked the shores,
With dignity,
For nearly a hundred years.

Beauty still radiates,
From her century-aged face.

Katie,
Beautiful Indian lady,

Grandmother of Pyramid Lake,
    Loved by all your people.

poem by Peter Wolf Toth
photo by Dirck Henderson

Katie Fraiser, Paiute, of Pyramid Lake

Indian Giver

Part One

California dedication of 27th Indian Monument in Desert Hot Springs. Created from giant sequoia; 43 feet tall; 8 feet wide; (10 miles from Palm Springs, photo by Jerry Skuse)

PART ONE

History books have seldom told of the genocide and extermination of the American Indian. One of the ways this was accomplished was through scalp bounty. By murdering and scalping 3 old Indian men, 2 women, and a boy, an amount of up to $1,500 could be collected, which was an enormous amount in 1763. The Dutch first practiced scalp bounty which was adopted at one time or another by most of the colonies. Because Indian scalp was much more valuable than animal furs, missionaries often kept a close eye on their flock. Even as recently as 1866 an Arizona county was offering $250 for each Apache scalp.

On May 20, 1978, Dennis Banks, his long black hair tied back from his face, arrived for the dedication of the California Indian Monument in Desert Hot Springs. He is chancellor of D.Q. University in Davis, CA, co-founder of the American Indian Movement, and was a participant at the Wounded Knee Incident in 1973.

We were preparing to dedicate the 43 foot tall, 8 foot wide sculpture of an Indian head that I carved out of a giant redwood during the last several months. A large crowd gathered for the ceremony.

The purpose of my art is to honor the Indian and to eliminate prejudice and injustice, as well as to alleviate poverty. My works are created as gifts, to raise the Nation's conscience to the plight of the American Indian. My goal is to sculpt at least 1 in each of the 50 states. I have received no government grants or money from a private individual for this project. This was my 27th monument after 6 years of travel.

Dennis Banks spoke eloquently of his people and how Americans devised ways to keep Indian lore. One thousand towns and thirty-two states claim names that have Indian meanings.

"This is the first time in my life I have seen anything so great, so tall, so beautiful," he said of the sculpture that towered above us.

As he spoke I could see the image of this great man's ancestors fighting the invading hordes of white men who were determined to take their homeland by any means, whether it be just or evil.

1

One of the final and most poignant tragedies in the Indian history happened on Dec. 29, 1890. Sioux chief Big Foot and some 300 men, women, and children were waiting to surrender to soldiers at Wounded Knee Creek, South Dakota. After some misunderstanding, the sound of gunfire echoed for the final time over the grassy plains. Bullets ripped through living flesh killing warriors, as well as innocent women and children. More than just the fighting ended there at the last massacre. Much of the Plains Indian's hope, spirit, and pride died there too. Along with them, all of the American Indian's fate was sealed. It was truly one of the greatest of tragedies in the annals of written history.

A Native American expressing her appreciation for the monument. (photo by Jerry Skuse)

Kathy and Peter Toth with Dennis Banks, being interviewed by a reporter from a local TV station. (photo by Jerry Skuse)

PART TWO

HUNGARY

My people, the Hungarians (Magyars), fought time after time against insurmountable odds also. In the 16th century a war raged against the Turks. Comparatively 30,000 hussars fought gallantly to the last man trying to defend Hungary against nearly 300,000 Turkish soldiers. They attacked in hordes, laying waste to most of the Hungarian Nation.

The fertile plains surrounding the mighty Danube River always seemed the center of numerous wars. It seems that wars could seldom be avoided. As in many other wars, Hungary was an unwilling participant in World War II. The Hungarians were forced to be an ally of Germany; either that or face Hitler's destructive war machines.

As the Russian troops advanced into Hungary in 1944-1945 the German soldiers were pushed back. The retreating German armies took everything with them: livestock, food, and all the valuables they could carry. Then, the so-called Russian liberators confiscated from the Hungarian people any remaining valuables, and took with them sinks and even toilet bowls. In spite of all this devastation, the Hungarians were faring well.

The terrible destruction of World War II was now only the nightmare of the past. The devastation of the cities of Europe was still very much in evidence in the rubble of broken bricks. The once majestic buildings were slowly being rebuilt.

Lives were slowly put back in order. The lack of food was by far the biggest problem, second only to the overtaxation and the oppression by the now Russian-controlled communist government. Food was scarce. It was normal to be hungry.

On a bitter cold morning in December 1947, just 21 days before Christmas, I was cast upon this earth; not of my choosing, but by the compelling force of life and my instinctive need to survive. I was alive and kicking, the 7th child born into a very religious family.

My life was a haze until the age of 4 or 5, when my time of awakening arrived. I was an individual person with thoughts and feelings of my own. My hard working parents seemed to labor unceasingly. My mother was pregnant with her 11th child. She gave me all the attention and love she could.

5

Surprisingly, she was able to give us ample love, even with all 10 of us children demanding her care.

Tony, Frank, and my sister Irene, were already laden with heavy responsibilities. All of us children were expected to pitch in and contribute our share in daily chores. We were taught responsibility at an early age.

My mother was a pretty, petite woman of German-Hungarian extraction. Because of her fair skin and light hair in her youth, she was given the nickname "Blondie". A city girl, she grew up in the beautiful capital city of Budapest. My father, strong and heavily muscled of Magyar ancestry, was brought up as a country boy, a farmer by birth. He was reared on the plains of Hungary, well acquainted with the hard work that was required to make the ground yield her fruit. My mother, not knowing anything about the grievous toil the ground demanded to be kept tame, had to learn the hard way when she married my father and moved to the country.

My father toiled from sunup to sundown in the orchards, then worked in a factory at night as an electrician. I don't know how he managed to keep on going with the little rest he got.

Life was difficult, made even more unbearable by the flagrant open thievery of our farm by the communists. It takes eight years to plant and cultivate a peach orchard to full maturity. My father took great pride in his farm. He fertilized the young peach trees by cleaning out and using the contents of the neighborhood outhouses. It was backbreaking work, but his reward was high. At the Hungarian Farm Produce Fair, he once won the highest award for the biggest, juiciest peach in the entire country. His award was a power tiller, a highly prized item. Since he was not a member of the communist party, he never saw any of his winnings. The communists gave the power tiller to someone in their party. To make things worse, because of envy of his orchards, they stole his land for the second time. He was simply told there was a mistake in the deed and the untamed land adjacent to his orchard was the actual property he owned. A further setback was my father's ill health which cost us the loss of our beautiful home.

A vacant wine storage building was now converted to our home. It was a simple, 4-room, earthen-floor house with no indoor plumbing, and was located at the edge of the village of Budaors by the foot of Stone Mountain. The kitchen consisted of a wood burning stove for cooking and it was also the only source of heat in the house. A large round table and 13 chairs, one for each of us, was the only furniture we had in the room.

As for our sleeping arrangements, my oldest brother's bed was placed in the foyer where the main entrance was located. It was very small and held little privacy for Tony with three doors leading from it. The third room was curtained off into two sections and eight of us slept in that room. Four of us boys slept on a bunkbed—Gabe and Endre on top, Frank and I on the bottom. My four sisters slept in similar arrangements on the other side of the curtain. The fourth room, which was also an extension of the kitchen, was the only one regularly heated by our cooking stove when wood or coal was available. That was the room where our parents slept with the two younger children, Julius and Esther.

I recall the cold winter nights when we tried to warm our feet by placing hot stones (that we called "Johnny stones") under our blankets. It was no real solution for our unheated room, where water would freeze, but surprisingly the warm stones and heavy blankets helped to keep us fairly comfortable. Before we went to sleep, it was common practice amongst us kids to tell spooky stories. At times they were so scary, I had trouble falling asleep.

Hungary consists mostly of prairies, but we were fortunate to live by the mountains. I was awed by the mysterious beauty of our surroundings, especially the stone-crowned mountain that stood in front of our house. About a quarter-of-a-mile behind the house was Horse Mountain, so named because it had the graceful sweep of a horse's back. North of it was an airstrip for small planes surrounded by a tall, thick forest of pine where we kids would often go to hike and gather wood for our stove.

In the early spring when all things suddenly came alive, the gentle slopes of the mountains were covered with beautiful wild flowers of many colors. I must confess that Stone Mountain was my first love. She held a certain mystery and fascination for me. On the higher slopes of the mountain stood the ruins of a monastery. The thick scarred walls still remained intact in places. Debris of broken stone was everywhere. Below the sagging floor was a maze of tunnels, rooms, and caves.

On Sunday afternoon all of us kids would take our lantern and explore the remaining ruins and the many long tunnels. It was such fun then, but when I was up there by myself, an eeriness emanated from the place. It was like a cemetery where perhaps many Hungarian soldiers were killed defending the mountain against the enemy.

My curiosity and desire to explore the surrounding mountain sides was hampered by the constant chores that had to be performed. I was given the nickname "Tutyi", meaning lazy, because at 7 years of age I just didn't take to hoeing and working in the fields as my brothers did. Consequently, I was given the job to keep watch of our 2 goats. While they grazed on the slopes, there was time for me to explore and enjoy the mountain leisurely.

As a child I loved birds and animals, and on numerous occasions would bring home wild creatures that had been found. My mother would get furious and scold me. How could she not love a young creature like the cute pink-nosed hedgehog I once found, as well as frogs, lizards, snakes, and bats? On one exciting adventure while browsing the mountain side, I spotted a large game bird with beautiful colors. My attempts to catch him failed when he ran and mysteriously disappeared behind a bush.

Directly across from our house at the base of Stone Mountain were many bombed out ruins. Here is where my hunting took place. Birds, rabbits, and other small animals would take shelter in the cool shade of the still standing walls. My brothers and I used to climb the walls of the ruins to get at bird nests. Sparrows and other birds were abundant there. Occasionally we'd smash bird eggs in our sister's hair, but mostly we'd boil and try to eat them. It was hard to get a bite out of a thimble size egg. Wild rabbit was bigger and tastier. I once cornered and caught one in the ruins and that evening we had rabbit stew. The delicacy was the head; my reward for the catch.

We raised many of our needed foods in our vegetable garden. From our two goats we had fresh milk and the few chickens occasionally laid eggs that we valued highly. Much of this had to be sold at market to pay the taxes. I knew too well the daily struggle to get food that was a part of our lives. In spite of all the hard work my parents and we children put forth on the few acres of peach orchards and vineyards that we owned, it was still not enough. Produce was an accepted payment for taxes and at times what precious little food we had was turned over to the government.

I remember watching my brothers hoeing the stony ground. As the burning sun rose high above our heads, we stopped to eat our meager lunch. At times it was only a piece of bread. We ran into the field to pluck up some wild onions to eat with it. As we sat down under the shade of a tree, my older brother Tony commented, "If only I could smell the lard on this bread!" You see, lard sandwiches were a treat to us, but that was when we had a lot to eat.

One morning while grazing the goats on top of Stone Mountain near the ruins of the monastery, a stranger appeared. As he approached me I noticed he was a middle aged man wearing a gray suit. From a distance, he seemed pleasant looking and I wondered what he was doing all alone on top of the mountain. It seemed to me that he belonged in a bank, store, or office. He was coming straight toward me. When he came within 50 yards, he beckoned me to come to him. I felt vulnerable alone with only 2 goats. Remembering my parent's warning never to trust strangers, I shouted nervously at the goats which started them running down the slope with me behind them. A safe distance was put between us and the stranger.

The following day the authorities combed Stone Mountain for two missing children from the community. Before the day ended, the mutilated bodies of the children were found in a cave by the monastery. It was possible that my encounter with yesterday's stranger could have been my last.

One year we built an earthen dam across the dry riverbed near our house which created a good size pond from the frequent spring rains. We snuck our mother's wooden washtub out and used it for a boat. After paddling to the other side, Endre, Frank, and Gabe jumped out which capsized the tub and threw me into the deep murky water. Grasping for air, I felt myself drowning. Miraculously my brothers were able to pull me out. None of us knew how to swim at the time.

The summer with all its adventures was now just a memory and school had been in session for almost 3 months. I hated school now as much as when it had started. It wasn't so much for my 3rd grade studies, but rather for the regimental discipline that was practiced.

I was always a free spirit and an individual in love with mountains, wild flowers, and all of God's nature. Rules were always hard for me to follow. My path to school carried me over the mountain and it was common for me to check out animal burrows and pick wild flowers. On rare occasions the school bell rang before my arrival. As punishment, the teacher would beat me with a stick. Even at home if I'd whistle a tune of an unreligious nature or not pray, my fervently religious parents would punish me further.

The late October sun was setting earlier every day. The leaves on the trees were turning brilliant reds, yellows, and oranges and the chill in the air brought a promise of an early winter. On my way home from school I noticed some strange activities on the side of the mountain. Hungarian soldiers were having combat practice. The blazing guns mesmerized me.

A week passed since the war games on the mountain. It was Friday, the last day of school for the week and I was so looking forward to having two days off.

That afternoon the teacher started acting strange. Classes were dismissed early and we were told to go straight home. On my way home, the distant rumble of shells exploding could be heard. It was a frightening, yet very exciting time. Reaching the safety of my family and home was a great comfort.

We didn't own a radio because in our house it was considered a sin to listen to it. My parent's strict religion taught us that "worldly" music was sinful. The latest shocking news of the revolution came from our neighbor's radio. The full-scale rebellion of the Hungarians had started. The Russian and Hungarian communists were being killed by the "freedom fighters" or were fleeing the city and country.

Our home was isolated 6 miles from the capital city of Budapest, so we were getting sketchy second-hand news at best. The constant thundering of war allowed us to know beyond a shadow of a doubt that the fighting was continuing.

The feeling was hard to explain on that fateful day of October 26, 1956. The excitement of the minute-by-minute unfolding destruction happening so close to our house was terrifying. I could understand the danger of fighting, but perhaps didn't fully comprehend the misery and pain it was bringing to the people. Approaching the age of 9, I was more excited at the thought of not having to go to school.

The deafening booms of the exploding shells from tanks and cannons kept us down in our root cellar. The earth would sometimes sway with the aftershock of heavy artillery that landed near our house.

The next few days brought an eerie calm to Hungary. We heard the happy news that the communists were driven out and Russia promised to give us our freedom. I was too young to understand the full scope of our freedom, but recall tales told by my older brother Endre. The following is his own account of what he experienced in downtown Budapest after the first phase of fighting was over.

"For as long as I live, I shall never forget that day! As the bus once again rolled through our village, I could again see the destruction that retaliation caused. But what I had once seen in Budapest was in no way comparable. The final stop of our bus was just inside the city limits of Buda, built on the one side of mighty river Danube. The closer we got, the more incredible the things were which we saw. Heaps of cobalt stones were piled high as the

streets were torn up to build crude barricades. Streetcars and busses were turned over and charred by flames. Burned and shelled out tanks littered the once beautiful city, now almost beyond recognition. The trail of misery and violence was everywhere. Here and there they still had some unburied bodies doused with clorox to check the outbreak of cholera, some covered with whatever clothes available.

As I passed with horror from place to place, I came to the burned out shell of a tank with its driver's body charred to resemble a charcoal form of a human. It was very much visible inside the twisted metal frame. Everyone we talked with told us stories of horror and terror that gripped the city the past week and a half. How literally thousands were killed, including groups of demonstrating children when they were simply run over by tanks as they marched in front of the main library. Indeed, many hundreds of freshly dug graves marked with small crosses dotted the city's streets and clustered about parks and larger unpaved areas. Many main avenues were completely blocked to all but pedestrian traffic as entire blocks of buildings were destroyed by the indiscriminate shellings of the enemy. The entire front walls of these buildings lay in ruin and I could even see inside the wrecked homes as floors and walls collapsed. Furniture, including a piano at one house, was clearly visible as they precariously hung among the ruins. As I slowly walked down these streets I thought, "O Lord, how many bodies those heaps of ruins are hiding from the eyes!"

After some hours of wandering among the ruins and charred remains of buildings, tanks, and transportation vehicles, I retraced my way toward home. I feared that with the coming darkness, more violence would erupt and I would be stuck without any means of getting to safety. It wasn't late yet as I reached the spacious place with its broad avenue where we usually boarded the bus for the last lap of our homeward journey. About another hour and I would be safely home. But, as I arrived at the bus stop, I simply was swept away by the great crowds lining both sides of this wide street. Certainly, I surmised, there is a reason for the gathering of this vast multitude, and without any hesitation, I just became one with them as they surged along. They crowded the broad sidewalks. They hung out of open windows and doors above and around us. Apparently in some anticipation, they were waiting for some great event to take place. Judging from these circumstances, I decided it must be something very important. Yes, this was the day I saw the greatest jubilant outburst of a nation welcoming a ragged army that was in part, responsible for this long awaited, but sadly, short lived victory. In five short days, through treachery and deception, the Russians regrouped and rearmed and came back under the cover of a Sunday night to crush the short lived liberty, fought for and paid for by the thousands who died. . .

But, on this day, it was still "freedom" and what a great display of enthusiasm. From the not too far distance came the sound of the now familiar noise. . .the rumbling of tanks. . .many of them. Normally it would have put fear and panic into the hearts of this multitude, but this day seemed different. The crowd must have known something that I didn't. But, if they were not afraid, why should I be? Before too long, though, I realized from the comments around me that the people were awaiting a tank column of the liberating Hungarian Army that so miraculously and unexpectedly defeated the Russians. Many of these tanks were captured through trickery or by violence, while others manned by the Hungarians, "defected" from the Hungarian Red Army to join the uprising. Now they were rumbling through the "liberated" city as victors of the revolution. Right along with them were those unnamed thousands who fought with anything they could grab, and if nothing was available, they used their hands. As the Russian armored cars and tanks rolled down the streets before they were forced to retreat, burning pillows were tossed at them from the open windows above. Stones and other heavy objects were used as missiles. Hillsides were greased so the steel plods of the tanks would be rendered useless. Overturned frying skillets with strings attached were utilized as fake field mines to thwart the advance of the oncoming tanks. While in desperation, those Russian or the Red Army's soldiers got out of their tanks and armored cars to investigate. They were immediately gunned down and their tanks taken over by the sometimes inexperienced revolutionaries. Often they quickly mastered the controls and quickly went off to face and to destroy the enemy, or to be destroyed by the oncoming enemy tanks. And so with tricks, bravery, and wisdom, within about ten days the advancing enemy was repelled and immobilized. But misery, violence and much destruction masked every spot they left behind. The Russian retaliation for any resistance and counter violence was the shelling and literal demolition of entire buildings and streets where freedom fighters were sheltered. Gaping holes and collapsed walls were everywhere with no regard to life or property in the communist anxiety to crush the rebellion. But now and for a few more days, it was in the past.

The dozen or so tanks and armored cars rolled up closer and closer on this beautiful afternoon. With their victorious personnel sitting and standing on top and on the sides and everywhere they could, the "freedom thirsty" multitude beginning to taste the sweetness of liberty went into a frenzy! Their shouts and cheers of joy and happiness will long live in my memory. Shortly after that, wonderful proof of victory was out of sight again. I took the bus to finish my homeward journey. After a few of the routine bus stops, my trip met with an unusual delay. It happened at a place where a tall bronze statue about 30 feet high, portraying a Russian soldier, was erected shortly after the liberation of Hungary in 1945. Now a crowd had surrounded its base as other people tied heavy ropes around the feet and arms of the statue. With great physical effort, cheered and urged on by the crowd, the great statue was pulled down after much struggle. Immediately it was attacked by the hundreds of bystanders with stones and hammers in their hands, smashing it into thousands of pieces which were carried away as souvenirs. I assume idleness must be boring, for I found myself also hacking away at the statue to carry away a piece of bronze with me. In the days following, after "freedom" was once again robbed from us, it caused me much fear knowing that if the communists would find that piece of bronze in our home, it would no doubt be used as evidence of our crime against the "people's government" and we would be severely punished. At that time though, it was no cause to worry. As far as I was concerned we were free and were going to remain that way! How sweet that thought was!

On that fateful Sunday night when the regrouped and rearmed Russians stole back into Budapest to crush the short lived, but so wonderful freedom, everything changed. Living close to one of the main roads leading into the city, we heard with fearful hearts, the rumble of advancing columns of tanks that shook the ground enough to rattle our windows. The morning news was terribly sad. Under the pretense of negotiations, the Russians lured, then captured and killed the two most famous leaders of the revolution. The Russians then came back under cover of darkness to destroy the small victorious forces holding the capital.

We could hear the big guns roaring as they spewed their fire and destruction over the land. After the first week of fighting, our food supply at home dwindled. My father went to the village store and stood in the long bread line waiting for the much needed food supplies. As the Russian tanks and armor carriers passed the store, they opened fire on the helpless hungry men, women, and children."

My father also told of tremendous destruction elsewhere.

"I dove into the ditch next to me and that's probably what saved my life. As I got up after the Russians were gone, I saw the dead lying all around me and heard the cries of the wounded. Those bullets were not only killing, but they exploded on impact, maiming the unfortunate victims or tearing off arms and legs. I helped one neighbor lady whose flesh was torn open by an exploding bullet. On one street limbs and parts of bodies were blown up, hanging in trees. It was horrible. . ."

It gave me chills just to listen to his account; the inhumanity and cruelty of man against man is astounding.

The fighting was now over and we tried to get on with the chores of everyday living. The huge number of Russian troops were no longer visible, but the tanks were placed on almost every corner, an obvious fact that the Russians were still very much around.

The ugly head of communist revenge was now in full swing. Brave freedom fighters were murdered in the name of justice. The freedom loving Hungarians took the path leading to the West. Two hundred thousand refugees escaped to the freedom of Austria in less than six weeks. Our own lives took a major turn when my sister Irene, age 16, and older brother Frank, age 15, also ran away. Their intent was to escape West to gain the ultimate dream of freedom.

We all worried that my brother and sister might have been captured or killed in their attempt to escape across the mine field and the Iron Curtain. After many anxious days and nights, we received a letter from Austria saying they were both safe. What a relief!

There were a lot of serious decisions for our family to make in the next few days. We had two choices, escape to the West, or stay in Hungary and have the family forever separated. Our plan was to escape to Austria as did Irene and Frank. Upon hearing the terrible stories of the many people killed or captured on the border we changed our mind. Just a few short weeks ago, the hated Iron Curtain between Austria and Hungary was completely torn up and the heavily mined area was cleared of the dangerous mines that could explode under the weight of a jack rabbit. Now it was again mined and the electric steel fence was back in place to stop the westward fleeing Hungarians. Then we heard some encouraging news that Yugoslavia had opened her border for the Hungarian refugees.

We decided to route our escape across the Yugoslavian border and from there we hoped to go to Vienna, Austria, to reunite the family once again. It was a painful decision on my parents' part to leave behind their many church friends and all that they worked so hard for. My parents also faced the risk of capture and imprisonment of family members. Their strong faith in God gave them confidence to carry out their plans.

My oldest brother, Tony, was obstinate and did not want to leave. At 17 he was willing to forsake his family to remain with the church, but was finally persuaded to come. Fear of burning in hell was a major part of our strict religious upbringing.

We children were told that we would just take a trip to a relative's house in Szeged, but I overheard my parent's conversation and was looking forward to our travels with much excitement. It was too hard for me to contain my enthusiasm of what lay ahead. I revealed my family's secret to Ferenc, my trusted friend, without realizing the potential jeopardy it may have put my family in. His father was on the police force. Ferenc was a true friend and kept my secret, otherwise it would have been jail for us all. In later years my letters to him of thanks for his confidence were unfortunately never answered.

Stone Mountain, Budaors, Hungary. Photo by Frank Toth

PART THREE

ESCAPING HUNGARY

We prepared for our odyssey on this cold January morning. With many layers of clothing on our backs and a few meager belongings in our hands, we slowly made our way past the mountains that I had grown to love. It was scary, yet exciting to leave our life behind and head out for unknown and strange lands. We had just recently butchered two pigs for our winter food supply and now all that good meat plus our two goats, a few chickens, and our dog was left behind. The realization just hit me that I may never see this beautiful place, the land of my birth again.

This memorable winter morning revealed a fresh blanket of white snow. We formed two groups which left separately. The one mile walk to the bus station seemed to take forever. We must have looked suspicious boarding the bus with bags and belongings in our hands, some tied to our backs. I took one final look back at the rugged landscape, especially Stone Mountain, and silently said my last goodbye. As we boarded the bus, I could see Turk's Jump Mountain in the distance. Legends say that a Turkish officer committed suicide off the 200 foot sheer cliffs. He blindfolded his horse and himself, then jumped to his death rather than face the humiliation of being captured by the Hungarian hussars. Hordes of Turks almost overran Europe in the 16th century.

We took the bus as far as possible, then transferred to a street car. Another hour passed and we were at the train station. All 9 of us children stood with mom as dad bought tickets. It was obvious to many onlookers where we were heading.

Our destination was Szeged, a town along the Yugoslavian border where we intended to cross to freedom. Even though Yugoslavia is a communist country, it's not a Russian satellite, therefore they allowed refugees to enter.

Since leaving Budapest we were joined by another family with four children and an older woman with her two grown daughters. As we sat awaiting the train's departure, a uniformed officer boarded. He looked at us and paused before moving on to find a seat. We were apprehensive and had reason to be. It didn't require a lot of guessing as to what our plans

15

were as our large group headed toward the border with our belongings. God must have been watching over us because miraculously we were not apprehended.

After arriving in the small village of Szeged, we went to my father's distant relative's house. This was a risky and dangerous thing to do in a communist controlled country. We couldn't be sure whether someone had reported the unusually large number of people going to this house. At any moment the police could come bursting in and haul us all off to prison charging us with treason by abandoning our country.

Our distant relative helped by putting us in contact with a former border guard that was involved in the illegal guidance of refugees across the Yugoslavian border. The guard agreed to lead us to freedom for payment and suggested that we wait till midnight before leaving the house to minimize the chance of getting caught. We were all very tired from the long train ride and this wait gave us a chance to get a little sleep.

About midnight our guide arrived and we filed out leaving the warmth and protection of the house. The night air was frigid. The bright moon shone on the newly fallen snow and illuminated the flat countryside. We had clear visibility for miles, but so did the border guards. The worse thought was that we knew they would not hesitate to use their guns, maybe even without warning. Many desperate refugees had armed themselves, determined to fight their way to freedom and if need be kill anyone that tried to stop them. This made the guards more eager to protect themselves, shooting first, asking questions later.

After a long walk our guide stopped and turned toward us. "This is as far as I will go," he said. "We are very close to the Yugoslavian border. Listen carefully! Go straight ahead."

He pointed toward a cluster of trees, one of the first we'd seen on the grassy plains. "You will soon cross a swampy area with thick reeds. Don't worry, it should be frozen over by now. Go straight through it because the border zigzags in this area and you might find yourself back in Hungary."

He then demanded to be paid for his services and took anything of value he could carry and all the money our group had. He ripped us off good, but we were in no position to argue or haggle over his outrageous demands. After confiscating all of our valuable possessions, the guide turned and walked back toward Szeged.

We were now moving steadily toward our freedom. My younger brother and sister were irritable. It was cold and the little ones were tired. We walked for some time before coming to the thickets and swampy area the guard warned us about. We thought of going around it, but after a few moments of hesitation remembered the guard's warning. More out of fear from being lost or captured than out of sound judgement, we proceeded into the swamp.

Soon we were engulfed by the thick marsh reeds growing 6 feet high in places. We couldn't tell how wide this forest of reeds was, or how long we would have to struggle in it. Would we be able to head in the right direction? Our guide had assured us the swamp was frozen over, but what if it wasn't? What if the ice gave way? The concentrated weight of 20 people wasn't something to be easily discounted. We stretched our arms in front of us to part the reeds and didn't spread out for fear of losing one of the children. It was a real struggle, accompanied with much uncertainty.

The younger kids were crying as my mother counted heads nervously to make sure no one was missing. Everyone seemed worried but me. I was enjoying this great adventure. It was frustrating for me to walk behind everyone at this slow pace, so I made a wide berth around the adults to get to the front of the group.

Suddenly, an eerie sound of cracking ice reached my ears! The night air was filled with the sound of terrifying gasps as the ice gave way. We dropped through to knee-deep water and mud. How much deeper it would get, we didn't know. How long can we last out in this cold dark swamp sopping wet? It was decided that we should proceed. The loud noise of the crushing ice could only be duplicated by a herd of elephants. Farther than we could see on this moonlit night, the loud sounds must have traveled. We could only hope no guards had spotted us yet, but if they were within a mile's distance, they must be headed our way by now. If we'd turn back we would be captured, but at least we wouldn't freeze to death. Returning to the village was out of the question, it was too far behind us. We continued going forward, farther into the dark unknown. How much longer we struggled with the reeds, ice, and the muddy water I don't remember. After what seemed like many dangerous hours, we regained footing on solid ground. As we reached the other side of the swamp, miraculously there were no guards waiting to capture us, but neither was there any sight of civilization that would have given us encouragement for our low spirits. The one thing that kept us going was what our guide told us before leaving.

"Shortly after you cross the swamp, you will be in Yugoslavia."

We didn't think of what could happen once we were in Yugoslavia. How far was the first village? Will someone really help us? Now these questions crowded our minds.

My shoes and pants were wet and by now my toes were numb from the cold. My adventurous spirit was waning and my energetic body now ached with fatigue.

We stumbled over a long narrow ditch. "This must be the border," someone said. There was no need for an Iron Curtain along Yugoslavia's border because until now, anyone crossing here would be sent back promptly. Since the border between Austria and Hungary was rebuilt, the U.S.A. made a deal to pay so much per refugee escaping to Yugoslavia. And now my dear reader, you understand why I owe a lot to this great country of America.

After many tiring hours of walking, we spotted the dark outline of a cabin in the distance. As my father walked ahead we prayed that we were out of Hungary. After several anxious minutes he returned.

"I can't understand what they say. We must be in Yugoslavia!"

A cheer of relief came from all of us at our success.

The couple from the cabin confirmed the good news that we were across the border on Yugoslavian soil. In spite of the language barrier, they understood our ordeal and helped anyway they could. The good-hearted couple provided us with hot drinks and warm shelter. It seemed to me we weren't the first refugees they had encountered. We took off our wet, muddy shoes and warmed our half frozen feet and cold bodies.

The kind Yugoslavian man went into town to notify the authorities to come and help. By midmorning a Yugoslavian patrol jeep transported us to a town by the city of Subotica. There a theater, with fresh straw on the floor, was already made into a temporary shelter which we shared with over 200 other Hungarian refugees.

The warm building and our bed of straw was a welcome relief. We layed down and quickly fell asleep. We awoke with the full realization that we were destitute. The little money and valuables we had were gone, confiscated by our guide. We were completely dependent on the Yugoslavian authorities, but with the aid of CARE and the generosity of the American people our needs were provided. Before the Russians closed the Yugoslavian border, 28,000 Hungarian refugees managed to escape.

After a few days of registration and classifications we were loaded on trains and were traveling again. Even though Hungary is only about the size of the state of Indiana, the farthest I remember traveling was to church in Budapest, about a 6 mile distance. Now we were suddenly traveling hundreds of miles across Yugoslavia.

The train had little heat if any, and we had to wear coats to keep warm. We rode through many cities and small villages. Farm houses dotted the white, snow covered fields that stretched as far as we could see. Our train was heading toward the snow covered Alps. The mighty steam engine bellowed black smoke from its tall chimney as it made its way over the high peaks. It was hard for me to believe that only a short time ago, we lived in the once peaceful, sleepy village of Budaors, and now were hundreds of miles from it.

As the train descended the montain side, someone yelled excitedly, "Look there, it's the ocean!"

A few miles below us the breathtaking Adriatic Sea glistened in the sunshine. It was like a dream! I was almost afraid to pinch myself for fear of awakening and finding myself back in Hungary.

The ground around us was no longer covered with snow. The climate changed slowly from frigid cold to very mild. After riding 3 days on the crowded train we had arrived by the shores of the Adriatic Sea. None of us had ever seen an ocean. Come to think of it, I hadn't even seen a large lake. Now here we were at a sea so vast that we couldn't see the other side.

We disembarked from the train and to my delight boarded a large seagoing ship and headed out to open water. Until now, the only boat I had ever ridden in was my mother's wooden washtub and that almost took my life. The big ship sailed smoothly over the choppy water of the Adriatic. We were told that Italy was only a few miles from us. Occasionally a fast moving border patrol boat with mounted guns passed near us. After what seemed like hours of cruising from Rijeka (Fiume), we arrived at the town of

Selce and were ushered to a nearby exclusive hotel where we were to remain for the next 3 months. The cleanliness of the hotel reminded me of our house in Hungary. My mother always swept and kept it immaculate, despite its dirt floors. Selce was a tourist resort now closed for the season. We stayed in private rooms in this luxurious hotel, quite a change for us poor displaced refugees. It wasn't hard to get used to the pleasant surroundings.

The food was nutritious, consisting mostly of fresh fish caught from the ocean. We never ate so much fish in our lives, but it was delicious and we had little to complain about. This was fine for us, but due to the lack of calcium and other needed nutrients, the smaller children were in poor health. Our kind Yugoslavian cook and her waiter-husband jeopardized their jobs by sneaking milk from the kitchen for the little ones.

As with all good things there are drawbacks. The adults were confined to the hotel grounds, able only to leave with a pass. The only restriction for us kids was the compulsory mathematic and writing courses that my older brother Tony, with the sanctification of my parents, taught us.

"When the question is popped, 'What is 2 x 9?' you are expected to answer '18' in seconds, even if I should wake you from sleep," bellowed the fierce voice of brother Tony, our teacher. Learning was the last thing on my mind with the excitement of an ocean in the back yard. I threatened to beat Tony up someday, but subconsciously understood the need for an education and tried to make the best of an unpleasant situation.

Tidal pools formed at low tide were my favorite places to catch small fish, crabs, snails, and starfish. Most of my available time though was spent fishing from a large stone pier that was close to our hotel. A safety pin, bent in the shape of a hook, and a short nylon string tied to the end of a stick was my only fishing pole. When a fish bit, I quickly yanked up and flipped him onto the dock, otherwise he'd slip off and get away. It was fun to observe the fish swimming in the crystal clear water. I have never seen clear water like the Adriatic before, nor ever again since.

The Adriatic seashore was a vacation of a lifetime. The mountainous coastline, as well as the sandy beaches with the fine hotel in Selce will long remain in my mind. Not only because of its beauty, but because this is where I fell in love with a girl for the first time.

I was really crazy about this pretty blonde girl who aroused hidden desires within my soul. From that day on, fishing and collecting shells were nearly forgotten. My time was spent with her on the rugged shore and secluded beaches. Younger kids like us (we were both 9 years old) were able to go far beyond the boundary of the hotel. The guard that kept an eye on everybody (for fear of us starting another rebellion I presume) wasn't worried about a few kids romping around. We had a lot of fun in more ways than one. Three months of heaven were spent by the Adriatic, two young Hungarian refugees in love, but she went to Belgium and I to America. . .

We prepared to leave for our next destination up in the wild mountain country of Socolak, near the city of Sarajevo. We boarded busses and continued our travel over some treacherous, narrow mountain roads. With nose pressed against the window my inquisitive brown eyes observed the

20

ever changing view. The bus's tires came dangerously close to the edge of the narrow road that had no guard rails which caused the passengers to gasp.

It was springtime in the mountains with budding trees and flowers everywhere, but for awhile the flowers were hardly noticed because I left my heart in Selce by the sea.

To our dismay, our new home was a rickety old building that was at one time used for World War II prisoner barracks. It was meagerly refurbished for us. What a sharp contrast from the lavish accommodations we enjoyed in the past 3 months. There were over 150 people who shared our room with two long rows of bunkbeds and very little space in between. Men, women, and children were packed like sardines in the room. Harsh pillows stuffed with coarse straw and itchy blankets were our only comfort. Precious little privacy was attained by hanging blankets between the bunkbeds. The bathroom was an enclosure with holes in the ground where you squatted down to do a job. Our new home left much to be desired and we occasionally longed for the comfort and privacy of our earthen-floor home left in Hungary. The rugged beauty of this wilderness was without equal even if our housing accommodations were crude. It wasn't long before I fell in love with this untamed part of Europe.

Eleven members of the Toth family in the hills of Yugoslavia. Peter is pictured in the bottom right corner.

The nights were long and dark up in this wild country. The stillness of the night air was occasionally broken by a distant howl. All the kids would gather around and listen attentively as my father told us frightening stories of how wolves tore their prey apart with their powerful jaws. He spoke with an authoritative voice as his dark eyes glistened in the faint light of the kerosene lamp. To keep the wolves away from camp he whittled for us kids a rattle that was intended to scare them away. Of course no wolves were ever sighted, but we had fun playing with it anyway. This was only one of the many toys he made. I would spend hours watching my father carve wood into human forms. He fascinated me with his art. For as many years as I can remember, he would carve toys for us kids since money was scarce.

The news spread with the fury of wild fire that a family of Gypsies were coming to our barracks. Because no one wanted them in their room, a big furor broke out.

I remember my first encounter with Gypsies back in Budaors, Hungary. One summer afternoon as Gabe and I were hauling buckets of water from the town well, we noticed a family of Gypsies moving into the bombed out ruins of a wine cellar across the road from our house. The father of the family came over to borrow some milk. I remember him as a dark complected, tall, handsome man whose dark eyes glanced at everything. Gypsies, my parents told us were a wandering people originating from somewhere in the Middle East. They prefer their own way of life and live in family groups. Hungarian Gypsies are known for their music; they are some of the finest musicians in the world. My parents also warned us to be leery of these people. Many times things may turn up missing when they are in the vicinity.

And now in Yugoslavia we encountered them again. The situation was unavoidable because the Gypsies had a right to move in. The decision was made to pull straws to see who would have to take them. Later when they settled in their room, the family was asked where they would like to go as their final destination. Someone overheard them say that since the barracks provided them with free food and shelter, they would like to stay "here". The Yugoslavian authorities promptly signed them up for America (the most difficult country to immigrate to).

We had much more freedom here in this remote wilderness. Several of us older kids went on a snake hunt with my father. During my search in a stone quarry, I spotted a large poisonous snake sunning himself on a boulder. I repeatedly yelled "snake" so loud that my voice was lost for days.

Mom was furious at dad for endangering us with the snake hunt. Her attention of late was focused on my feverish youngest brother Julius. His persistent illness started a rumor that he had cholera or some other contagious disease. Consequently, our whole family was quarantined to the medical ward of the barracks. I hated the hospital atmosphere, especially since we shared the room with a young lady that had recurring nightmares about her brother being killed by the Russians. She'd wake up in the middle of the night screaming. It was nerve-racking and very sad to witness this poor girl's vivid nightmares.

Julius's health was deteriorating rapidly and my mother feared for his life. The only medical person in the barracks was a nurse who finally diagnosed his symptoms as possible whooping cough and urged us to rush him to the hospital. My father and Endre carried Julius several miles over the rugged terrain to the nearest medical facility. There was but one doctor on the entire hospital staff. He was most kind and sympathetic and went out of his way to help my little brother. After a few days in the hospital with proper medical care, his high fever abated and his cough greatly diminished.

My mom was relieved when she was able to bring Julius home to the overcrowded barracks. The hospital was a new building constructed from U.S. funds, but the lack of running water and the terrible overcrowding made it a "horrible" place to be. The toilets were overflowing with human waste and flies were everywhere. My mother experienced an even more horrifying sight, a stillborn infant was left in the corner of the room with hundreds of flies covering it.

Julius's health greatly improved and life went on. After 2 more months we received the good news that our visas cleared and we would soon be leaving for Vienna, Austria.

Traveling was now a way of life for us and though it was at times tiring, I savored every minute of it. Our train took us through Zagreb and the rugged Yugoslavian back country. On the 4th day we arrived in Vienna. My brother Frank, and sister Irene, were there to welcome us. Our family was reunited once more.

It was a unique experience to live in this world famous city. At night Vienna glowed like a jewel, but my heart and dreams were on mountain tops, crystal clear oceans, and forests—where nature still reigned supreme. These several months of travel gave me a different perspective on life. My memory fails me of how or when I first heard of the American Indians, but in the course of our travel, through books and personal accounts of people, my interest was captivated.

Life in Austria was better than anywhere else. One of the things I enjoyed most was the tropical fruit now available. We were aware of such luxuries in Hungary, but couldn't afford them. On occasions my sisters and mom used modern appliances which saved time and made life much easier.

At first we lived in the basement of the Nazarene Church, the faith that my parents belonged to. (In America the church is called the Apostolic Christian Church.) These good Christian people helped us out everywhere we went.

We then moved into the Vienna camp that was housing hundreds of Hungarian refugees. Things were much better here than in the Yugoslavian camp. The rooms were smaller, housing only 25 to 30 people each and we had our freedom to come and go.

Though food and lodging was given to us, clothing and other needed items were in short supply. Consequently, the grownups went searching for work while us younger kids were enrolled in Vienna's public school.

It was traumatic to be placed in school. Since none of us spoke the German language, all the kids seemed to be talking 100 m.p.h. What helped me to pick up the language was listening to the class and extra tutoring. Besides a language barrier, there were many other obstacles to conquer. I belonged to a minority group in school, faced at times with contempt and prejudice by some of the Austrian kids. Making friends quickly solved most of my problems. Soon I felt accepted by almost everyone.

As we waited for our visas to clear, the Hungarian Apostolic Christian Church in Akron, Ohio worked to help make our dreams come true, to immigrate to the United States.

After living in Vienna for over a year, the joyous news came that our visas to the U.S. had cleared. It had taken all this time for them to investigate for moral, mental, and physical defects. The U.S. Immigration Service carefully screened and accepted only those who could be an asset to this country.

In October of 1958, we moved to Salzburg, the highland of Austria, to wait the final leg of our journey to America. This city was like a distribution center for many refugees. We occupied our time by visiting a nearby Austrian castle and touring the beautiful city of Salzburg. We lived close to the area where they filmed "The Sound of Music" starring Julie Andrews.

It was December, 1958, nearly 2 years after fleeing Hungary when we finally began packing for our trip to America. By bus we went to Munich, Germany, traveling on the Autobahn through the famous Black Forest. At Munich's airport we boarded an outdated U.S. Army plane. My excitement and train of thought was on flying above the clouds toward our new country. The 6 huge propellers roared and I held my breath as we took off. The plane flew so high that buildings became small match boxes, then vanished from view. Thousands of feet over the Atlantic Ocean the cloud formations looked like the North Pole. The plane's motion and the anxiety of flying gave me an upset stomach. It was a good thing there was a bathroom aboard.

*It hardly seemed possible that our plane was landing in New York. It seemed like just yesterday when we lived under the tyranny of the communists. Although in recent years our lives in Hungary had improved, it wasn't long ago when my father, killed and out of hunger, ate a cat. Our donkey fell victim to hard times, not really his, but ours. In 1952 the hungry and growing Toth family had little food, so my father butchered the donkey so that we could live.

I remember how my brother Tony, in his hunger and desperation, wished that he could only smell the lard on his bread. As one of the younger members of the Toth family, my most vivid memories are of better times when we had the rarity of chicken eggs in the house. But then again, how could I ever forget the chewy cow udder my mom once cooked for us. Believe me dear readers, if you're hungry, cow udder or a lard sandwich is great food.

It was daylight when we landed at New York's Idlewild Airport. We got off the plane and took our first steps on the soil we dreamed of for so long. Once again we rode the train, but this time through the back country of Pennsylvania "America" to a new home and life that awaited us in Akron, Ohio.

Front page of Akron Beacon Journal, December 1958, Akron, Ohio

STANDING BESIDE *their family at Idlewild Airport after landing on a plane from Munich, West Germany, are Antal Toth, 45, and his wife, Iren, 43, with their 11 children. Center, foreground, is Eszter, 4. Other children (left to right) are Guyla, 6; Sarolta, 7; Szuszanna, 8; Peter, 10; Gabor, 12; Eva, 14; Ferenc, 17; Iren, 18; Antal Jr., 19; and Endre, 16.*

PART FOUR

ARRIVING IN AKRON, OHIO

My parents were happy that after two years of travel we finally came to peaceful Akron, Ohio where we could settle down. Now life might be boring for me since our adventure was over.

Mr. & Mrs. Hunyadi, their 9 kids, and many members of the church welcomed us with open arms. We were displaced and homeless and yet they accepted us like family. We were driven in big cars to our new home that was cleaned, recarpeted, painted, and furnished by the generous people of the Hungarian Apostolic Christian Church of Akron, our American sponsors. Our Pastor, Mr. George Hunyadi, put a thousand dollars down on our house. They, along with the church people, helped us in any way they could.

Our church was unique from most because Mr. Hunyadi was just one of the several ministers of the church. None of the ministers were paid by the church for their work, but lived off of their professions in other fields.

Standing on the porch, I could see the happiness in my mother's blue eyes as she gazed upon her new home. The big white house looked inviting. We entered the front door and began exploring the many rooms of the two story house. The spacious, well equipped kitchen was a delight to my mother. Off of the dining room was a large living room with comfortable sofas. We proceeded to the second story where there were 3 large bedrooms and a bathroom with a deep porcelain tub.

From the stairway window my eyes caught something thrilling in the back yard. A big lake washed the edge of our property.

"Look at that big lake!" I said with jubilance to my younger sister Shirley who was standing beside me. "I'll teach you how to swim."

In the Adriatic my attempts to swim failed miserably. Then in a little pond in Vienna, Austria, I succeeded at a few short strokes. The only place in the pond that was over my head was a strip about 5 feet wide in the center. All day long, with the help of my older brothers, I practiced swimming acrossed it. My courage and swimming ability improved with time.

Suddenly I realized that adventure and exploration need not stop. The near 100 acre lake by the back yard was to be my future adventure.

25

The day had been long and tiring and we were all in need of sleep. The house was still full of well-meaning people, joyful at our arrival and it was only common courtesy to stay awake.

Earlier in the day several newsmen met us at the train station and now more came through the front door with cameras flashing. My sisters were asked to stare at an electric iron as if they had never seen such a thing before. Next, they asked me and a couple of the younger kids to act as if we were grabbing wildly at oranges and bananas in a bowl. How my brothers and sisters felt, I don't know. As for me, my exhaustion was now topped with humiliation. Before the picture was taken, I turned my hand inward, thus it appeared that my hands grabbed away from the fruits. Destitutes, perhaps we were, but I had plenty of pride left.

It's true that we came a long way and were thankful for our good fortune to be in America. But despite our lower standard of living in Hungary, coming from an earthen-floor home, we considered ourselves upper class people with high ideals. We were only beaten down temporarily by the communist's system that was forced on us in the old country by the hated Russians.

A picture of our family appeared on the front page of the Beacon Journal. It was accompanied with a lengthy article explaining that we were the largest family ever to immigrate to Akron.

Our church friends helped us adjust to the new lifestyle in America. We were told the do's and don'ts of everyday living and became needlessly afraid and apprehensive about the violent ways of the black people and other minorities. There was also the poisonous plants we were to look out for, like poison ivy and sumac. One lady even went so far as to tell us not to inhale the fragrance of some flowers, less we get sick.

We never received any welfare, but supported ourselves by acquiring any available jobs, however menial, for the older members of the family. This was very difficult because few places hired anyone with little comprehension of the English language.

It was our family's custom (as was many Europeans) to form a common kitty. At the end of every week all earned money was put in it and my mom budgeted the spending. In less than a year, to the amazement of Mrs. Hunyadi, my mother proudly paid back, in cash, the $1,000 down payment on our house.

Before the dreaded school enrollment came about, I had a chance to check out the lake by our back yard. I tried my luck at fishing and caught several bluegills and goldfish. Large goldfish were very abundant. Sometimes traveling in schools of 100, they turned the water scarlet. Summit Lake, as I learned, was polluted by the large rubber factories in the city. Their pollutant waste and chemicals kept the water from freezing and many species of water foul would make this lake their migrating stopover and some their winter home. My biggest fascination was drawn to these hundreds of migrating ducks and geese.

The inevitable came and we were enrolled in school. It is hard to start in a new school for any kid, but not being able to speak much English made things even worse. I had never finished third grade, never entered fourth, and yet they placed me in the fifth grade.

Tibor, my Hungarian friend from Austria who was the same age as me, came to the United States with his family a few weeks earlier than we did and settled here. He explained to me one day that he felt strange in his class. "You know, Peter," he said, "these Americans are sure small!" Tibor should have been in the fifth grade with me, but it turned out they put him in the first grade without him realizing it. No wonder the kids seemed so small to him.

My first American teacher was Mrs. Luders; a kind, elderly, soft spoken woman. Not knowing what she was saying distressed me and I began feeling sorry for myself. As soon as school was out I would dash for the woods and swamps by Summit Lake. I found comfort and peace among nature. Many of the kids must have thought me strange and who could blame them? It takes a lot of effort to adjust to a new country.

My brothers and sisters had their own difficulties at school. It seemed like the language problem, however short lived, appeared infinitely larger than it really was. Ultimately we all had to deal with and overcome it.

To help my English a system was devised where each member of the class took turns sitting by me and helped me read a first grade book. After two weeks the words had meaning and we went on to second, third, and higher grade books. A new world opened through my knowledge of English.

In a few months I thought myself capable of talking, reading, and expressing myself verbally as well as anyone else. One day our teacher brought in a tape recorder and we all took turns speaking into it. I was shocked to hear my speech when the tape was replayed. My English was so different from everyones that I found it hard to believe it was my voice talking. After that day much effort was given to losing this strange accent, but nothing seemed to work and I started to develop a complex.

Those moments when kids teased me about my accent were terribly embarrassing, sometimes it even got me into fights. Even in the sixth grade, the teacher singled me out for a special class of kids that had speech defects. It made me feel like a "real dummy".

Like many of my sixth grade classmates I became a school patrolman whose job it was to see to the safety and orderly conduct of the children. One of my assignments was to keep the kids on the sidewalk. I often yelled out to them, "Keep off the grrrrass!" rolling my r's in the process. Some of the children jeered and laughed at my speech problem.

In the Hungarian language it is mandatory to roll the r's. This was a most difficult process for me to learn and now a most difficult thing to unlearn. It was over a year before I spoke reasonably good English with little accent.

In Junior High School, body building and weight lifting became my hobby which gave my small frame the bulk and size it needed. Even more important than my relatively strong physique, was the self-assurance derived from it. There is virtually nothing in this world that, in time, I can't succeed at or overcome. No task is beyond my capacity. Sure there is always someone that's bigger, stronger, smarter, and better looking than you, but if you get your face shoved in the dirt, as I have many times, don't give up. Be proud of who you are, if not you, who will be? Strive to be honorable and the very best you can be.

There was a time when I was known around school as a tough Hunky who showed little fear from anybody. My muscular appearance helped to keep me out of fights. Most kids seemed afraid to challenge me, but it was impossible to bluff my way all the time.

One of my few fights began on a hot afternoon in school as I was in line to get a drink at the water fountain. A heavy-set bully cut in front of me and a push, shove, and insulting words ensued. With a promise of a fight after school we parted. Later while I was combing my hair in the bathroom, old bully Lucas walked in.

"After school, Peter!" he sneered as a couple of his friends laughed in the background.

I was nervous and scared of the upcoming fight, after all, Lucas was much bigger than me. His cool posture made me angry at myself.

"Now Lucas!" I yelled in anger and slugged him in the face. Blood poured from his nose as we boxed and wrestled on the bathroom floor. This fight was my clear victory and soon afterwards we became good friends.

My early struggles were never forgotten. Consequently, I would always stick up for the weaker, picked-on kids and help them out against bullies whenever possible. I learned first hand and understood the indignities faced by someone that is a little different. Usually it's the insecure and inferior person that will try to walk all over you by teasing and making fun of you. In this way he generates a false sense of superiority about himself. One must never allow himself to be intimidated by anyone.

My earlier years were divided up between school, church, weight lifting, pets, and the great outdoors. I longed to explore the swamps and mysterious lagoons of Summit Lake, unattainable by any other means but a boat. My dream was to someday own one. Opportunity came knocking. One day a couple of local punks tried to con my brother Tony into buying their old wooden boat. They thought they'd really pull a good one over on us by trying to hide the fact that it leaked. I knew it leaked all along, but didn't care and helped them talk Tony into buying it.

The exploration of Summit Lake finally began. Tony was excited, but I felt like Jacques Cousteau setting out on an ocean voyage. Gabe and I paddled while Tony bailed out the small amount of accumulating water. We had fun collecting many fishing bobbers, balls, and other floating items. We even found a little red rowboat that needed a new bottom. Later we pulled it home and after many days of repair, it became my own boat.

I discovered a small swampy island near our house. Because the island looked so forbidding in the evening against the murky water and swamps, I decided to name it "Black Island". A pretty neighbor girl came to visit and helped me plant flowers around the island. Wood and other building materials were towed behind my little red rowboat which was used for building my shack on the island. It was built lower than the tall cattails to keep people from discovering it.

Once while trying to secure the towline on some boards in a secluded wooded section of the lake directly across from our house, a gang of black kids attacked me. Stones and other missiles were thrown at me, at least one big stone hit me in the chest. Several guys jumped in the water and grabbed for the back of the boat. I feared for my life and thought they'd catch me for sure, steal my boat, beat, or even kill me. With unrealized strength and speed, I managed to reach the safety of deep water. After catching my breath from a safe distance it was my chance to cuss them back.

The 1960's were turbulent times; hate and anger was rampant. Blacks were demonstrating in the streets, and some cities were literally looted and burned. Whites were dragged from their cars, beaten, and some even killed simply because they were white. It's ironic that although I had dangerous and sometimes life threatening encounters with blacks, one of my best friends was a black. People should not be judged by the color of their skin, creed, or nationality. Had the gang of kids on the lake been white, they may have done the same thing to a black because any group of people can turn into an ugly mob, unthinking, unfeeling, and destructive.

My early teens was also the time in my life for romance. To the great pleasure of my parents I would be in church Sundays, Thursdays, and sometimes even Tuesdays for youth group. I had a strong calling—the two beautiful daughters of the minister, Rosemary and Violet. These two girls really lit up my life. My heart sank at least a foot when they didn't make it to church. I didn't know which one was loved most, but my heart would have settled for either. Rosemary was admired from a distance, but Violet seemed to reciprocate my infatuation. The romantic fool that I was, gifts of wild flowers and a couple of small turtles were given to her. Oh, those innocent days of wine and roses, I mean "turtles and wild flowers."

Religion was always a mystery to me. If God is kind and good as the Bible claims, how can he allow his people to suffer pain, torture, and misery? If he is merciful, how can he condemn people to be tortured in hell like my parents often preached to us?

My parent's church was full of some of the best people I have ever known. The Hungarian church in Akron has many teachings that to this day I firmly believe in, but some of their customs don't agree with me. One such is that in this church men sit together as a group on one side of the aisle and the women on the other. For members it is normal for men to greet, embrace and kiss each other as it is for women, but it is forbidden for a man to embrace and kiss a woman. Also, when a man asks a woman to marry him, it's done through the minister.

My love for God's creation never ceased. When it wasn't girls, it was my many pets. The many pigeons, dogs (Vites and Mityas), a hawk, three coons, a golden pheasant, as well as other pets, were barely tolerated by my parents. They caused me much difficulties. Our neighbor, Mrs. Ruth Kohari, was usually very understanding toward us, but my many pets wore her patience thin.

One cold winter morning in 1962, I walked down to the lake to see if there were any new ducks or geese. An ugly chemical spill that looked like oil and tar slicks covered much of the water. My fear was for the health and safety of the ducks, which was well founded because the ducks were getting the oily mess all over them.

Peter, age 13, feeding his ducks at Summit Lake.

In the next few days tragedy struck my feathery friends. The shores of Summit Lake were now thickly covered with a black, oily substance. The mallard and white ducks were least adversely affected, but divers like the grebe, coot, and the beautiful little buffleheads were so thickly covered with oily tar that they lost most of their buoyancy and could barely stay afloat.

I watched their pathetic attempt to hide among the reeds, cattails, and bushes. Many fell victim to dogs, muskrats, and other predators, while others froze from the lack of protective feathers. With anger and frustration at the factories for not doing anything about the much suffering and death they caused, I decided on a one-man crusade.

Most of the remaining daylight after school was spent capturing and trying to clean the helpless ducks. A cleaning station was made out of our basement and before long over a dozen ducks were being cared for. My mom ordered me to take them out in the cold garage, but as soon as she turned her back, they were snuck back in. It made me want to cry to see these delicate creatures immobilized, sick and dying from the chemicals dumped by the factories. Despite my most thorough effort at trying to save them, most of them still died.

*My brother Julius, friend Tommy Hillrich, and I drove to our recently purchased farm 65 miles from Akron to fish and hunt. When my thoughts drifted to the helpless Summit Lake ducks dying, my gun was lowered never to be raised again.

Death touches us all, as it ultimately must. Joey Hillrich, Tommy's brother, was my schoolmate and friend. Just a few days ago we met on the beach. His death came suddenly; a handsome, intelligent, proud Marine who hardly lived at all and now he was gone.

The day we buried Joey was the longest day of my life. After the tears are shed, life must go on. It was his death that made me realize how precious and fleeting life is and how we should savor, respect, and make the most of it by making our own contributions. I wanted something of me to remain behind after my departure from this life.

Every season has its beauty, like a warm spring day when all things come alive with a promise of renewal. When flowers bloom and young birds take to wing, there is so much to live for, and for some of us so short a time. It is so good to be alive; God, how I wish I could live forever.

*Irene, my oldest sister was the first one in our family to get married. I suspect not so much for love, but to free herself from our strict religious parents and their many stringent rules. Through Irene's husband, Joe Vankos, we became acquainted with Sherman Schumacher, a man that became a friend of the family known as Uncle Sherm. He was to us the ideal image of a great American. Sherm gave my brother Gabe and I jobs helping with lawn work and making jeep trails in his beloved 250 acre valley. Later, he donated this acreage, valued at over a quarter-of-a-million, to be preserved forever in its natural state as a city park for Akron. Even to this day, I remember how he would treat his wife Mary, a delicate pretty lady, with the utmost respect. One could hardly tell if their honeymoon had ever ended. Sherm was then and still is today, a most positive influence in my life.

Each year my family had to fill out lengthy forms because we were not citizens. Our Hungarian citizenship was lost due to our desertion and the number of years we'd been away. In 1968 it was an honor for me to become a citizen of the United States. Every day I am grateful to be in America and live under the best system of government in the world. My fellow citizens, I pray that we will never trust Russia because a nation with no honor cannot be trusted.

Upon turning 16, my summer was spent working at King Machine, a local machine shop. It was a good feeling to work side-by-side with grown men and bring home a substantial paycheck for the family kitty. It made me feel like an adult. At the end of the summer, before registering for the tenth grade, my father's health took a turn for the worse. I stayed on at the shop. It was a tough decision to continue working to help the family meet the many bills that had to be paid.

1962 Toth family picture taken at home on Manchester Road in Akron, Ohio. Peter, age 15, pictured on top right.

1975—Toth sisters, bottom left: Zsuzsanna (other artist of the family), Mother Toth, Esther. Top: Irene, Eva, Shirley.

My father's stay in the hospital was long and upon his release the doctor suggested peace and quiet. Our farm became his recuperating sanctuary for the next two years. Sixty-five miles now divided the family. In order that my father would not be alone, my youngest brother Julius, and sister Esther, went to live with him. It was a difficult transition for them to leave friends and attend a little country school. Also, it was hard on my mother to divide her time between the family in both the city and the country. She drove the 65 miles twice a week to bring food and share her motherly love. On her drive out to the farm, she would frequently make a stop at the country school and Julius and Esther would come running across the schoolyard with outstretched arms yelling, "Mom! Mom! It's so good to see you!"

Now many years later the old farmhouse lawn is choked full of weeds where once well-trimmed grass and beautiful flowers grew. On rare occasions my mother still visits the farm and as she drives by the country school, she can still see little Julius and Esther running out with open arms to greet her.

My high school education continued in the evening which enabled me to work and study at the same time. A few years later, in order to further my knowledge of this world, I enrolled at the University of Akron for evening courses. Psychology was my main subject and the intent of my education was not a degree, but to learn and have greater understanding of myself, life, and the people around me. Life at times seemed so complex. Education was a tool to help erase some of my many ignorances.

Much time was now spent at libraries where the shelves are chocked full of knowledge about virtually every subject. History was always one of my favorite subjects, so my interest in the American Indian grew. So many facts and details were left out of our history books. The "Flamingo Feather" was my favorite book on Indians. It's strange, but the Indians and my people seemed to have a lot in common as far as injustice is concerned.

My time was never spent in bars, but rather at the Arena Roller Rink in Barberton, where for awhile I was quite popular. Most of my friends would never have suspected by my actions that some girls made me feel shy and awkward. A big change in my life came about with the purchase of a large orange, 500cc, Suzuki motorcycle. My shyness was mostly overcome and several girls were attracted to me.

My mother looked upon my girlfriends with displeasure. Her religion mandated that a man must not even look upon a woman with normal desires unless he marries her first. My mom wanted me to marry a girl of the church. I never thought much of the Hungarian churches rules, however I have respect for a person with high morals and ethics and try to live my life accordingly.

Peter standing beside his first motorcycle.

Peter sits down to lunch with his friend Ron, a co-worker at Flexi-Grip Machine Shop.

The big city of Akron, with a population of 254,000, was my hometown for over 10 years. I found my schooling stimulating, but my job gave me a feeling of stagnation, a feeling of wasting my life away.

Work in the machine shop came easy for me. My four older brothers had paved the way with their willingness for hard work at King Machine. I hardly had to ask for a job. Since tough working Hungarians like us were hard to come by, they almost came and got me.

After three years on the job, an offer came to work for higher pay at Flexi-Grip, through my brother Endre. My new job consisted of fine repairs on golf grip molds. Working on the milling machine, lathe, and press was interesting at first, but was not very challenging to me. Although some people find working there rewarding (and my opinion has no bearing on that), it's just something I didn't care for.

It's hard to put into words my dream of freedom and travel, something I longed for, for so many years. The decision of giving up my good secure job and throwing my fate to the wind was difficult for me.

For the past five years my obligation of helping out the family financially was fulfilled. Due to my father's illness my earnings from the machine shops went to supporting my parents and younger brother and sisters. Fortunately, my father's health returned and he was able to resume working. After five years of monotonous hard work I finally had full control of my money, to do with as I pleased. For the first time in my life I was in a position to make decisions for myself.

The first thing I had to do was to break my family bonds. It was my desire to do something meaningful with my life and not be stuck forever in a machine shop. I wanted to see the country and perhaps eventually the world, as I did in my youth.

It's very difficult to leave everything behind, but I decided that life was elsewhere for me. The guys in the machine shop laughed at me when they heard about my plans to travel.

The time came to prepare myself financially. Though I was making good money, nearly $14,000 a year (in 1970 that was good money), it still took a long time to save up the needed thousands of dollars for my odyssey.

At times I was having second thoughts about leaving, but my departure date was set for the latter part of 1971. Perhaps subconsciously I was hoping something or somebody would change my mind. My girlfriend, Jan, was mad at me so I couldn't look to her for help. Her anger at my planned departure, as well as other problems, like her old boyfriend and the pretty blonde whom I was seeing of late, helped to break us up. I was heartbroken, but my new girlfriend Becki comforted me. My determination for travel and adventure was unhampered. This was to be the last year for me at the Flexi-Grip Machine Shop and studies at Akron University.

With part of my accumulated cash I bought a blue Dodge maxi-van, the very best my money could afford. Even though it was a basic stripped down model, I was very proud of it. For added height and uniqueness, I decided to utilize the hull of an inverted 14 foot motor boat as a permanent roof. First the seats and all excess weight was removed, then the remaining shell

36

was fitted on top of the van. This was then reinforced on top with about 100 bolts which united the van and the boat permanently. It was a triumphant feeling when I cut away the original roof of the van and sealed it against leakage. All the extra head space above made the van twice as large. For visibility and distinction, fifteen portholes were added.

An icebox, stove, sink, cabinets, drawers, and a comfortable bed was installed. For my personal enjoyment I purchased a portable nineteen inch, black and white TV and placed it in the back where the bed was located. Since my parents thought TV was evil, we were never allowed to watch it as kids, so it was a real treat for me now.

Because of my love for the sea and my fondness for eerie stories about lost ships, I decided the most appropriate name for my motor home would be the "Ghost Ship". The "Ghost Ship" was destined to travel the shores of the Atlantic, Pacific, and the Gulf of Mexico.

Peter beside his creation "The Ghost Ship," his home for over 5 years. (Photo by Harold Haven, The Chattanooga Times)

As the time grew nearer for my departure, I started getting cold feet, but there was never any serious thought of backing out. A dream looks so beautiful from a distance, but when you come right up to it and realize the impractical sides, it's so easy to feel disillusioned. I would be traveling alone with much personal risk and danger. Many dark lonely nights lay ahead, but that's what adventure is all about.

As December approached, my departure was at hand. My resignation was finally handed in. After over 5 years at the Flexi-Grip Machine Shop, I was leaving to the disbelief of my foreman and co-workers. They had no other alternative but to believe now.

The difficult task of deciding what to take and what to leave behind on my trip bore down on me. The great thrill of packing the Ghost Ship made the reality of my adventure overpowering. I equipped her with all the bare necessities which included most of my earthly possessions. Several pairs of blue jeans, shorts, shoes, boots, gloves, shirts, sweaters, thermal underwear, coats, sheets, blankets, and pillows were neatly stacked above the bed on specially constructed shelves. Many books were also packed in. If ever I was going to read them all, surely it would make a genius out of me. Special handling was required for my tackle box, fishing rods, and a rifle that I took for protection. A skillet, pots and pans, kitchenware and all kinds of art supplies, knives, a snake bite kit, dozens of bandages and seemingly hundreds of other things I never needed or used were packed. After a trip to the supermarket, I stowed 100 pounds or more of canned food and other emergency rations in every nook and cranny. The Ghost Ship moaned under the heavy weight, but surprisingly the load was digested in an orderly fashion in her hull. As a remembrance of my hard years of entrapment in the machine shop, I took my hammer and several favorite chisels.

Besides all of my possessions, I was taking Curly, a brown miniature poodle, that was a parting gift from my girlfriend Becki Kawczk.

It was a cold January morning when I said goodby to Becki. Leaving a pretty blonde girl with tears in her eyes in the early morning light was at the time, the hardest thing I ever did.

PART FIVE

EARLY TRAVELS

The excitement of finally having my dream come true was temporarily dampened by the overwhelming loneliness and loss that enveloped me. The constant demands of my pet poodle, Curly, brought me back to reality. Several stops were made to see to his comfort.

My first priority was to put 1,000 miles between Ohio and myself by heading south to get away from the cold.

The Ghost Ship sped swiftly down Interstate 71. At a point less than sixty miles from home it began to drizzle and the van started wobbling on the wet road. My fingers froze to the steering wheel. With the thought of losing control, I instinctively jerked the wheel back to the right. That just made things worse. The back tires started skidding sideways on the wet pavement. With a firm hand and a level head the van was brought back under control. It was a nightmarish thought to envision myself upside down with a wrecked van so close to home after all my dreams of traveling.

Through the traffic of Mansfield and Columbus, the Ghost Ship moved unencumbered, but it was a harrowing experience dodging cars, trucks, and buses going through Cincinnati. We were all driving as a closely knit group, at times exceeding 70 mph. It was a difficult maneuver just to get into the exit lane which took me to Interstate 75.

It seemed like an endless road, especially to a person who has never done much traveling by himself. I have traveled thousands of miles on planes, boats, and trains, but it was always with my family.

Finally the state of Ohio was left behind. Kentucky, with its sparsely populated land, was a welcoming difference. The rolling hills and meadows still looked green in the waning afternoon light. The January weather was warmer here. As the sun settled over the countryside, the long and tiring day came to an end. I would have driven beyond midnight had it not been for my fidgety dog. He needed to be taken for a walk so we stopped at a convenient rest area.

The huge, well lit rest area was crawling with trucks, campers, and cars; a real hobo junction. The neatly trimmed grass looked freshly cut and picnic tables rested every fifty feet. After Curly came back from investigating the

39

grounds, he ungraciously turned his nose up at his bowl of food. Thoroughly exhausted, I climbed into bed and with Curly bedded on the floor, we instantly fell asleep. This was my first night in the Ghost Ship, which was to be my home for the next five years.

Early the next morning my journey continued. The weather, up to this point in time, had been in my favor, but now all hell broke loose. It rained down in sheets. Driving was made even worse by a compulsory detour from Interstate 75 which took narrow winding roads through little towns because this part of I-75 was not yet finished. Visibility was hindered further by the constant spraying of water on my windshield by trucks that passed me continuously.

As the beautiful foothills of the Smoky Mountains of Tennessee came into view the rain eased up a bit.

On the second day of the journey we entered Georgia. The burning of Atlanta on Sherman's march to the sea took place here in 1864 during the Civil War. In some ways I can understand the devastation better coming from a war-torn Hungary, ravaged in 1956 by the Russians.

Now facing us was the long monotonous journey over the flat unchanging countryside of central and southern Georgia. The weather was becoming increasingly warmer. Palm trees swaying in the summer breeze was my dream throughout the over 1,000 mile trip south.

After a day and a half of hard driving, we entered Florida. Soon after crossing the state line, it was almost like getting a second chance at summer. I rolled down the windows, soaked up the warm rays of the sun, and enjoyed the scenery of green grass and palm trees dotting the roadside. The warmer weather seemed to have improved Curly's contempt for the long hours of travel.

We exited off Interstate 75 and headed east on Interstate 10 toward the great Atlantic Ocean. The first huge body of water I had ever known was the Adriatic Sea. When calm, it was so crystal clear you could see 20 feet down. It was my destiny to see the ocean again, this time the Atlantic.

We pulled into Jacksonville Beach. The familiar sea air filled my nostrils. It was an overwhelming feeling to be by the sea again. I donned my swim trunks, ran into the salty blue waves, and dove in. The water was cold and refreshing, a bit cloudy from the pounding surf, but every bit as vast and beautiful as I remembered the ocean to be.

Curly was handy when it came to making friends, especially meeting girls. We were strolling on the beach when I noticed a pretty brunette stretched out on a beach towel sunbathing. Her pink bikini accentuated a terrific tan. After pointing Curly toward her, he sprinted off and introduced himself by licking her face. Startled, she jumped up! A quick apology was made for my unruly dog's behavior and before long we were on a first name basis. Had Becki known how handy "Curly Joe" was in meeting girls, she would never have given him to me.

We stayed as close to the ocean as possible, moving slowly south on Highway A1A. Each day was spent swimming, surfing, and soaking up the sun while lazying around the beach. With a tropical breeze blowing gently in my face, a snooze was enjoyed under the shade of the palm trees. Perhaps we had too much of a good thing. One day while surfing, some fine particles of sand got in my eyes.

As our journey continued toward Titusville, my eyes became inflamed. It was getting late, so I drove into an apartment building parking lot and camped for the night.

The next morning everything was blurred. Some kids playing nearby were asked for help in finding a doctor's office or nearest hospital. They called their mother who directed me to a nearby clinic.

A doctor examined my eyes and assured me that it was just a passing condition and gave me some ointment for them. I was told to relax for a few days and rest my eyes.

The next two days were spent in the parking lot. Curly ate his dogfood, while I lived off my survival kit of canned foods which consisted mostly of pork and beans. My meals were supplemented by fish I occasionally caught in a nearby river. The aroma of cooking fish and my persistent presence must have annoyed someone in the building because the next morning the slam of a car door awakened me. It was followed by heavy footsteps and a loud knock on my door.

"This is the police! Is anyone in there?"

"One minute!" I yelled and quickly dressed. As I opened the door the fuzzy outline of a man in a police uniform appeared.

"What is your business here?" he questioned. "There's been a complaint that you've taken up a parking space for over two days now. You can't stay here!"

With a profound calmness the problem with my eyes was explained to the officer. After he took a closer look at my eyes and saw the medication he was sympathetic toward my dilemma.

With a kind voice he said, "Stay here as long as you need and take care of those eyes. Don't get on the road and cause any wrecks."

The next morning my eyes were greatly improved and anxiously we moved on. Slowly heading south, my determination grew to cling tooth and nail to my savings. By sleeping in the Ghost Ship, buying food at supermarkets to cook my own meals, and living off the land whenever possible, I saved a lot of money.

We passed through Vero Beach, Palm Beach, and Ft. Lauderdale. The traffic was nearly always congested, except for the late night and early morning hours. A plan was devised to nap and sunbathe on the beach during the day and drive at night.

It took over ten days to travel the length of the East coast of Florida. Traveling leisurely without any schedules made it difficult to keep an accurate track of time. Days seemed to flow together, soon even weeks passed almost unnoticed.

My freedom was enjoyed, but cops began watching me when I stayed for more than a couple of days in an area. It was a fact, I was different from ordinary people, perhaps a classy bum with some money, but a bum at best.

There are a lot of people on the move in this country. I met a few young people who traveled with nothing but the clothes on their backs. Most are young men and boys. There are few girls really "traveling", most that I encountered were runaways. My heart goes out to them because they are the victims, many times forced into prostitution by pimps, or grabbed by deviates and are never seen again. The young boys are equally victimized by homosexuals who offer them free meals and a place to stay. Often they get more than they bargained for, some are messed up for life at the hands of sexual perverts.

There are many migrant workers who follow the seasons to pick crops where and when available. Most transients I ran into though were sad, old men who liked their wine and always found me an easy sucker for quick change. Paranoia seemed to exist between them and the law. Perhaps that's the reason they are constantly on the move.

We drove into Miami Beach, a city to itself. The huge hotels looked like skyscrapers; a tourist trap for sure. Our stay was brief and then continued toward the Keys.

Highway 1 extends over the ocean. Long bridges connect the numerous islands all the way out to Key West. In this scenic beauty, the Gulf of Mexico is consummated with the Atlantic, like the unity between man and woman.

A premonition of the Ghost Ship falling off the bridge into the ocean worried me during my travels here. All my earthly possessions would sink beneath the waves. Even though my van was paid for, I never carried insurance on it because of my belief that the premiums always outweighed the benefits. Life is a gamble. Fortunately, my many premonitions of oncoming disaster never materialized.

After many days of travel, I was getting used to the ways of the road. The compact size of my home on wheels was both an asset, as well as a liability. The bare necessities were made do in so far as modern conveniences were concerned. The stove was real handy in frying up eggs and heating up canned food, but not much good for cooking large meals. The icebox was a nuisance. A large block of ice that should have lasted two to four days melted in a few short hours and its drain would constantly clog and flood the Ghost Ship. My sink was made quite functional by a manual pump which produced running water. A porta pottie was never purchased because of its large size and the van's lack of space. In my case a bucket was more functional and a milk carton served well as a urinal. When dumping, no one was the wiser; they thought it was milk. A natural setting in the woods was preferable to public restrooms and way stations. Bathing was no problem while it was warm. Sponge baths or a dip in a pond kept me adequately clean.

Despite the cramped living quarters, the Ghost Ship's small size, in comparison to a larger vehicle, was an asset in regards to parking it or maneuvering it through heavy traffic. Another benefit was good gas mileage.

Our journey on Highway 41 carried us toward Naples on the West coast of Florida. When the setting sun cast its last rays on the swampy everglades the outline of a Seminole village came into view. This was my first chance to stop at an Indian village. When the army tried to forceably remove the Seminoles west of the Mississippi, they resisted, bringing on the seven year Seminole War. Failing to capture their indomitable leader, Osceola, in battle, General T.S. Jesup treacherously seized him under a flag of truce in October 1837. Four months later he died in prison, supposedly from sickness. The war continued for an additional four years. Here in this village lived some of their descendants. Proud people to this day, not admitting defeat.

After leaving the Indian village, I drove into the enclosing darkness. The stillness of the endless swamps was occasionally broken by the lonely call of a bull alligator. His cry echoed into the vast emptiness. Because the swamp air was hot and humid, the windows were rolled down. The night suddenly erupted with strange sounds. In my mind the Seminole war of 1835-1842 was reconstructed. The very road driven on came alive with the savage war cries of the Seminole Indians as they held their ground in combat with the U.S. Army. The marshy everglades became drenched in human blood as they defended their land. Seminole infants were even sacrificed, enabling their mothers to replace the shrinking number of warriors. This was indeed a one-sided war, a small unbending tribe of Indians fighting against a powerful nation.

The van's piercing headlights pushed through the ominous darkness which seemed like a huge black cave swallowing us up.

On the outskirts of Naples was a dumpy looking gas station with a large sign "regular gas 29.9". It was my forced habit to take advantage of low gas prices and this was the lowest in a long while.

An old man with a deeply tanned, weather-beaten face and curly white hair beneath a blue seafarer hat emerged slowly from the station door. He reminded me of a storybook sea captain. The old man waited on a blue sedan that pulled in before me.

"Hey man, that's a cool van. Did you design it yourself?" said a voice.

"Sure did," was my reply, startled at his intrusion on my private thoughts. Many people asked me questions about the design of the Ghost Ship.

The voice revealed an immaculately dressed boyish looking young man wearing a pale blue shirt with tight fitting pants. His dark brown hair was neatly parted to the right.

"You're from Ohio, aren't you?"

"Yep, from Akron."

"It's been a long time since I've seen my buddies from Ohio. Your Ohio plates urged me to say hello. Hey, let me buy you a beer and let's talk about home."

His over friendliness was somewhat strange, but I didn't think much of it at the time.

"Thanks for the invitation, but I'm too tired from traveling."

"Come on!" He was almost pleading with me. "I have a car and will give you a tour of the town. Been living here for three years and know this area pretty well."

Naples looked interesting. Should my decision be to stay a day or two he might be able to show me a few points of interest. Well, why not? If he should try to rob me, I'll flatten him.

With Curly on guard duty, the van was left at the gas station and I climbed in his fancy mercury sedan. Something about him just didn't seem right which caused me to be uneasy. As we drove down the street, he spoke of Naples—the historical sites, the good fishing in the Gulf, and about the many retired people living here.

"Any girls around?" I asked.

"Very few, mostly just older women."

"Too bad for you. This doesn't sound like my kind of place."

After driving around for some 20 minutes, his conversation always came back to men. He turned off on a dark, secondary street.

"You really think it's bad down here with only a few girls?" he asked. "A guy can do a lot of the same things for you that a girl can."

I tried to ignore the last remark, but the truth was coming out at last. He talked about a local bartender who did jobs on guys and he didn't have to spell out that the bartender was not a woman. His interest was more than friendly toward me. My premonition of this weird person was only too true. He slowed down on the dimly lit street.

"Hey, what the hell is this!" my deep voice allowed the anger within me to slowly erupt.

"You're a good-looking guy," he said defensively. "Can you blame me for trying to pick you up? I can take care of your needs."

As he described his desire to perform perverted oral sex, I almost slugged him. It took a lot of restraint to contain my anger.

Homosexuality has always been hard for me to understand. One might say I was very naive and perhaps led a sheltered life, but I don't think that was the case. It seemed I was luckier than most and never ran into them. It wasn't until the age of 16 that I realized that queer meant more than funny or strange. It was a sickening shock to me then and now that a man could desire a man. I always thought it was the law of nature that every guy wanted to court and love a soft, feminine woman. Even the Bible condemns homosexuality. God destroyed Sodom and Gomorrah because of this evil.

The homosexual cowered against his door. If I should beat the hell out of him, what would it prove? Besides, the return route to the van was unfamiliar to me. Logic took over.

"Get this damn car moving! Now!"

"OK! OK! If that's what you want!"

He turned the car around and we headed back to the gas station. It was difficult to be open-minded enough to try to understand what makes this guy tick, but upon cooling off my curiosity grew. Since I studied psychology, my interest was to try and figure him out.

"What made you decide to proposition me?"

Defensively he said, "I thought you might be lonely traveling by yourself. I just don't ask 'any' guy walking down the street, besides your good-looking and sexy. There is no need for you to feel threatened."

Again, my stomach felt weak, it's true he threatened me—like anyone that was about to vomit on me would.

"When a girl calls me sexy, it's flattering, but coming from you it makes me nauseous."

He told me he was divorced and had a son which was hard to believe. His marriage of convenience was a facade so that no one would suspect his clandestine meetings with male lovers. He went on to explain that women are dirty. It is presumed he meant the female menstrual cycle. My limited observation is that some men are just not mature enough to handle a real woman, consequently they seek the companionship of men.

"Tell me, how can I keep the likes of you from harassing me again?"

He thought for awhile, "You can't. If someone likes you, he'll try to convince you."

"About convincing, what would have happened if I had been ten years old, my sexual drive hardly defined?"

Without hesitation he answered, "I would have convinced you."

"Let me tell you, should you ever try to do something with my nephew or my buddy's ten year old son, I'd beat you within an inch of your life."

"I'm not a child abuser!" he said defensively. "I don't do things like that."

I questioned his sincerity. Though this encounter had been repulsive, it had taught me a good lesson—to be leery of over friendly guys.

The thought of this encounter happening to a young impressionable child worried me. It is so important that parents know where their children are going and who they're with. Always know what company they keep.

We arrived back at the gas station. As I walked toward my van, he yelled at me with a disappointed voice, "Listen, don't judge us gays too harshly! We are just trying to lead normal lives like everybody else."

The word "gay" struck me as odd. Does he really think he's "gay"? "Normal"? Personally, I feel there's no gaiety about him. He seemed like a sad, confused, miserable human being to me. To this day I refuse to call a homosexual "gay"!

*Living off the land seldom produced satisfying meals. Coconuts that I knocked off a tree were too green to eat and after most of the day was spent gathering pinfish, a form of ocean clam, only a small handful of edible meat was attained.

A few miles south of Fort Myers on a secluded beach, I camped for the night. A cool breeze drifted through the back window stroking my body on its pressing journey to eternity. The curtains danced with a ghostly rhythm as I sank to a deep sleep.

The melody of singing birds and the morning sun awakened me, none too soon, from a nightmare of being back at the dirty machine shop. The room was full of dust from polishing which burned my lungs and blinded my eyes. I punched my time card and saw myself turn old and gray. What a living hell! I wiped the sleep from my eyes; it was a relief to be awake and free to go where I want and do as I please.

My intent was to get an early start for a day of fishing in the shallow bay.

After digging out my fishing pole and lures, I put on a faded pair of cut offs and tennis shoes to protect my feet from getting cut on the sharp coral and set off for my fishing adventure. The water was warm and very clear. Schools of mackerel and other small fish followed in my wake as I waded farther and farther from shore. They darted ahead of me just out of reach. I threw my lure in the middle of the school and after several good jerks, snagged a couple of them.

It was strange being able to wade out so far into the Gulf. Now and then the water would reach up to my chin, but mostly it was about 3 to 4 feet deep. Suddenly, all the fish disappeared. Then I saw a huge form coming straight for me. It must have been six feet long, though it seemed more like ten feet at the time. Terror gripped me! I froze motionless in the water. All the stories I read about sharks and now I was face to face with one. To swim for shore would be a futile attempt, even in this shallow water. If he was after me, he could catch me a hundred times before I'd even get close to shore. The thought of yelling for help crossed my mind, but there was no one in sight but Curly. With fear in my heart, I gripped my fishing pole as a weapon, but it would be like beating a ferocious dog with a straw. My thoughts turned to the fish on my stringer. Could that be the source of attraction? Were they bleeding? The eerie silence churned within me and brought on fears of dying in the watery grave of the Gulf of Mexico. Worse still than death, was the thought of being mangled by the cruel jaws of a hungry killer. I had read many stories of hapless victims literally torn apart by a frenzied shark.

It seemed an eternity as he circled clockwise around me; his black fin never broke the surface. I clenched the fishing pole until my knuckles turned white. Sweat rolled off my forehead as I anticipated his attack.

Suddenly, remembering stories of how dolphins kill sharks by butting them to death, I prayed for one to appear.

The large dark blue form lingered perhaps a few more seconds which seemed like a lifetime. As quickly as he came, he disappeared. With haste, I headed for shore. Somehow fishing just didn't seem very important anymore, especially since I came so close to being caught for lunch myself.

Despite my potentially dangerous encounter with the shark, I hold no malice for them. They are, after all, created for the purpose of filling the needed ecological niche in the water, like the vultures and scavenging hyenas fulfill on land. Without sharks feeding on sick fish and other carcasses, the oceans would perhaps die out through rampant diseases. One must learn to respect the dangers, as well as the beauties of the sea.

On our way north in search for human companionship, I stopped at a crowded beach. On the north end of the beach an attractive, fair haired, young woman who was basking herself in the hot sun caught my eye. I began devising a way to meet her. The more I schemed of telling her how pretty she was and what a lonely traveler I was, the more garbled my thoughts became. As I walked toward her, she raised her head and smiled at me which was totally unexpected and momentarily intimidated me. I chickened out and walked right by her.

Since my first attempt to communicate failed miserably, I decided to use the "old trusted dog routine." Curly tugged on the leash as I pointed him north toward the pretty girl. He circled around and headed south to a blanket with three dignified elderly ladies. As they sunbathed and chattered idly, he sniffed them once or twice, then raised his leg high and hosed down the outstretched legs. The wails and screams—I've never seen such commotion!

"Young man! Is this your dog?" the raspy voice of the infuriated woman asked.

"Who, me? That's not my dog!" I turned away with hasty steps. From a safe distance I called Curly. My plans to meet the pretty young girl were momentarily forgotten.

As I drove out of the parking lot, I could see the pretty blonde girl from the corner of my eye, raising her arm as if to wave to me. To this day I often wonder, "Did she just straighten her hair, or was she really waving goodby to me?" Perhaps she too was lonely like me.

Most of northern Florida is covered by pine forests. The strong odor of paper mills can be detected for miles in this area.

The quiet town of Port St. Joe, on the northwest panhandle of Florida, wasn't always this quiet. It was one of the bustling port cities back in the 1800's. Relentless storms filled the harbor with sand and it was a seaport no more. Many people left the city in search of new jobs. Though its hayday and glory is now past, thanks to the ingenuity of its remaining people, the town is striving well.

As night fell we pulled into a little park, close to where the great wharf once was, and prepared to spend the night. Out on the dark water, I could still see the remnants of the docks. Old rotten pile logs protruding from beneath the dark sea still attest to its great past.

As darkness engulfed my Ghost Ship, I felt watched by a thousand eyes. Even Curly seemed uneasy. That restless night my mind created ghosts of pirates marching out of the darkness along with the brawling sailors, drinking, swearing, and boasting of their conquests. It was a place of violence and excitement. Past history of fearless men who risked their lives in the often stormy seas are now mostly forgotten.

The piercing rays of the morning sun shining through the porthole window of the Ghost Ship forced me out of my strange dreams. Thoughts of my girlfriend, Becki, made me a little homesick, so that morning I wrote her a long letter.

Three young guys drove up to the pier in a red chevy truck with a motor boat in tow. I watched as they backed the boat down the ramp expertly and decided to shoot the breeze with them.

"Hey guys, how do you catch fish around here?"

The tallest of the three, with reddish hair, seemed to be in charge. He looked at me and said with a southern drawl, "You'll never catch anything here. You have to go out a ways."

"Well, hope you guys have better luck than me," I said hoping they'd ask me to come along.

After talking among themselves the younger of the three turned to me, "If you'd like to come fishing, my brother said you're welcome to join us."

Not being one for hesitation I jumped at the chance. Off we were trolling the Gulf of Mexico. The boat was small, but served its purpose well for catching smaller fish. As my line tightened, I jerked with all my might. The moment's excitement reminded me of "Islands In The Stream", a book written by my favorite author, Ernest Hemingway. I imagined that it was a huge swordfish on my line, nearly pulling me off the boat, even if it was only a two pound mackerel.

In less than an hour we caught nearly a dozen fish. When the fish quit biting in one area, we'd follow the flocks of seagulls and the fish started biting again. It seemed to always work. In exchange for the day's fishing, I entertained the guys with stories of my travels and adventures. Before the day was over, we caught about twenty sea trout, 4 to 8 pounds each, and a dozen other edible varieties.

The guys who were perhaps descendants of sailors of the old Port St. Joe were really decent and I thanked them for inviting me fishing. They refused my offer of gas money and gave me a good part of the day's catch. I was eating fish for the next three days.

The beautiful beaches of Panama City hold unhappy memories for Curly and me. I haven't decided yet who, if either of us, came out ahead. After leaving Curly locked in the van, I joined some newly acquired friends at a gathering. The hours passed quickly, as I enjoyed being in the company of friendly people. Most of my time was spent visiting with a young girl who reminded me a lot of Becki. She was interested in my travels and as the evening ended, she accompanied me back to the van to see the famous Ghost Ship.

As I opened the door, a terrible stench reached my nose. Curly acted guilty as he huddled on the bed. My green velvet bedspread was covered with brown paw marks, as was the front seat, dashboard, and the whole length of my van.

Angrily I threw Curly outside, scolding him loudly. He caused me nothing but problems, that undeserving dog! I felt like beating some sense in him.

Too angry to be embarrassed with the condition of the Ghost Ship, I temporarily forgot about my ladyfriend, whom I rudely left standing outside. After realizing my ill manner, I climbed out to apologize for my behavior. The surprise was on me. There was no one to apologize to. I was left abandoned with my stinking Ghost Ship.

The tedious and unpleasant task of cleaning up the mess began. Into a bucket of cold water I added cups of Tide and Ajax detergent and started scrubbing the carpet. It was well after midnight before I was through. The bad odor still persisted, but by sprinkling my Musk cologne all over the carpet, it helped to disguise the still lingering smells.

With my anger released, I thought of the run-down condition of Curly due to traveling and my heart went out to him. It really wasn't his fault that he got sick. I called for him, but he was nowhere in sight. During the next three days I met a beautiful southern gal at the college in Panama City who helped to search for my little buddy, but with no luck. (Clara and I were to have a warm relationship in future years.)

After 4 memorable weeks of sun, beaches, adventures, and the loss of my companion, I sadly left Florida behind.

The Ghost Ship rumbled through Alabama, Mississippi, and finally over the border of Louisiana.

On my way to New Orleans many young people spoke to me with excitement of the upcoming Mardi Gras. Their conversation reeled with the anticipation of this special celebration. I watched them as they thumbed rides along the roads for the past 150 miles.

When I saw New Orleans for the first time, the city didn't seem much different than other large metropolises. In the distance the sun's rays reflected off the world famous Superdome. The downtown area of the city took on a unique flavor. The character of New Orleans came alive. The architecture of the many 18th century buildings was unique. Wrought iron fences encompassed spacious green lawns in this exclusive section of town. The street suddenly narrowed till there was barely enough room for one vehicle to pass through. Two story buildings sporting large decorative balconies lined the streets. Throngs of people were all about, milling on the sidewalks and peering down from the balconies. Street vendors loudly announced their goods as people collected around their carts. The smell of food and incense hung in the air. This place reminded me of being back in Europe again. I caught a glimpse of a horse drawn buggy coming down Bourbon Street. This was the French Quarter that I had heard so much about.

Slowly I inched my way forward, looking over peoples' heads from the vantage point of the high seat of my Ghost Ship. One end of the street was blocked off and a large crowd had gathered. Police were keeping the crowds behind barricades. Cheers came from the many spectators as the first float came around the far end of the block. This must be the Mardi Gras—I made it here just in time.

Once the Ghost Ship was parked in a safe spot, I explored the many facets of the French Quarter. I peered into the all night shops, restaurants, and topless bars and watched with fascination the ghostly looking nude women. Strangely enough, I met a young man from Akron, Ohio who was a neighbor of my friend, Sherm Schumacher. After a few hours of walking around, I returned to the van and drove to a quiet safe neighborhood and camped for the night.

To avoid any harassment by the police, I was up and on my way at the crack of dawn. I explored other parts of the city, especially the city park. Its huge oak trees, laden with Spanish moss, provided shade from the heat of the day and created a country atmosphere. A noisy group of kids played football on the closely trimmed grass, so a search was made for a quieter section of the park.

At the edge of a pond, I turned off the motor and observed the beautiful scenery. Several mallard ducks rippled the smooth surface of the water. An old man was fishing with his grandson on the far side of the pond. The little boy's laughter reached my ears as the old man played silly antics persuading giggles from him. A young couple passed in front of me hand in hand, totally unaware of anything except each other. It was a quiet, but somehow lonely spot.

My thoughts were interrupted as a car pulled up near me. A young girl in her middle 20's stepped out and proceeded to unlock the trunk of her car and remove a folded up bicycle. As she bent over, her long brown hair rolled off her shoulders and swept the bumper. She was an average-looking girl of medium height with a learned quality about her. I thought she looked sexy in her beige, tight-fitting sweater, which revealed an ample bustline. The bike was quickly assembled and she rode off through the park.

The Ghost Ship needed a thorough cleaning, so that afternoon held the tedious job of washing off the journey's accumulated dust. Upon its completion, the cleaning continued inside. A nasty habit of mine was leaving items where I dropped them. In other words, I am not very good at picking up after myself. It seemed like every couple of days the interior of the Ghost Ship desperately needed a woman's touch.

While washing the porthole windows, I saw the young woman on the bike return. As she drove by, I stuck my head out through the door and boldly said "hello". She circled back and introduced herself. Jan asked me if I was here for the Mardi Gras. I told her of my dislike for large crowds, but might stay for a couple of days anyway. We parted at dusk, but the following day I heard her familiar voice once again.

"Hi there Pete. How you doing today?"

We talked as if we were old friends.

"Sure hope I can convince you to stay around for the big parades. They will be starting before the end of the week."

"I'm beginning to like New Orleans. You know, I might stay awhile."

She invited me to drive my Ghost Ship to the protective shelter of her home. Jan lived on the second floor of a huge 18th century two-story mansion. A five foot tall wrought iron fence surrounded the grounds. After we pulled in the drive, she opened the heavy steel gate and we drove in. Beyond the gate everything was draped by the cool patchy shadows of trees and the well trimmed shrubs. The cobblestone drive which extended halfway around the building was more like a giant patio. I was amazed at the huge building with large white pillars at its front entrance. It looked more like a museum and it was beyond me how one family could own such a big house.

Two big dogs, with tails wagging, came running to meet Jan, but as soon as they saw me they started barking and growling. Now I'm not generally afraid of dogs, but I was a bit apprehensive that they might attack me. Jan held them at bay while her landlord, a tall thin man with silvery hair, came running out and locked the dogs in the backyard.

Jan ushered me toward the safety of her apartment. We walked to the back of the house and climbed the narrow wooden steps. When we got to the top to the balcony overlooking the backyard, we could see the dogs running around below like lions on the prowl.

Dusk was approaching as we entered the side door that led to her apartment. We felt our way through the now dark hall.

"Boy this place looks spooky. Do you always leave the door unlocked? Aren't you afraid someone might come in here and get you? They could be waiting for you in the dark."

"No," Jan said confidently, "this place is safe. The dogs protect it. Believe me, my landlord and the five foot high fence keeps everyone out."

The large empty hall and adjacent rooms gave me a feeling of uneasiness and I even suggested to Jan that we check the place over to make sure that no one was in there. She just laughed.

"There's nothing to worry about, Pete," she said calmly.

The irony of it was, here I was thinking of searching for someone, when for all Jan knew, I could have been a maniac myself. She had a great trust for me and her judgment of character was good.

"Why don't they rent out some of these large empty rooms?"

"Heck, the landlord doesn't need money. The only reason he rents me the upstairs is because he knows my parents. They're good friends."

After walking through several rooms we came to the back entrance of her apartment which led into the bathroom. This room was so large that it seemed more like a living room. On the linoleum covered floor set an antique cream colored tub that stood on four legs with a large blue towel hung over its side. Pantyhose hung unevenly from the towel rack.

We stepped into a large living room covered with thick brown shag carpet. A comfortable couch and a TV were partly hidden by the many plants; this room, as the other ones, looked more like a greenhouse with plants everywhere. The spacious apartment had a certain feminine charm. Though a bit untidy it had a kind of warm, lived in look. Jan made me feel very comfortable as we played chess and talked most of the evening.

A month had elapsed since I had had a real bath so before the evening had ended, I relaxed in a refreshing tub of hot water. Sponge baths are quite efficient for cleansing, but no comparison to the comforts and enjoyment of a tub.

The next morning we checked the time for the arrival of the large floats and parades. We rode bicycles and viewed the thousands of people lining the parade route. Suddenly there was a roar from the crowd as the marching bands came into view.

Half a dozen bands passed before the huge floats came into sight. There were four floats in all. The first was a dragon shooting flames and smoke from his nostrils. People who rode on top of the float threw souvenirs to the crowds. Suddenly a coin came rolling by our bikes. Six people rushed for it, but Jan quickly managed to stomp her foot over it. Proudly she showed me an aluminum coin the size of a silver dollar.

As Jan watched my bike, I pushed my way into the crowd. A dozen black kids came running along the side of the float yelling, "Hey, mister! Hey, mister! Throw me a doubloon!" Their voices together echoed with the throngs.

Many of the spectators reached their hands high in the air begging. The result was many aluminum coins and hundreds of brightly colored beads were thrown to them.

Before long I was getting the hang of it by pushing, shoving, and fighting for coins, beads, and other collectible items. That evening we went home with many souvenirs. My posterior was so sore from the small seat of the bike that the next day I couldn't even sit down, so we followed the gala procession on foot.

The better part of the next ten days were spent chasing after the wild and colorful parades. The floats, one more elaborate than the next, went clanging by as we mingled with the throngs of happy exuberant people. We collected many more doubloons, piles of beads, and other collectibles of the Mardi Gras.

The next morning I said goodby to my intelligent friend and was on my way heading west. I had spent two weeks in New Orleans with Jan. She was a kind understanding person and it was hard to say goodby to her.

It took the better part of the day to make my way through Baton Rouge, Crowley, Lake Charles, and Port Arthur before arriving on the beautiful beaches of Galveston, Texas. A friendly bulldog that I found lost on the beaches became my new traveling companion.

It was here that an attractive redhead wanted to travel to California with me. She confided in me of the trouble she was having with her beautiful girlfriend who stole all her boyfriends away. She tried to prevent me from meeting her for fear it might happen again. So many people in this world have insecurities like this pretty redhead. Many of us go through life being too critical of our shortcomings, while in reality, everybody has their faults. We should try to be satisfied with being the best we can be and to be proud of ourselves.

On the day of my departure we had plans to meet on the beach. I waited for her, but she didn't show.

Because of the gas war in Galveston, the gasoline price was 19.9 a gallon, low even for February 1972. I filled up before heading south toward Mexico.

Corpus Christi sticks out in my mind because this is where a second homosexual accosted me. Again I had to be tormented with ugly suggestive remarks. Since I promised myself that the next homosexual that bothered me would get knocked on his can, I doubled up my fist. The tall sickly-looking man appeared to be near 50 years old. He might have a heart attack if I hit him too hard or worse yet he might even die. I changed my mind and just got the hell out of there.

That same day I drove into Brownsville which is separated by the Rio Grande from Matamoros, Mexico. The only difference between these 2 towns was the language. In Mexico signs were in Spanish, in Brownsville they were in English. My observation was that people were the same on both sides of the border. Besides a few tourists, they seemed to be mostly Mexican—a dark complected and handsome people. The majority of them had Indian ancestry.

After finding a parking place close to the border entrance, I parked the Ghost Ship, tied Bull out with plenty of food and water, and put him on guard duty. My next two days were spent commuting across the border using the mass transit system and trusted legs. I didn't drive into Mexico for fear of the border guards tearing apart the van searching for contrabands I didn't have.

Contrary to reports I heard, no one bothered me except for some kids that tried to sell me their sister for $20. I sat on a bench in the well landscaped city square of Matamoros and ate a dinner of fruits. Many people here were friendly and my heart went out to them because of the poverty they were forced to live in. As most tourists, I indulged in buying some inexpensive souvenirs.

On my way back to the border, a taxi-driver tried to sell me grass and assorted drugs. Since I don't believe in artificial stimulants (I'm crazy enough without drugs), this offer was declined. Undercover cops try to sell drugs to unwary Americans and throw them in jail as they cross the border with the goods.

When traveling alone for a long while one loses his sense of identity. Earlier I arranged with Becki to send my mail to Brownsville and with her letters, I regained my identity once more.

On my leisure trip through the vastness of Texas, New Mexico, and Arizona, I often thought about Becki and the good times we spent at her parent's house watching Star Trek and my all time favorite nature show Wild Kingdom. Becki's mother, Mrs. Kawczk, always treated me like a member of the family especially since my own parents and half my family moved to southern California.

The wonders of the southwest deserts with its huge cactus and wind blown sand captivated me. This was a place of beauty and tranquility, but still foreign to a northeasterner who was used to green meadows and many trees. At times I felt out of place, a foreigner to this desert region.

Ever so slowly I was getting tired of this endless arid wasteland. The sun has parched the land until the vegetation matches the coloration of the brown hillsides. It was beyond me how a dead-looking place like this could be so teaming with life—many deer, coyote, and other creatures abound here.

54

A crane lowers as Toth directs the now half-finished Indian monument onto steel rods which protrude from a cement base. This process is used to reinforce and help preserve the wooden sculptures on a permanent foundation. This method allows air to circulate around the monument and has been in use since late 1974. (photo by Robert Bower, The Post-Register)

PART SIX – MONUMENTS

NO. 1 MONUMENT (STONE)
La Jolla, California—Feb. 1972

After nearly 2 months of traveling, I drove into California. It was a good feeling to be so near home—even if I'd never been here in my life.

A fog bank rolled in obstructing my first view of the Pacific, but as I wound north toward La Jolla (a San Diego suburb) where my parents and brother Tony, wife Erika, and kids lived, the fog slowly rose. From about a quarter-of-a-mile distance, I finally got my first glimpse of the majestic Pacific.

Two blocks from the ocean I stopped at my brother's home where his older children Becka, Donny, and Lydia came running out to greet me. "Uncle Pete! Uncle Pete!" My mom and dad who owned the house next door were happy to see me too.

It was great to see everyone. The kids had sure grown since two years ago when I saw them last.

Surrounding my parent's and Tony's spacious homes were tropical gardens with beautiful flowers of assorted colors which were my mom's pride and joy.

The next few weeks were spent by the Pacific. The sandy beaches were outlined with rugged cliffs that in places rose to a height of fifty feet. A lot of my time was spent down here walking Bull and fishing with my brother's kids.

One evening while I was at Wind & Sea Beach watching the sunset, a protruding cliff caught my attention. In the fading light I saw a shadowy image of a face in the stone. That image haunted me for days.

There were tales of a place called Sunset Cliffs where girls bathed in the buff. This sounded like my kind of place and once I discovered it, much of my time was spent there. It seemed the weekends were the best time to go girl-watching. On weekdays a guy had to be careful of homosexuals hanging around. Nudity is considered sinful by many religious people, but to me there is nothing evil about the human body. God's creation, especially barebreasted women, have always been greatly admired.

On a Sunday morning while everyone in the family was at church, Bull

55

and I were at Sunset Cliffs beach swimming, sunbathing, and girl-watching. Suddenly the peaceful morning was shattered! I heard whistles blowing and cops started coming down trying to arrest us. It seemed like the cops were scampering after the good-looking naked chicks. I don't blame them, I'd have done the same thing too.

In all the confusion and the mass arrest I got away, but Bull got lost. Most of the afternoon and the next several days were spent searching for him, but to no avail.

With the loss of my pet Bull, and the closing of the nudist beaches, Sunset Cliff and Black's Beach, my interest turned to the cliffside with the hidden face.

One evening while cleaning the van I came across my machine shop chisels and hammer. Why not try to use these chisels on the stone cliff where an image of a face haunted me? After all, they won't be used in the shop again.

I took my tools to the beach and examined the cliffside. I didn't have any idea of where or how to begin, so I went ahead and practiced on a small version first. Its completion encouraged me to begin on the cliff. With chisels in hand I started chipping away.

Weeks were spent on the cliffside. At times I felt like giving up, the work was hard and the progress slow. Frustration and anger at my lack of skill was at times my sole motivation, but the figure of the haunting face slowly emerged from the stone. The left cheek was marred with a line from natural erosion, but I just left it natural to give him more character.

My girlfriend, Becki, and I missed each other so she flew out to see me. At the San Diego airport she hugged me.

"Peter, you look so different!" she said. "The sun has really bleached out your hair and you've a great tan. It's like hugging a stranger!"

"Well, you're looking great yourself," I told her.

We were both happy to see each other and had nearly a half year to catch up on. She could only stay a week because of her secretarial job, so our short time was spent at Sea World, the San Diego Zoo, and other attractions.

I could hardly wait to see the expression on Becki's face when she saw my sculpture.

"I didn't know you could sculpt, Pete!" she said with amazement.

"Well, neither did I."

We spent a lot of time on the beach. Part of this time she watched me work on the cliff and occasionally we'd go in for a swim.

One day we watched three guys body surfing at the La Jolla Cove. Since I was a good swimmer, why not try body surfing? Shortly after joining the group, a rip tide carried me dangerously close to the rocky shore. I didn't realize that the other guys had flippers on and effortlessly outmaneuvered the wild surf. The waves were getting bigger and the strong currents carried me within a few feet of the rugged shoreline. By now I was at the mercy of the rip tide, helplessly bounced against the rocks by the raging sea. There was hardly time for fear, I thought the Pacific was going to claim me as its next victim. (Many people had drowned at this cove I was told.) Luckily for me, an observant lifeguard helped to pull me out and saved my life. Safe on shore I mostly felt silly and terribly embarrassed. All this time Becki never realized the danger I was in.

A couple of days before Becki had to go home an unpleasant episode occurred. After a late movie, we parked the Ghost Ship close to the cove and fell asleep listening to the roar of the ocean. Sometime after midnight we were awakened by loud voices and the flashing light of a police car. The California cops harassed Becki almost to tears and demanded her I.D. and I had a gun pointed at me like a criminal. After this episode Becki was probably ready to go home, but she still cried at the airport.

After Becki flew home I continued working on the large stone sculpture.

The La Jolla newspaper ran a picture of my haunting face sculpture with a caption under it "Mysterious Sculpture—Who made it and why?" They called it a scarfaced Indian.

My sculpture of the "haunting face" may very well have been an Indian, but at the time it could have been white, black, or yellow. The race didn't seem important. Perhaps the paper spoke the truth though; subconsciously I may have sculpted an Indian. I have always felt that the Indians were victims of long abuse and injustice. Even as a boy in Europe I heard of these noble people.

My sculpture "haunting face" with his new found name "scarfaced Indian" and slight fame thanks to the La Jolla newspaper, started attracting more and more visitors. Most people were complimentary and some even amazed. All of a sudden I was considered by some people a sculptor. What a joke! I hardly knew what I was doing!

Not everyone was complimentary though. A young bearded man stopped by and threatened to call the cops on me for defacing the cliffs. Sure enough a police officer appeared the next morning and told me of the complaint he received, but then voiced his approval for my work.

Ever since Becki left, Doris, an attractive, dark complected Ecuadorean girl began stopping by to see me. We grew very fond of each other.

In early May I was finished with the sculpture and Becki's birthday was coming up, so I prepared for my trip back to Ohio. It was hard to say goodby to my family and Doris, who was all broken up about my leaving. She wanted us to get married and settle down in California. Marriage was out of the question until my late 20's because my freedom was too important to give up at this time. I wasn't mature enough for such a major step in my life. I cared for and thought highly of Doris, but I loved Becki.

As a farewell gift from my niece I received a gray squab (baby pigeon) that she found abandoned at the entrance of the San Diego Zoo. No one wanted the poor thing, so guess who was stuck with him?

The Ghost Ship was on the move again, first north to San Francisco, then east across the deserts and mountains.

Somehow the desert and the open space sets a person to thinking and dreaming of great inventions—of houses and even castles to build and books to write. So many things I dreamed of accomplishing.

Haunting face emerging from cliffside. (Photo by the La Jolla Light)

Toth beside finished stone sculpture at Wind & Sea Beach, La Jolla, California. His first sculpture was referred to as the "scarfaced Indian" by the local people.

Beyond the high cliffs and sand blown dunes my mind sees the shadowy figures of the first inhabitants silhouetted against the great canyons. The image of a proud Apache Indian Chief sitting on his painted pony captures my romantic fantasies. When I think of freedom, pride, and dignity, my mind shifts toward the Indians.

On the flat plains of Wyoming and Nebraska, wheat and other crops have replaced the once perennial buffalo grass. Now that the extinction of the great buffalo herds was a near success, herds of cattle graze on the remnants of the open prairies.

Grand Island, Lincoln and Omaha—I've seen all these towns and admired many, but I would rather have seen the Indians free like the wind, hunting the endless herds of buffalo. It saddens me to see these proud people stripped of pride and some reduced to poverty.

Even before I drove into Iowa, the capital of the cornbelt, tiny raindrops fell like tears. I felt an emptiness that's hard to explain and I longed for the understanding smile of a familiar friendly face.

Somewhere east of Fort Wayne, Indiana, I pulled into a country cemetery to rest for a short time. It had been raining for two days, but now the mist that enveloped me stopped momentarily. About twenty headstones of heavy granite and numerous worn markers were visible. The lush green grass, interlaced by tiny wild flowers, flourished in the spring dampness. This was the most peaceful and attractive place I'd seen for many miles.

As the shadows fell, the darkness stole the light of day and the cemetery took on a sad and desolate appearance. The rain drizzled once more, the eeriness of the cemetery unnerved me and this angered me. I cursed the dead that seemed to beckon at my Ghost Ship door. A cemetery with monuments to the dead is a waste. It's the monuments to the living that count. It's wrong to waste good fertile land. People say respect the dead, but it is more important to respect the living. Respect LIFE! We should not try to preserve our remains, but return it to earth. After I'm gone, my living organs will be donated to the sick and less fortunate, and my remains are to be cremated and the ashes cast on a field of wild flowers, so that in death, I may yet nurture life.

This night was restless—the rain wept tears of grief and the wind moaned of past sorrows. I wished I had found a place other than this cemetery to rest my weary soul.

In the morning the sunshine came bursting through.

NO. 2 MONUMENT (WOOD)
AKRON, OHIO—SUMMER OF 1972

After thousands of miles of travel, I was back in Akron and elated at being home. It was May 15th and still most of the trees had not yet leafed. A

60

Akron, Ohio Indian Monument in Sand Run Park. Plywood temporarily attached to top to protect artist from rain. Elm. (photo by Tom Kaib, Plain Dealer)

strange feeling came over me as if I'd been away for ages. Before I left Akron, it was the greatest place to live, but now my perspective had changed. Somehow this place just didn't feel right. The smoke from the rubber factories lingered in the heavy air. Things I never seemed to notice before were now apparent. Buildings looked in need of paint or repair. Was it the city or me that changed? Perhaps for the first time I was seeing things as they really were.

The excitement of running into an old friend was a real possibility, but no one stopped, waved, or said hello.

Becki was overjoyed to see me and even liked the baby pigeon. I made it home just in time for her 20th birthday.

The next few days we drove around re-exploring Akron and its outlying suburbs. It was great to be home, but I felt a little out of place, somewhat like a stranger, even around my remaining family and friends. Where I belonged was not yet clear to me, but I knew it wasn't Akron. It was as if I had outgrown my hometown. I knew, however sad it might be, that my destiny lied elsewhere.

Becki jeopardized her job and spent a warm spring afternoon with me. We drove to the house on Manchester Rd. where I grew up and gazed at Summit Lake, the place where Black Island and a lot of my earlier adventures took place.

Now progress had changed the scenery. Dredging machines had ripped out the swamps and Black Island disappeared beneath the murky waters. Progress had destroyed much of the nesting grounds of the ducks and other wildlife. Some of the cattails are now coming back to provide the needed shelter.

Becki worked five days a week, so this gave me a lot of time to search the area for cliffs or large stones to sculpt.

To save rent, the Ghost Ship remained my home, and was parked mostly by Becki's parent's house. This at times put a strain on my relationship with her brother Paul, but most of the time I got along well with the Kawczk family.

One day while driving through Barberton (a suburb of Akron) I spotted a large maple tree stump beside the road. That evening it was all I could think about. Since I had trouble finding stone, why not use wood?

The stump was on city property and the next day an understanding was worked out with the Barberton city fathers. The finished sculpture would be a gift to the public, like the stone one was in California, so my chiseling began. Working in wood was a pleasant experience. It was much easier chiseling than stone and the unique grain, color, and fragrance pleased me. My media had taken a drastic change from stone to wood—ironically my chisels stayed the same. It was awkward cutting wood with a heavy steel chisel, but after I ground the cutting edge to razor sharpness, it then sunk into the wood with little effort.

After two weeks the stump was transformed into a unique sculpture. Many people came by to see it. Some called it a Native American and others weren't sure what it was, but they seemed to like it all the same. The local newspaper (Akron Beacon Journal) came out to interview me. I told them of my stone, scarfaced Indian in California and my traveling adventures.

A Chip Off Old Stump

Four weeks ago Peter Toth started chipping away at a maple tree stump on Sixth st. in Barberton and his finished product (right) is a sculptured head that has become a tourist attraction as it looks out across Lake Anna. A pigeon, which Toth calls "Chicken," perched on his shoulder as he whittled away and atop the finished work. Toth, 24, is a self-taught artist born in Europe and a resident of this area for the past 13 years. He is a graduate of Norton High School and attended Akron University. Toth lives in a van and likes to travel. He has carved a stone face in a mountain in California and his goal is to sculpt some landmark in each of the 50 states.

When the newspaper article was published many more people came out to meet me. It was an uplifting and flattering feeling to have such favorable response from so many people. It left me with a positive feeling and a new found zeal for working in wood.

Some people asked me to make them private sculptures. I was on cloud 9 and really felt that at least some of my money problems were solved. With hammer swinging, the chips flew most of the summer as I worked on several carvings, some three to eight feet high. But soon I found out that although people enjoyed my sculptures, they liked their money better. One man, for whom I finished a sculpture on his Portage Lake property (beside his $50,000 home), told me afterwards that for payment he'd let me swim anytime in the lake. All my hard work barely payed for the fuel and upkeep of driving the Ghost Ship around.

Eagle created from ponderosa pine, 3 feet high.

(Left to right) 2 ft. cedar abstract, 1 ft. oak Indian, 2 ft. walnut bearded man. Toth sustains himself through the sale of small sculptures. (Photos by Chris Kennell)

Because money wasn't coming in, at times the thought of getting a job crossed my mind, but then I wouldn't be able to give 100% of my time to sculpting. Sculpting was exhausting, but so self-gratifying. From here on, almost none of my sculptings were done for commission, but were done because of a pressing inner need to be creative. After working all day long on a large sculpture, I'd still be fired up with adrenalin because there was a bear, a snake, eagle, elephant, bearded man, or some kind of figure I just "had" to liberate from the wood. Often I would stay up all hours of the night creating nudes, animals, and abstract figures conjured up from the depth of my mind. Creating meant so much more to me than any money or security.

One such abstract creation was "Octobird", a thin, many legged octopuslike creature with a birdlike face. It stood about 3 feet high. One day an older couple stopped in and examined my sculptures and were drawn to Octobird. I needed money for gas and worried about them finding the price too high. Consequently, I asked $85 for it. That $85 meant so much to me because it was one of the first sculptures sold. To celebrate I took Becki out to a restaurant and splurged on a $1.25 chicken dinner. Later friends of the couple told me they would probably have paid several hundred for Octobird, had I not wanted to sell it.

Money was really tight; I did have savings, but that was for my travels. Money was going out, but little was coming in. A local boutique encouraged me to make small carvings for them which I left on consignment. People just loved them, they told me, but few were sold. I was beginning to realize the meaning of a starving artist.

In late July Becki and I took a leisure drive through Akron's Sand Run Park when at the edge of a clearing we spotted a large dead elm tree. After an extensive study of the main trunk, I saw the figure of an Indian in the still solid elm. Some pictures of my other sculptures were shown to the Parks Department who agreed to help remove the top of the tree and my next three months were spent carving on the big twelve foot stump.

At first there was some doubt in my mind, "Could I really liberate the image of an Indian?" Little time was wasted dwelling about my insecurities. With hammer and chisel in hand, I flung myself against the elm and began to work fervently.

By now my trial and error method of sculpting was improving a little. Even though I read much on stone and wood carving, it was still hard for me to apply a book's principles. Small flimsy wood chisels, with plastic and wood handles, quickly fell apart under the relentless pounding of my five-pound steel hammer. I then made a couple of wider steel chisels and gouges which proved very useful and durable. These new tools made my work easier.

Chips were flying and in a couple of months the elm started looking more and more like the Indian that I first envisioned. Becki gave me a lot of hell for spending too much time away from her. She accused me of being married to my work. Some days I was so involved in sculpting that all sense of time was lost and even lunch was often forgotten. I practically lived in Sand

Run Park and worked on a composite of the area Indians.

One evening an attractive girl came by and swore that the unfinished Indian had talked to her. I don't know if she was stoned or not, but it was flattering that she thought the Indian was lifelike enough to speak to her.

A most important idea came to me. If my Indian sculptures could speak to this young girl, then it could speak to others. How many countless others? A trail of these whispering giants across this country could speak to millions of people of the atrocities committed against the Indians.

"I WILL MAKE ONE SCULPTURE OF AN INDIAN IN EACH OF THE FIFTY STATES TO HONOR THEM."

For a long time it was my desire to contribute to humanity. I have always felt that the Indian was a victim of long abuse, prejudice and injustice. The idea of contributing to the Indian cause was brewing in the back of my mind for a long time, perhaps years, but now I declared it to be so and talked about it publicly.

"No one gives a damn about the Indian," was the feedback from many people. "Do something more positive and accepted like statues of the pilgrims. Now that's something the country would admire you for."

There are many motivating factors involved in a person's decisions and goals in life, whether it be conscious or subconscious. Because of my own family's past oppression by the communists, I hoped to alleviate some of the problems of the downtrodden. Here was my opportunity to immortalize the good names of some of my heroes like Chief Joseph of the Nez Perce and Osceola of the Seminole, as well as all the Indian people, past and present, that suffered.

One of my modern day heroes, John F. Kennedy, said, "Ask not what your country can do for you, but what you can do for your country." This was a chance to give of myself to America, the greatest country in the world.

*As the Ohio monument was near finished, Tom Kaib, a reporter from the Cleveland Plain Dealer, wrote a story on my work and a color picture of my Indian sculpture appeared on the front cover of the Sunday Plain Dealer Magazine.

Most everyone had favorable comments about the sculpture and the meaning it portrayed. There's always the exception though. A young ecology fanatic, as I later perceived him to be, came and glared at me, and after a few minutes finally spoke.

"Why the hell are you destroying the tree?" he growled.

"How can I destroy something that died years ago?"

Not expecting that rebuttal, he stepped back for a second.

"Well anyway, you should have let it rot away. I like to see trees rot away naturally in the woods," he said defensively.

I met many fine people who wished to help my cause. Some even offered money which to their surprise, I didn't accept. Somehow, I felt that the monument wouldn't be much of a gift if donations were taken.

A middle-aged gentleman by the name of John Stanley visited me on many occasions. He was a real talker who charmed the people with his wit and information about my work. His beard, which looked a little like Colonel Sander's, gave him an artistic look. People often shook his hand. "You're doing a fine job, sir," they complimented him. They must have thought me to be his young apprentice. I didn't mind the attention John received and encouraged him not to keep explaining he wasn't the artist, but to simply say "Thank you."

Portage Trail, a couple blocks from the Indian monument, was the trail used by many Indians to carry their canoes between the lakes. The Ohio Valley was regarded by most Indians as a neutral hunting ground. The Delaware and Wyandot (Huron) Indians were widely known in the area, so I decided to name the monument Delawot. It was in honor of all the Indians, past and present, that lived in and around the state of Ohio.

People with little knowledge of the Ohio Indians have often told me that no Indians have lived in Ohio. They were much surprised to find out that many tribes lived here. To name a few, there was the Erie, Wyandot (Huron), Ottawa, Oneida, Shawnee, Miami, and Conestoga.

The Shawnees raised a famous son, Tecumseh, born near Springfield, Ohio. He grew up to become a great Shawnee Chief with a vision of unifying a vast Indian confederacy. Tirelessly he visited many tribes from the Great Lakes to the Gulf of Mexico, but met limited success. Tecumseh was a hero to his people and so feared by his enemies that the mere mention of his name (as a participant in fighting) was said to have won battles.

Tecumseh was respected for his bravery and humanitarianism. Because his father and two brothers were killed in battles with whites, he hated all settlers. (One brother was killed fighting beside Tecumseh in the well documented Mad Anthony Wayne's Battle of the Fallen Timber.) He would never harm women or children and was against the tribal tradition of torturing the prisoners and influenced his people to do away with all torture. In his failure and disillusionment in unifying the fragmented tribes, he joined the British Army and was commissioned a brigadier general. At the age of 45, in 1813, Tecumseh was killed at the head of his warriors in the fight against American Naval Officer, Oliver H. Perry. General W. Harrison called Tecumseh an uncommon genius and one of the most admired leaders in our history.

At one time the Ohio Valley was the heart of the ancient Hopewell culture. Little is known of these mound-builders except that they had a well organized society, led by the elite, upper class. Archaeologists believe that over 2000 years ago they had craft unions or guilds for carvers and traders.

Perhaps even more mysterious was the Adina culture that pushed their way into Ohio, Pennsylvania, and New York some 3000 years ago. These ancients were giants; archaeologists claim women near 6 feet tall and men 7 feet. It is believed the Adina culture was destroyed or assimilated some fifteen centuries later by the more powerful Hopewell. We can only speculate what happened to them, the mystery continues unsolved.

Joanne Dobbins helped to bring about the small dedication ceremony of the sculpture. With the Ohio Indian monument now finished, my plan was to follow the seasons—go south in winter and north in summer.

Here's Becky Kawczk with two other Toth sculptures, a Madonna in Barberton and an Indian head at Lake Milton.

NO. 3 MONUMENT
De LAND, FLORIDA—JAN. 1973

The cold winter loomed ahead so my logical decision was to head for Florida. Becki worked out a plan with her boss to take an early vacation and drive down with me. Her companionship made the prior long lonesome road an enjoyable trip.

Her employer was getting tired of giving her time off. In late May she took a few days off and drove to Cape Cod, Massachusetts with me. Here we acquired a seagull with a broken wing that became my pet.

Now, on this long trip south, the seagull and pigeon were getting on Becki's nerves and she had a hard time adjusting to roughing it in the Ghost Ship. She was anxious to get to sunny Florida for a week's vacation to recuperate from her parent's divorce.

We had a blast on our vacation on Florida's East coast around Daytona Beach. One morning while collecting seashells, we found a large fish, about 4 feet head-to-fin. It was a bit decomposed. Holding my nose, I tied a rope on his tail and dragged him a little distance behind me.

People gasped, "You caught that fish?"

"Sure did!" was my reply. I may have caught him out of the water, dead and stinking, but caught he was, nonetheless.

The wind whipped up and it turned cold. The damp ocean air made the cool wind really chilly, so we put on coats and sweaters. Even in Florida it gets cold at times in the winter.

We spotted a number of large trees around Daytona, cypress and oak, but because of the lack of leaves, it was hard to determine if they were dead or alive.

Becki's vacation was over and she had to get back to work, so I put her on a jet and sent her off with a kiss. My search went ahead in full gear for a suitable dead tree to make the monument from.

A state park west of Daytona looked promising; the park's director seemed quite impressed and desirable to have my monument for his park. We just couldn't find a large enough tree among the thousands of small diameter oaks and pine.

Still searching and a bit disappointed, I drove around and wound up in De Land. Beside the Stetson University's parking lot, I spotted a medium size oak stump. My decision was to use this for the Florida monument.

Early the next day I went to see the Dean of the University and with his blessing was chiseling on the stump the same day. The size of this sculpture was less than 10 feet in height and near 30 inches in diameter. Still I was elated because this was the third state where my monument would stand in honor of the Indians.

Since this sculpture would be smaller, in the future I would make another one for Florida, much larger.

Stetson University is nestled among the pine forests of east central Florida. Founded in 1883, it's the state's oldest institution of higher education. This University is named in honor of John B. Stetson, the famous hat manufacturer. The College of Law was organized in 1900, the first law school in Florida. More than 30 buildings house the activities of the De Land Campus.

Never having lived on campus before, I observed the daily life of the live-in student and found it was mostly routine. I didn't miss much by living at home while attending classes at the University of Akron. Even though the Ghost Ship was my home, I was given permission to use the University's facilities and took advantage of the inexpensive lunches in the cafeteria.

Several families in De Land invited me for meals and this helped to reduce my grocery bills. A Hungarian family had me over for a great chicken paprikas dinner. This Hungarian dish reminded me of those very special occasions back in Hungary when my mother would cook goulash and paprikas for the hungry Toth family. Although in those hard times, the only meat in the stew was enough to give it flavor, certainly not like the American version with several pounds of meat.

Much of my research on Florida's history was done at the University's elaborate library. Osceola and the Seminoles first came to mind because of their intensive resistance against the forces of the U.S. military during 1835-1842. They fought years of fierce battles in the everglade swamps of Florida. Still most Indians that were not killed were forcibly removed to Oklahoma. Even today some Seminoles refuse to admit defeat and live on a reservation in southern Florida.

The three major tribes that vanished from Florida were the Calusa, Timucua, and the Apalachee. The Calusa gained wealth from gold that washed ashore from Spanish shipwrecks. These Indians were seafarers who established regular trade with Havana by the year 1600. They dominated the Gulf Coast from their village Tampa (some 70 miles south of the modern city) to the Keys. In the 18th century, defeated, they were driven into the Keys and by 1763 the tribe numbering 350 was removed to Havana by the English. The small number of Indians that remained, lost their tribal identity. The once powerful Calusa suffered the same fate as the Timucua and Apalachee—vanished into oblivion.

The warm subtropical climate of Florida attracted many settlers. In his search for the fantasized "Fountain of Youth", Ponce de Leon was the first European to see Florida in 1513. France, Spain, and Britain settled, fought over, and claimed Florida. Spain finally ceded Florida to the U.S. in 1819.

*Looking back, I must have been a strange sight sculpting with a big hammer and chisel on an Indian with two pet birds watching me. I made friends quickly though and was invited to dances and parties. Some evenings when I wasn't working on my small carvings, I'd be playing chess with the local students.

During my one month stay in De Land, I worked long hours on the sculpture, at times from sunup till sundown. Slowly the form of an Indian brave appeared.

Several of my student friends told me about the art professor that was on vacation and would be back in a few days.

70

"Man, won't he be impressed!" one of the students said. "None of his students ever made a sculpture so impressive and large. He'll be out here every day watching your progress and advising you."

The professor never showed; not once during my stay.

Later that year, they thought so highly of my Indian monument that it was pictured on the front cover of the Stetson University yearbook. It was an honor for my work, as well as the American Indian cause.

Some of the feedback from the students was that the art professor was outraged! As one of my friends later told me, "He called your Indian a worthless junk and wondered why they didn't pick one of his sculptures for the cover, or at least one of his student's works." Now I understood why the professor never came out to visit me.

In a little over a month's time I was finished with the sculpture and headed toward my next state. Georgia was on my mind.

NO. 4 MONUMENT
COLQUITT, GEORGIA—FEB. 1973

It was still the dead of winter in early February, but strangely enough I was heading north. Georgia is a big state with many important cities. Such were Atlanta, Columbus, Macon, and Savannah, but I was looking more at the smaller southern cities like Albany, Bainbridge, Valdosta, and Waycross by the Okefenakee Swamps. There must be a suitable location for an Indian sculpture somewhere in Georgia.

Though I entered Georgia blindly, my eyes were on Lake Seminole, bordered by Bainbridge, Georgia and Chattahoochee, Florida. The lake was beautiful, but too isolated to place my monument there.

My search continued for a tree through many towns without much luck. On my way north toward Blakely on Highway 27,.I wound up in the small town of Colquitt. In front of a youth center was the largest oak tree that I'd seen in a long while. My decision was immediate to use the big dying oak for an Indian monument. After a lengthy meeting with Charles Bevis and the town's officials, work started on the big oak. It was agreed that the Ghost Ship could be parked beside the youth center building and water and electricity furnished.

The February weather was surprisingly warm, near 80 degrees. In the following days there was little warning as northern gales deposited several inches of snow. Some people seemed confused at the white slippery stuff, while others were elated and made snowmen and took pictures of the rare snow. People told me that it snows in Colquitt once every ten years or so. It had to snow just when I was here. This crazy cold weather finally caught up with me from the North. Fortunately, the snow didn't last long and in a couple of days the sun's warmth melted the small remaining patches.

Northern Georgia is a little colder and has more frequent snow in the winter, but the over five million people living in this state experience a hot and humid climate much of the year.

De Land, Florida Indian Monument located on campus at Stetson University. Oak.

"War Cries"
Peter's oak creation is on display at the Lincoln Indian Center in Lincoln,
Nebraska (height 4 ft.)

Colquitt, Georgia Indian Monument. Charles Bevis standing at base beside Highway 27. Oak.

As in most warm climate areas, a large number of Indians lived in Georgia. The Cherokees extended into the North, while the Apalachicola, Yamasee, and Hitchiti lived in the South. The powerful Creek Confederacy controlled most of central Georgia and Alabama. As in most eastern states in the 1700-1800's, the Indians were tricked to sell their land, or if that did not work some excuse was made to move them forcibly.

The "Indian Removal Act" was signed into law by ex-Indian fighter President Andrew Jackson on May 28, 1830, followed by much sorrow, tears, and death to thousands of Indians on the force march to Oklahoma. History remembers this sad event as the "Trail of Tears." The Indian tribes of Georgia, as well as all tribes east of the Mississippi River, were to cede their land in exchange for territory in the West.

With my thoughts on the many injustices done to the Indian, I worked fervently chipping away at the thick oak bark. A big friendly black man came to cut out the top of the tree. The huge branches were dropped to the ground, leaving a 23 foot high, 4 foot diameter stump.

During my two month stay in Colquitt sculpting on the Indian, I came to know many of the over 2,000 people in this community. Some seemed a bit puzzled at my presence. A local girlfriend told me rumors were circulating around the local beauty parlor that I was an undercover agent on a spying mission and just doing my sculpting as a cover-up. What I could have possibly been spying on in a little town is beyond me.

People came by often and asked many questions about my project. One morning while working off a 20 foot ladder, my support rope came loose and in a split second I plummeted to the ground, fortunately landing on my feet unhurt. A man across the street watched wide-eyed and turned away in disgust. It was apparent that he thought I was showing off. What he didn't realize is what a lucky klutz I was—my neck could have been broken.

It was a fact that I was a northerner in the land of the rebels and detected animosity against the Yankees in a few people. With my past travels in the South, I have seen the evidence in graveyards and still felt the scars of the Civil War.

At a neighboring roller skating rink I was refused entry because my hair was too long; a thing long overlooked up North by the year 1973. As soon as people understood my mission of the whispering giants, even the ones that seemed indifferent, literally opened their doors to me. Many asked me over for dinner. The unmatched southern hospitality was in full evidence.

One neighbor lady asked me over for chitlings—fried hog guts cut in small bits that smelled most unsavory. I decided chicken was more my style of food.

"Don't worry, Pete," she assured me. "You have to acquire a taste for chitling."

A friend, Wally, invited me over to her family's house on the outskirts of town. Her mother Faye, father, and family just about adopted me. Some of the finest and best home cooked meals I ever had were with the Roberts. Her brother Brad and I fished with a gill net in a swollen creek and caught several good sized fish. Brad told me of the time a 3 foot alligator was tangled in his net. With a knife he cut him loose. It seemed like no matter what part of the nation or the world one might live in, adventure and excitement can always be found.

For over a month I had been working on the monument and in the course of that time several newspapers interviewed me and wrote complimentary articles on my endeavor to honor the Indians. One Cherokee Indian lady took much pain in interviewing me for a magazine.

"You know, Peter," she said, "my observation is that people are most proud of their Indian heritage when it's only 10 to 40%, in contrast to full-blooded Indians who may at times tragically feel less proud of their heritage.

As the monument was nearly finished Doug Odom, a blonde man from Dothan, Alabama stopped by. He was most impressed with my work and tried hard to convince me to make the next Indian monument for his hometown.

"You can choose the spot and we'll have it placed there for you," he assured me. "If you should decide to make it for Dothan, we'll see to it that everything will be provided, log, varnish, et cetera. Also, we can probably get Governor George Wallace for the dedication."

The Indian monument was now finished for Georgia, so with my invitation to Dothan, Alabama, I set to packing and sadly said goodby to all the good friends I made in Colquitt. It was like leaving my hometown behind.

Throughout my travels many people have asked me, "Peter, what state did you like the most?" I would often explain that it would be unfair for me to make a choice because each state influenced me differently. On this subject my decision would weigh heavily on the pretty ladies I would meet.

Somehow I always romanticized about the South and admit with no regret that my heart was left in Georgia. She was warm, gentle, pretty as a dream and how well I hid my sorrow when it was time to go. She stood alone and watched me go with the rising sun and the sparkling morning dew. The yellow wild flowers growing around the old oak tree and the emptiness in my heart beckoned my return, but the overpowering mission of the whispering giants and the long lonesome road carried me away. . . .

NO. 5 MONUMENT
DOTHAN, ALABAMA—APRIL, 1973

This was my second visit to Alabama, so I didn't feel like a complete stranger. Dothan is a city of over 36,000, located in the southeastern part of the state. It was quite a change from my last two small towns. Dothan was a fair size modern city, but even with the heavier traffic and more people, it had a small town flavor.

In a week we had a large oak tree located that had to be removed because of impending construction. A new building was to be erected on the site. Even before the tree was cut, I was debarking it and chiseling into the still green wood. The sticky sap bled from the tree and got in my hair and all

Dothan, Alabama Indian Monument, located downtown beside the Houston Memorial Library. Oak.

over my clothes. The city crew used a cherry picker to cut the top off and my work went ahead in full gear on the remaining 20 foot oak.

My sculpting took place between two large buildings. Consequently, the visibility to the passing motorists was very poor, however the news media really took an interest. For a time, the local cable TV ran daily pictures of the monument along with extensive TV and newspaper coverage.

I was forced to pay the price of a celebrity. Several girls visited me; none more frequently than two cute blonde girls. Almost every day, like clockwork, they would stop by after school to say "hi" to me, giggle, and carry on. These two girls (whom I thought were twins) couldn't have been more than 14 years old, but by their action of crowding me, literally rubbing up against me, it was a fair assumption they both had a crush on me. Unfortunately they were too young and much overweight. It was presenting a problem. It would have been very easy to tell them not to crowd me or even to get lost, but I just didn't have the heart to be cruel (they were too sweet).

Once or twice a week a class of twenty to fifty kids would come out to view my work and ask me questions on my endeavors. After such a session, a cute little black girl (5th grade) gave me a note with a phone number informing me that she had a pretty older sister and if I'd marry her then I would be her brother-in-law. I was surprised at her forwardness, but was also flattered that she wanted to be part of my life.

Many kids, as well as adults, were very kind. A delicious steak dinner was prepared for me by a Sioux Indian woman. A special "thanks" goes to the Lazy Daisy Garden Club whose members took turns bringing me lunch when they heard that my weakness was girls and food. In spite of all these good meals, I didn't gain any weight, probably because the extra calories were burned off from hard work.

The Indians of Alabama had little to worry about concerning obesity because their demanding hard way of life kept them lean. The Coushatta and Alibamu (the state of Alabama is named after them) were displaced and now live in Texas.

The powerful Creek Confederacy consisted of roughly 24,000 people, some of whom had mixed heritage of Spanish, French, and English blood. Though a peaceful agricultural people, they still listened with interest when Tecumseh came amongst them. The great Shawnee Chief mistakenly thought his mother was a Creek and the tribe was proud to be related by blood to this great leader.

Despite their very civilized way of life, they were constantly threatened by the white settlers who called them savages and came flocking to their tribal land. Their 100 or so towns had well built homes even to white settler's standards and soon their Creek homelands were illegally occupied.

About a quarter of the tribe did go on the warpath. In 1813, one thousand warriors wiped out Fort Mims. All but 36 of the 570 inhabitants, including women and children, were massacred. This brought out General Andrew Jackson (not yet President) who marched on the Creeks killing thousands of them in his wake. Finally, when he became President, he perpetrated the final removal of the Creeks, as well as all Indians whether warlike or peaceful, on the forced march west of the Mississippi River called the Trail of Tears. This monument in a small way, will honor all these people who were defending what was legally theirs in the only way they knew how.

Friends from Georgia invited me to drive to an excavated Kolomoki mound where skeletal remains were on display.

A storm started to bear down on Dothan the following day and a twister touched down only a few blocks from me. The rains caused floods, but luckily for me, the only inconvenience was all that rain which slowed my work.

It was almost May when the Indian monument was near completion. The next step was to secure the best location to move the giant sculpture. My choice was to place it on the circle highway around the city, or by the main library. We ran into much resistance and red tape from the highway department, so the decision was to place it in front of the Houston Memorial Library (across the street from the post office).

My impending departure was near, so we had a small dedication with the Mayor and other dignitaries. Governor George Wallace was unable to attend. The previous year an assassin's bullet crippled him as he was campaigning for the Presidency.

Preparations were made to leave. A sculpture was bartered for a tuneup of the Ghost Ship. My seagull was placed in his traveling box, but the pet pigeon would not be coming with me because earlier he decided to take his freedom and flew away. I took mine now and headed north. It was hard to leave all my Georgia and Alabama friends, but my destiny was elsewhere, besides, Becki awaited my return.

TRAVELING

Driving the long trip to Ohio was slow and monotonous, but as I got into Columbus, Georgia, the tempo picked up some. As I cautiously drove through heavy traffic, there was a sudden loud thud and my Ghost Ship lunged forward. Doggone, some fool ran into me! I hit the brakes, stopped to see who hit me, and prepared to call the police. The man that hit me just kept on going.

"You #&?$!" I yelled at him. I jumped back in my seat and tore off after him, cautiously running two red lights. After about a mile chase, I caught up with the bum as he pulled into a tavern parking lot.

"What the hell you doing? You crashed into me and then took off!"

"The dent wasn't too bad," the half inebriated man muttered.

"Not bad!" I said angrily. "Only about $100 damage!"

He told me that he had no money, but he'd be glad to send me his social security check. What was I to do? If the police are called then I'd be stuck here for at least hours or even days testifying in court against this unsavory character.

With the man's promise to send money for the damage, I exchanged addresses and moved on. Not surprisingly, nothing was ever heard from him. The dent wasn't that bad and it wouldn't be too expensive to fix, but what made me so angry was the fact that he just took off and left the scene without even saying he was sorry.

After two more days of hard driving I was back in Ohio in time for Becki's birthday.

We had a happy reunion as Becki told me how much she missed me in the last few months we'd been apart. I assured her that she was missed too, but there was a change coming. There was a guilty feeling deep inside me because of the other girls in different states. We had an agreement that we could both date because it would be unfair if she'd sit home and be lonely while I traveled.

I must admit the girls I met during my travels were driving a wedge between Becki and me. A feeble attempt was made on my behalf to hide the love letters from girls and the fact that occasionally they were answered.

The short time spent in Ohio found me working on abstract and small Indian sculptures that would be used in the future for gas money, as well as something to barter with.

It was during this Ohio visit that I acquired my prized pet crow. He was found in the woods near Doylestown on a search for a supply of wood. Crows are surprisingly very intelligent and this bird soon grew attached to me.

NO. 6 MONUMENT
SHARON, PENNSYLVANIA, I-80 REST AREA
JUNE, 1973

Becki wanted me to stay with her longer, but I had to head for my next state. The closest state to Akron, Ohio was Pennsylvania, so I packed my hammers, chisels, seagull, and baby crow into the Ghost Ship and kissed Becki goodby once again.

Interstate 80 took me toward Pennsylvania and after the smoky steel mills of Youngstown, Ohio, the Ghost Ship crossed into the quiet countryside of my next state.

My first stop was the town of Sharon. After talking with the city officials about my plans they seemed quite receptive and promised to search for a large log.

For several days I drove around the western part of the state conducting my own search from the huge city of Pittsburgh, to the small town of Mercer.

The Keystone State is the 4th most populated state with 11,750,000 residents. Most of the people live on the eastern side of the state in and around the large cities of Philadelphia, Harrisburg, Reading, and Scranton. People here are mostly white, a little over 8% are black and very few are native people (Indians).

Pennsylvania Indian Monument in early stages at its original site in the town of Sharon. It is now permanently displayed at the Rest Area on I-80 by the Ohio border. Elm. (photo by Charles F. Porter, Harold)

Delaware, Susquehanna, and Munsee are some of the Indians that called Pennsylvania their home, some lived here for many hundreds of years before the white man's arrival. One of the most important Indians of the mid 1700's was Chief Shikellamy, an Oneida living in Philadelphia, who conducted many missions of great importance between the Iroquois council and the Pennsylvania governors. He was a real diplomat for his people and settled many disputes, but still the Indians lost their land. Many paid the ultimate price, their lives.

The great Indian wars are now but past history and many Native Americans suffered much humiliation and defeat. Some suffer even today and this is the reason that I was preparing to make the monument to these noble people.

A large dead elm was found near Sharon and my work began. The hot summer days were cooled off by an occasional dip in the nearby Shenango Reservoir. Fortunately, this large body of water was less than half-a-mile from where I was working.

As the sculpture was taking shape, Becki visited me on the weekends. It was a long drive for her to make alone, but we wanted to spend some time together and it was hard for me to get away. Her visits were always pleasurable and I'd proudly show her my progress on the sculpture. It was hard to see her go home Sundays, but in another week she'd return. I loved her very much and often worried for her safety driving alone on the highways.

Many people were coming by to see how the monument was taking shape. Large chips were being removed from the log when I noticed a lady driving slightly over the center line. She seemed so preoccupied watching me chiseling that she touched bumpers with an oncoming car. I felt in some way responsible because the minor accident was probably caused by the sight of my big wooden Indian bust. It must have seemed strange to people to see me sculpting with two big birds watching. They would sit side-by-side on a small log comically trying to ignore each other. The traffic increased, especially after the local paper and a TV talk show interviewed me and my strange pets.

These pets of mine have given me many memories. One hot afternoon I recall sitting down on a nearby log when a loud squawk and a cushioned object was felt under me. Quickly I jumped up to see a flutter of black feathers and an angrily protesting crow jumping around. I felt bad and thought for sure I'd injured the poor bird. After all, 180 pounds on top of a young crow is a deadly crushing weight. Thank heavens he survived, but didn't trust me sitting close to him again.

On some hot afternoons I could be found down at the swimming hole skinny-dipping with a couple of the neighborhood girls. During one such escapade a uniformed man appeared on the shore and started talking to me. In the back of my mind I could read the local headlines, "Sculptor caught skinny-dipping with local girls." The girls quickly moved out to deeper water to hide their nakedness. Their lack of clothes was quite apparent with female undergarments littering the two large outcropping boulders

Toth's unique traveling companions. (photo by Charles F. Porter, Herald)

near shore. The park cop told me how much he liked my sculpture. What relief! He could have caused us a lot of problems, but just left with a grin on his face, probably remembering some of the pranks he pulled when he was young.

As the weeks went by the Indian took on a finished look. The smaller carvings made in the evenings were used to barter with for needed supplies. Others were sold for cash to help pay for food and gas.

This monument was to be moved to the Welcome Center on Interstate 80 (on the northwest corner of Pennsylvania). I was still waiting for the highway dept. to move it, but it was taking them too long and Dunkirk, New York, was awaiting my arrival.

It Happened This Week---by davis

Comic of Toth sculpture that appeared in the local Sharon newspaper.

Finished Pennsylvania sculpture at I-80 rest area. At the taking of picture it was near 20 feet tall, but is now half buried in concrete. (photo by Mrs. James L. Kidwell)

After brushing on the last coat of wood preservative, I said my goodbyes to everyone and drove to the swimming hole one final time. My journey was postponed till dusk because of the heat. That afternoon was spent swimming and in the evening after much hesitation, I drove back to the monument. Two of the neighborhood girls came running out to meet me with hugs and kisses. It was heartwarming to be missed so much; leaving Pennsylvania behind was hard to do.

NO. 7 MONUMENT
DUNKIRK, NEW YORK—AUG., 1973

It seemed like such a long drive to New York state—the road stretched out endlessly. My thoughts drifted to Becki and her anger that my work took me away from her. She was angry about so many things and I couldn't blame her frustration of my obsession with the monuments. My continuous flirtation with girls would be the end of us someday.

The night air was cold and refreshing and kept me from falling asleep as I made my way toward Dunkirk. The rolling hills and flat meadows were similar to my home state of Ohio. It has been my personal experience that most of New York state is quite flat, except for the eastern part where the beautiful Adirondack and Catskill Mountains are located.

Smoking the Peace Pipe.

Dunkirk, New York Indian Monument. Elm. (photo by The Evening Observer)

Besides the mountains, other attractions are New York City, Niagara Falls, Lake Erie, and many historical sites that tourists come flocking to see each year.

The "Empire State" with nearly 18,000,000 people ranks only second in population to California. Contrary to some people's beliefs, New York state, unlike burgeoning New York City, is not overcrowded, but somewhat sparsely populated, especially the northern and central part of the state which has some of the most picturesque parks and countryside. A few areas have retained the natural beauty of the Indian era.

Many of today's Indian people live side-by-side with whites. New York is one of the few eastern states that still has reservations. Most of the Iroquois live on state reservations totaling 87,000 acres in this state. The Mohawk, Cayuga, Oneida, Onondaga, and Seneca were the original five tribes formed into the League of Iroquois. It has been called the first League of Nations. When the Tuscaroras migrated north from North Carolina, they were adopted into the Confederacy which then became the League of Six Nations. It is said to have been founded in the middle 1500's by Deganawidah. Much fighting among the Indians brought on starvation and ruin, but Deganawidah had a dream of uniting the warring tribes and spent much time making his dream a reality.

The Iroquois Confederacy stood above all in war and no tribes north of Mexico ever equaled them. They developed a high civilization with safeguards for ensuring the peace.

The Iroquois held the balance and control of the entire state of New York and their power extended even to the royal courts of Europe. Iroquois chiefs were routinely taken to these countries and treated as royalties. They were also wooed by some of the colonies.

The League of the Iroquois inspired Benjamin Franklin to copy it in planning the federation of States.

It was a rule of the Confederacy that all action taken must be unanimous. With the outbreak of the American Revolution, the decision as to where the Confederacy loyalty should remain was split. Because of the split, the League was dissolved and the tribes went their separate ways. The first League of Nations reigning as the great lords of the forests came to an end.

The Iroquis, as well as many other tribes of New York state, have contributed much to the past and present history of our great Nation. Skenandoah, an Oneida, was loyal to the American Revolution and fought against England, helping the Americans in the border conflicts along the Mohawk River and secured valuable information about English troop movements.

Thayendanega (Joseph Brant) was a colonel in the British army and was the first Mohawk to read and write. Handsome Lake, a Seneca, was a religious teacher attaining great honor in the eyes of his people. He became one of the greatest of Indian prophets.

George Washington is honored by the Seneca even to this day because of his honorable treatment of the Iroquois.

Many Mohawks live in the "Gowanus district" of Brooklyn. These are the skilled high-steel workers who find steady high salaried jobs on construction of some of our tallest buildings and high bridges. With a few individual exceptions, the Mohawks have no fear of "cat walking" along steel girders or working at dizzying heights. Mohawks follow this dangerous vocation as a tribal trade. Many have worked on the Empire State Building, Mackinac and Verrazano bridges, as well as many other giant structures.

Other Indian groups that were mostly forced out or destroyed were the Wappinger Confederacy which consisted of the Kitchawank, Manhattan, Sintsink, Wappinger, and the Wecquaesgeet. The Delaware Confederacy consisting of the Munsee, and thirteen Algonquian groups of Long Island which were the Canarsee, Corchaug, Manhasset, Massapequa, Matinecock, Merrick, Montauk, Nesaquake, Patchogue, Rockaway, Secatogue, Setauket and Shinnecock shared the land of New York. New York also consisted of two miscellaneous tribes, the Mahican and Erie.

So much history passed beneath my tires as I was nearing my destination. A couple of miles outside the city of Dunkirk, population 15,000 located about 40 miles southwest of Buffalo on the shores of Lake Erie, I stepped out to get a closer view of the Great Lake. It was like an ocean so large that I could not see the other side. The water was clear and warm, a great place for a refreshing dip from the sweltering summer heat that was sure to follow the sunrise.

Soon after I got into town the Mayor and city officers showed me the large dead elm that I was to use to sculpt the monument. Since the dead elm tree was still rooted, it was decided to cut the top out and eventually move it to the Waterworks Park. Meanwhile, I unpacked my hammer and chisel and started my seventh monument.

There was no payment involved in my creating this monument and since I had been traveling for nearly two years now, money was tight. But my dream and mission was too important to me to allow money to slow me down. Even if I had to exist on beans and bread, I would finish my mission. Somehow I survived those early days of hardship and hope. It made me a better man.

That afternoon several neighbors gathered around wondering what I was doing.

"You trying to cut down the tree with a chisel?" one inquisitive voice asked.

"Yep! Gonna make some firewood!" I replied jokingly. Soon friends were made and a sympathic neighbor let me throw a long extension cord to his house for electricity. This was a practice I was getting used to. Most of my neighbors didn't accept money for the electricity used, but I paid their kindness back by giving them one of my small carvings.

Dunkirk was a friendly college town and people were good to me, but I never felt that same overwhelming hospitality that was found down south. It wasn't long before a couple of girls started hanging around. They were quickly dispersed by the arrival of Becki who would visit me on the weekends. It was good to have Becki with me even if it was for a few hours a week. We went swimming at Lake Erie Public Beach and had a good time.

There were good reviews from the nearby city of Buffalo and local

DEAN WILLIAMS, right, president of the Seneca Indian Nation, spoke to a large crowd Sunday afternoon as the Indian sculpture was dedicated in Dunkirk. Also pictured are Les Maybee (center) Seneca historian and Dunkirk Mayor Clem Lutz.—(OBSERVER Photo)

CEREMONIAL DANCING AND SINGING added Indian lore and culture to the dedication Sunday afternoon of an Indian sculpture in Dunkirk.—(OBSERVER Photo)

newspapers, radio, and TV. As the news of my work got out, Dean Williams, President of the Seneca Indian Nation, invited me to the reservation. It was a bit disappointing when I found there was no Indian village, as I perceived it to be, but just a lot of modern houses there. Mr. Williams and I had an interesting discussion about his people and after inviting him to the upcoming dedication, I left him with a warm handshake and a gift of one of my small carvings.

While working on the monuments I met many Native Americans, one in particular was a very attractive Seneca Indian girl. We talked in depth of what really happened at Wounded Knee on February 27, 1973 and how the press tried to destroy the credibility of Dennis Banks and the rest of the participating Indians. It was refreshing to talk to such an intelligent young lady who personally witnessed the Wounded Knee Occupation of 73.

Nearly two months had slipped away and with the monument finished and fall coming on I couldn't wait the two weeks for the dedication and had to leave for my next state. I said goodby to my Indian and white friends and headed back to Ohio.

NO. 8 MONUMENT
WHEELING, WEST VIRGINIA—OCT. 1973

Briefly I returned home to Akron to spend a little time with Becki before starting off east toward West Virginia. Moundsville invited me to do my next monument there and it sounded like an ideal town (named for the Indian burial mounds located there). Upon arriving and exploring the community in depth it occurred to me that this area may not be best suitable for my monument. One of the drawbacks was the lack of visibility because not that many people drove through here. With this conclusion I swung the Ghost Ship around and headed toward Wheeling.

It took a meeting with the city's Mayor and councilmen before the search for a large log was under way. A large dead elm was found and my work began.

Wheeling strangely had me reminiscing of southern California. The many beautiful homes on the hillside and winding steep roads had me wondering how cars made it up the steep driveways in the wintertime. One thing missing though was the ocean. I fell in love with this beautiful mountain state and its people.

Quite a number of kids and adults came to watch as I progressed with the giant (nearly 5 ft. in diameter) sculpture.

The Braiding family, who lived down the street, became my good friends and invited me to dinner on several occasions. Each day after school their pretty little seven year old daughter, Amy, came to see if I needed ice for my icebox or fresh drinking water. She was a great little friend who swept out the Ghost Ship and was always ready to help me anyway she could. Even Becki came to know and like little Amy on her weekend visits.

Wheeling, West Virginia Indian Monument. Adjacent to the courthouse in downtown Wheeling. Elm. (photo by the City of Wheeling)

I wanted to drive to Akron to save Becki all the commuting back and forth, but fall was here and winter was soon to follow, so I had to put all my time in finishing the monument before the snow came. When Becki could pry me away from my work we'd drive around the countryside to enjoy the exceptionally beautiful fall colors.

One day an old man appeared and told me about his hobbies and boasted of his wealth. Being rather poor, I asked him to help me out, not by giving me money, but by buying one of my modestly priced small sculptures. The old tightwad said he might, but never did. The old man, like many people, liked my work and the poignant idea behind it, but when it came to shelling out money, it was often no go.

West Virginia's population of 1,860,000 people live in a rugged mountainous setting. The Allegheny Mountains in the west cover two-thirds of the state.

When Virginia seceded in 1861, the Wheeling Convention created a new state and named it after the Indian tribe living there, the Kanawha. Later the name was changed to West Virginia. The Moneton tribe of Indians were probably met by the early explorers of this state like George Washington in 1753 and Daniel Boone. The Delaware, Shawnee, and Tutelo Indians probably hunted and traveled the picturesque, rugged Allegheny Mountains, as they did the Ohio Valley.

As in many parts of the country the Indian history in this state is scantily documented. Ancient Hopewell Indians built their mounds beside the Ohio River in West Virginia, as well as in many other states. Today the Indian is remembered in the whispering mountain pines, names of counties, towns, and rivers, but mostly he is lost in oblivion.

Many Indian cultures are lost forever, but the many contributions of the Indian are with us today. The domesticated wild food plants that today yield two-fifths of the world's agricultural products—corn, tobacco, potatoes, peanuts, cotton, and many other plants are contributions from the Indian. The yearly yield of corn in the United States alone is between four and five billion bushels. About three billion pounds of peanuts are harvested each year. Potatoes are the world's most widely grown staple food. Thirty-two billion pounds are grown annually in the United States. Millions of tons of tomatoes are grown throughout the world. All these and more are gifts of the Indians.

Many of the roads of today were established Indian trails and portages—the overland way between lakes and rivers. The Indians not only created these passes, but also discovered where precious minerals, like gold and silver, could be found. We are much indebted to these Native Americans.

It was October and the northern wind began to blow when I finally finished the monument. As in the previous states, I had to bypass the dedication once again. It had to be moved to its final destination—downtown Wheeling beside the courthouse.

I said goodby to friends and headed back to Ohio. It was a great feeling to have finished six states this year—Florida, Georgia, Alabama, Pennsylvania, New York, and West Virginia. I realized that next year might be different, the states may be much farther apart, or perhaps the work in each of the states may take longer.

My brief stay in Akron was spent visiting Becki and my remaining family. With the weather turning much colder, I prepared to travel south to a warmer climate.

NO. 9 MONUMENT
CLEVELAND, TENNESSEE—DEC. 1973

Again the trip south was long and lonely. I searched for low priced gas; with my limited funds every penny counted. By now I grew accustomed to making every cent count. It was hard for me to stop in a restaurant and spend good money, when I could purchase nearly twice that amount in a grocery store. My idea of splurging was to buy extra milk. Surprisingly I had more cash stashed away for emergency money (that was saved from my machine shop days) than many people had in banks.

One advantage of making little money was my lack of worry about paying taxes. Many times throughout my travels I'd meet people on welfare or collecting unemployment. When these same people heard of my financial predicament they urged me to do likewise. Sure, I was eligible for food stamps, unemployment, or some form of welfare, but I was always too proud to even seriously contemplate any handout. My feeling was that I was my own keeper, a healthy able-bodied person quite capable of making it on my own.

Thirty miles north of Chattanooga, by Interstate 75, I stopped in Cleveland, Tennessee, a town of about 24,000 where I was invited to make my ninth monument. It was near here (in Red Clay) that the Cherokees met for the last time prior to their removal to Oklahoma.

Back in the 1700's the great Cherokee Nation occupied all of the southwest Allegheny mountain region of Virginia, the Carolinas, parts of Tennessee, northern Georgia and northeastern Alabama. Unfortunately an unanticipated enemy, smallpox, nearly wiped out half the tribe. Today most Cherokees live in Oklahoma though there is an eastern band that lives on a 56,000 acre reservation in the Great Smoky Mountains of North Carolina.

A famous and contributing leader of the Cherokee was Sequoyah. After he taught himself to read and write he devised the Cherokee alphabet which made possible a written system of communication for his people.

The "Trail of Tears" was a dark and sad chapter in our country's history. Cherokees, Creeks, Choctaws, and other regional Indians were forced to leave their homes and most of their earthly possessions behind. Thousands died from exhaustion and the elements of that cruel force march west of the Mississippi into Oklahoma. Many Cherokees wept openly as the soldiers prodded them along like cattle. It must have been hard for them to see the immensely beautiful Smoky Mountains fade from sight.

Cleveland, Tennessee Indian Monument in front of the main library. Oak.
(photo by Pete McCollin)

The fertile land of Cumberland Valley, Tennessee was the traditional center of the Shawnee Indians. The Ohio Valley (Tennessee being the southern most part) had been the heart of the Hopewell burial mounds culture, an advanced great confederacy that had its greatest development from 400 B.C. to A.D. 400.

The Hopewell had vanished from the face of America upon the white man's arrival in the area of Tennessee. They found this land thinly occupied by Indians, a hunting ground and battlefield open to all.

And now I worked on a large dead oak tree, trying to capture the composite likeness of the past Indians that lived here.

Cleveland, Tennessee was most unlike the old smelly congested Ohio city of the same name. It is a city of serenity, with the Smokies in the background and unlimited recreation areas all around—Signal Mountain, Harrison's Bay, and many more.

On the second week the limbs of the large oak were cut off and it quickly took on the shape of an Indian. I had no problem getting all the things I needed—ladders, preservative, et cetera.

Lee College was two blocks down the street and frequently my lunch was eaten in their cafeteria. The art professor invited me to give a lecture to his students on my sculpture and it was a most interesting experience. After that day I felt right at home on campus.

Working on the Indian from the vantage point of 20 feet above the ground, I noticed a pond partly hidden by thick bushes. At sundown, with a couple of artificial lures and fishing pole in hand, I made my way quietly toward the pond that was rumored to be well-stocked. The pond was in the spacious yard of a neighbor and to keep from being seen, I would fish from the cover of the bushes. In less than fifteen minutes a big trout was on my line, so to keep him from splashing around, possibly giving my presence away, I quickly pulled him to shore and grabbed him. The fish jumped and one of the lure's exposed hooks embedded into the fleshy part of my index finger. To prevent him from further jumping, forcing the hook deeper in me, I squeezed the life out of him.

In the fading light I made my way back through the thick underbrush. The fish got hung up in a bush, which drove the hook even deeper into my finger.

It was a relief to climb inside the well-lit Ghost Ship. After removing the fish from the lure, I tried to jerk the hook out of the tip of my finger.

"Youch!" The pain was excruciating!

I contemplated going to a hospital, but to pay an extravagant amount of money to a doctor and still feel the pain, didn't make sense to me. The hell with it, I decided to operate on myself. To minimize the pain, a wire was tightened around my finger. When the finger was numb it was washed with alcohol to prevent infection. With a wire cutter I cut away the remaining lure. All that was now left was a quarter inch wire of the hook protruding from my finger. I decided the best course of action was to push the embedded barb through so that it would come out the other side. When I pushed it the sharp point could not pierce my callused skin. As I continued to push the hook, to my horror, it disappeared beneath my flesh.

About this time, three middle-aged men appeared at my open door.

"Can we come in?" a voice inquired.

Before I had a chance to say anything, all 3 of them filed in.

"We're from the Baptist church. Would you mind if we pray over you?"

"It's OK," I told them.

My operation continued with a sharp knife and nail clipper as the TV blared in the background and the men prayed over me! With the nail clipper I cut away at the callused skin where the barb was trying to come through. By putting pressure on my finger, the point of the barb appeared at my now torn flesh. I steadily attached the nail clippers to the protruding tip and with a final jerk, the hook pulled free. After washing the wound thoroughly the Baptists departed.

The fine Baptist Christians invited me for dinner and treated me with the utmost southern hospitality, but I had several unpleasant run-ins with some of them. My guess is, one look at me and they all wanted to save me from this sinful life.

One evening a professor from Lee College invited me to a banquet held at the local Holiday Inn. The dinner was good, but then the preaching started and went on and on. The crowd started murmuring and the preacher asked people to come up so that he could lay his hands on them. His eyes commanded me to come to the alter. I must have looked like a real sinner to him dressed in my patched old blue jeans while everyone else was in a suit and tie, but my sins are no more than the next guy's. I couldn't stand the preacher's haranguing any longer and walked out the door.

A tall lanky girl awaited my return at the Ghost Ship.

"Where've you been, Peter? I've waited for a long time, let's get started on your drawing lessons."

She was sweet with a talent for drawing that I admired. We sat on the bed, the only flat surface in the Ghost Ship and my first lesson in pencil drawing began.

Debbie came to see me often. She was shy, but I really liked her, even if we made a strange looking couple. She was 6 feet tall—3 inches taller than me.

Late one evening there was a loud pounding on my door.

"I'm here for my daughter! Where's Debbie?" a low voice growled.

"Coming daddy," she said meekly.

"I don't want my daughter seeing you anymore!" he said angrily.

"Sir, she is almost 20 years old and besides, she is teaching me portrait drawing."

He went off pushing Debbie toward their car. The next day Debbie asked me over for dinner. Her father and the whole family were surprisingly very friendly to me that evening. She explained the problem of her older sister getting pregnant and having to get married, consequently they were very strict with her.

Christmas 1973 was a sunny and fairly warm day in Tennessee. I enjoyed a fine Christmas with my neighbors. It never failed to amaze me how

*This old man with a flowing beard was made from a weathered cedar
fence post for a South Dakota couple. (1½ feet tall, sold for $200)*

strangers not only accepted me, but were also good to me. I can't thank all these giving, wonderful friends enough.

Food and gasoline were two things I had to have and both were ever increasing in price. Gas was selling for as high as 39ᶜ a gallon. Quite a jump from the 19.9 I bought it for in 1972 hardly a year ago in Galveston, Texas. To cut back on fuel costs I decided to buy a motorcycle large enough to ride on the road, but light enough to carry on the back bumper of my Ghost Ship. With the money received from the sale of my previous big motorcycle in Ohio, I bought a 175 Kawasaki. This gave me a cheap form of recreation and transportation. The Ghost Ship was now parked permanently on the site until I was ready to leave the state.

The big Indian head was now finished. During the last two days in Cleveland, several people came by asking to buy small carvings. It was a good thing several were on hand to barter or sell. One lady gave me a 20-inch bike because she liked my work and in return was given a small carving.

A taxi driver bought a $65 carving with a $12 downpayment. He was to send me the rest of the money, but never did. Most people that I trusted with payments though, seldom ripped me off. Things were looking better, I had enough gas and food money to get to my next state.

At 3 a.m. the morning mist enveloped the Ghost Ship as it disappeared heading south toward Florida. Misty-eyed I glanced back at the peaceful town of Cleveland and felt like it was my hometown being left behind.

NO. 10 MONUMENT
PUNTA GORDA, FLORIDA—JAN. 1974

On my way to Florida a prearranged rendezvous took place at the airport in Atlanta, Georgia. I fought the traffic to the airport and to save money, parked the Ghost Ship in the pilot's reserved space. It was all worthwhile when Becki emerged from the big jet.

"So good to see you, Peter!" Becki hurried to embrace me. We got her suitecase and went back to the van where the crow and seagull greeted us. It was a pleasant trip through Georgia and Florida. We even stopped at Disney World, but the entrance fee was too high, so we pushed toward our destination of Punta Gorda.

The next day we drove into the Holiday Inn parking lot in the quiet little town of Punta Gorda, population 3,800. One of the biggest stumps I'd ever seen was next to the parking lot, over 20 feet tall and more than 5 feet across. The remaining sawed off branches were bigger than most trees.

Prior arrangements were made with the owner, Fred Babcock, and we moved into a plush room reserved at no cost at the Holiday Inn. What a change after living in the cramped van.

With hammer and chisel in hand, the endless possibilities of making an Indian from the giant stump were contemplated.

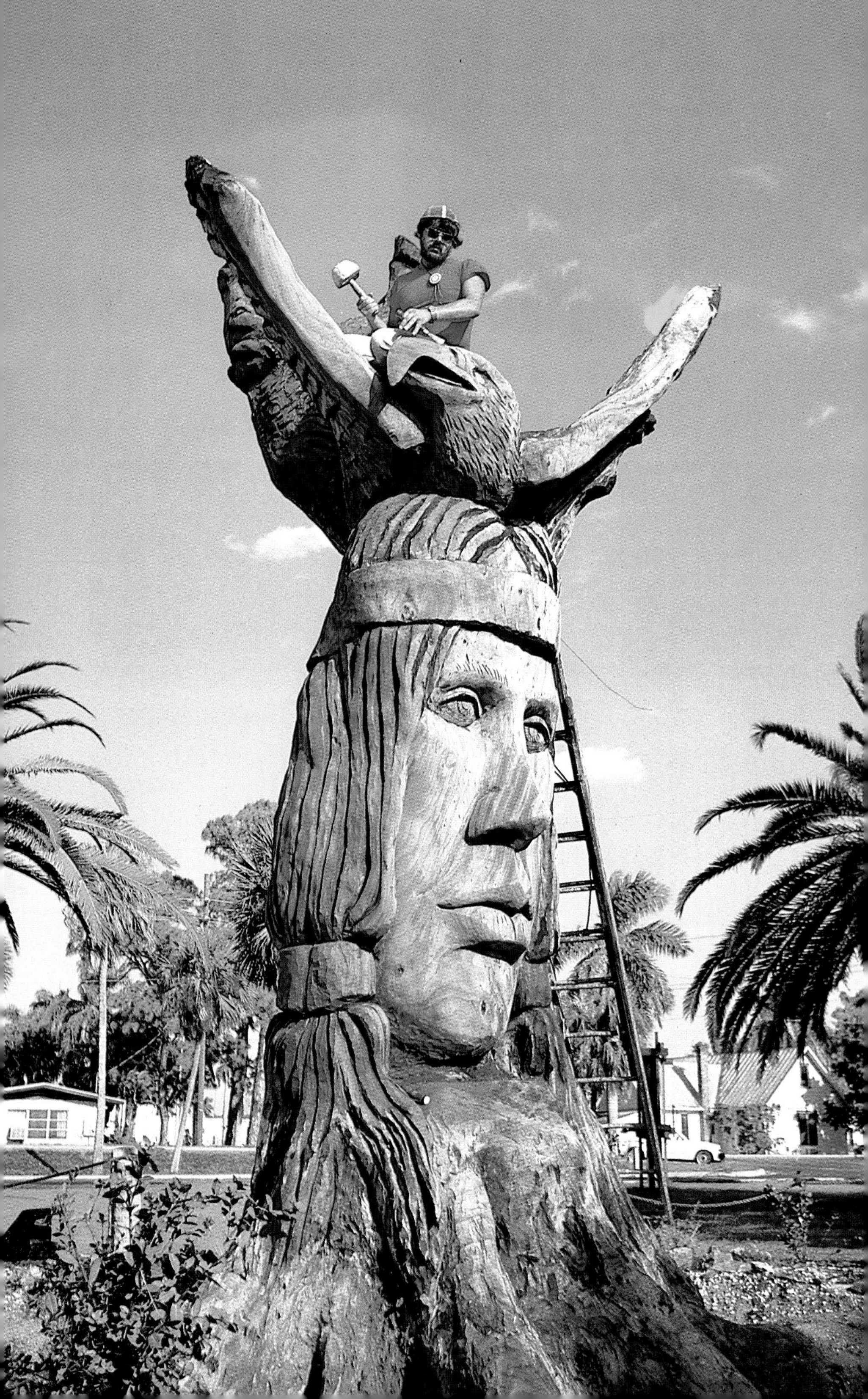

1974

Black

would

ke it

Back view of Florida's Indian Monument, brave and dying bison on his back with legs in the air. (photo by Rick Barry, Tribune)

Punta Gorda, Florida Indian Monument, working on the eagle, Front view of Indian maiden with eagle on top. (Ear Tree, Photo by Kathy Toth)

97

Though I am not one to be awed by titles or great wealth, I was grateful to Fred Babcock who contacted me a year ago after seeing a news article on my Georgia sculpture. He asked me to come down to Florida to sculpt an Indian from the huge dead tree stump. What an opportunity to be in Florida for the winter and to make my second Indian monument for this state. This one would be much larger than the one in De Land.

What surprised me is how a man like Fred Babcock, with great wealth could be concerned with a struggling artist and his dream. This giant stump would be the biggest challenge of my career so far and I just couldn't wait to sink my chisel into it. This monument would be most significant, not only because of its huge size, but also because it's the tenth one, a major obstacle to overcome on my way to one in all the fifty states. To add more history, it was reported that this tree was planted by Harvey Firestone and Thomas Edison who spent their winter vacations here.

In no time at all I saw the image of an Indian. This sculpting was unique from all the rest (and the only one) because I accepted monetary remuneration for it. I suppose the simplest thing to do would have been to finish the Indian and be on my way, but I saw more in this wood. Much more! Besides the Indian brave, I saw an Indian maiden on the opposite side and the top large branches revealed a giant eagle intertwined with a dying bison. These three extra figures on the massive elaborate sculpture were not done for monetary purpose, but rather for the remembrance of the once plentiful bison and eagle, and my personal artistic pleasure.

My chisel cut into the reddish tropical wood, known locally as an ear tree because of the large beanlike fruit it produces. Long days were spent chiseling on the massive sculpture and before long the shape of the giant bison with his legs and belly pointing toward the sky appeared. On the opposite side the eagle with spread wings futilely attempted to fly. The Indian maiden and brave also emerged from the wood.

Occasionally we swam in the Gulf of Mexico, but Becki was afraid of sharks and stingrays, so preferred the motel pool. To save money we heated TV dinners and other precooked food in our room in a small toaster-oven. Becki would frequently smoke up the room and hall, so the maid would tease her.

"The crazy blonde is cooking again."

The crow and seagull seemed quite content with Florida and an old Irish setter that recently adopted me. They were referred to as my "family". Though they were a headache at times, I enjoyed their company.

Becki liked vacationing with me in Florida, but after a hurtful disagreement she walked off into the night. Her absence worried me and fears that some maniac may have raped or even killed her crossed my mind. She finally came in about 3 a.m. Relieved at her safety, but angry at her lengthy absence provoked another argument and I sent her home.

The monument was nearing completion. Because of the TV and newspaper publicity, I had many people flocking out to view my sculpture. Several civic-minded groups and colleges invited me as a guest speaker.

Girls came to flirt with me, some younger than 14 years of age. One lady that was staying at the Holiday Inn, over 60 years old, winked at me and repeated her room number several times in the course of our conversation. She may have been looking for a young lover, but however attractive she was, like the 14 year old girls, she was ruled out—too young and too old. It seemed all women fell madly in love with me, under six and over sixty, just my luck!

It was early May, 90 degrees of sweltering heat, but the work had to be finished. Another bucket of water was poured on my head to cool the burning heat and the chiseling continued.

As in previous states neighbors brought me fruits, cookies, and other goodies. Two brothers came by frequently to see how the monument was shaping up. After we became good friends, the younger brother confided in me of his bout with cancer and the loss of his right eye, now replaced with a glass one. His 16-year old blonde sister was looking forward to meeting me as soon as she was released from a Minnesota clinic, where she was undergoing some extensive chemotherapy treatment for cancer. When she came home, unfortunately it was in a coffin. I attended her funeral. God in his mercy took away a delicate creature, destroying one of the beautiful flowers of humanity.

There was a telegram waiting for me at the lobby desk—a large package to be delivered that afternoon. I wondered what the mystery package would be. Five foot, five inches of it arrived. It was Becki. She came in time to spend the last two weeks in Florida with me and to help pack for the long drive back to Ohio.

Fred Babcock was a cordial unpretentious guy. I met him on several occasions when he drove his '57 cadillac to town. Before we left, Fred invited us to his 100,000 acre ranch. Somehow I couldn't help but admire him. Fred cooked up a wild boar that was shot on his ranch. This important man went out of his way to cook me a delicious meal. Me—the guest of honor!

Jokingly I told him, "Fred, I think I'll hire you as my personal cook. This was one of the finest meals I ever ate."

With the monument finished, we headed home with a load of wood that nearly filled the Ghost Ship. Once home Becki inherited my Irish setter and went back to work, while my task of hauling in a good supply of walnut, oak, and maple to my basement studio began. Since my parents had returned to their home in Ohio, a section of the basement had become my studio. Every time I came home from a different state, several of my favorite carvings (some were models of the large monuments), as well as good seasoned wood came with me. The basement was steadily filling up.

My mother was apprehensive about all the wood, however neatly it may have been stacked in her basement. She was afraid that termites or other wood destroying pests would infest the house, but to put it outside meant it would crack beyond my being able to carve it.

The summer just slipped away as I worked in my studio waiting for replies from letters written to different states about making monuments for them. Before long September rolled around. I packed the Ghost Ship and headed toward the West Coast.

TRAVELING

It was a wonderful feeling to be back on the road again, especially since Becki decided to come with me. We had a lot of differences and these next few months of travel were to prove if we could tolerate each other. Also, this was a chance for us to explore the states and locations for future monuments.

The first state that we checked out was Indiana—Fort Wayne had great possibilities. In Illinois, Peoria and the Illinois River area looked promising. Davenport or Des Moines, Iowa and Lincoln or Omaha, Nebraska were noted. Our fascination was with South Dakota, the big Pine Ridge Reservation, historical Wounded Knee, and the famous Black Hills. The road to Mount Rushmore was disguised by many cheap looking tourist traps, but still it was well worth the trip. The guide at Mt. Rushmore tried to discourage us from visiting the Crazy Horse Sculpture located nearby. This sculpture to the Indians fascinated me the most.

We paid a gate fee and drove up to the studio to get a closer view of the mountain sculpture. Becki was surprised with the big spacious studio. We met Ruth, the pleasant wife of Korczak Ziolowski. Her sons were hauling new equipment and Korczak's lunch up to the mountain and invited me to ride along. We piled in the truck and drove the mile of rugged road up the side of the mountain. It was a great feeling to be on top of the mammoth unfinished sculpture. I just never realized how big it really was and the tremendous amount of work already done. How could anyone not admire a man with such an undertaking? Korczak had quite a reputation for being tough—he fought four men at one time in the local bar. He is perhaps the greatest sculptor alive today.

It was an experience meeting him as he drove up in his jeep. A man, as rugged looking as the mountain he stood on, gave hell to his sons for being late. To infuriate him further, one son backed up the truck to turn it around and hopelessly hung it up on a protruding boulder. Korczak was reputed as calling his sons "honey", but now he called them everything but honey. Angrily he grabbed a jack and started raising the front end of the truck to free it.

"You gotta put the jack on the back bumper to get it free," I said.

He just glared at me, boiling with anger. "You ¢-$*!," he yelled. "Who the hell are you to tell me how to do anything on my mountain?"

For a minute I thought we might get into a fight, but it was only a verbal bout and one-sided at that. Korczak was over 60 and with his weather-beaten face and long beard he looked like a cross between Santa Claus and a grizzly bear, favoring the grizzly bear by a long shot.

Late that afternoon I was asked to meet him in his private office. Becki waited patiently as Korczak and I discussed our mutual work to honor the Indians. It surprised me what a nice guy he really was. He had great respect for the Indians and their culture and allowed Dennis Banks, Russell Means, and other Wounded Knee participants of 1973 to camp on his land. We talked of his ambitious project. He told me that he never expected to finish

Crazy Horse, but his sons, after his death, probably would. As for my Indian sculpture, Korczak flattered me.

"You know, Peter," he said, "the monument you made in Florida looks just like my best friend, Ben Black Elk, who was Crazy Horse's cousin."

"Korczak, if you really think it looks like him, why not write it on the picture?"

He wrote in ink, "Ben Black Elk, he would of liked it and so do I—Korczak."

Now if ever anyone asks me about the Crazy Horse Mountain Sculptor in South Dakota, I tell him about my encounter with Korczak and show them the picture with his signature.

As we drove west that evening, I went over all the advice that Korczak gave me. "Don't let anyone tell you this style or that style is best. Be yourself and you will succeed," were the echoing words of wisdom given me by one of the greatest sculptors of today.

NO. 11 MONUMENT
VANCOUVER, WASHINGTON—OCTOBER 1974

We traveled one thousand miles of monotonous flat plains, intriguing dry deserts, and spectacular jagged cliffs. The tree-covered beauty of the Rocky Mountain country of Montana and Idaho made us fall in love, over and over again, with this great country of America. The road was long and tiring, but well worth the effort, especially when we came into view of the magnificent snow-covered Mount Rainier in central Washington. We were awed by this great creation of God; the over 14,000 foot peak was above the clouds which created an angelic halo-look. We spent most of that day driving through Chinook Pass on Highway 410 and stopped occasionally to admire the most breathtaking mountains we had ever seen.

After driving through Olympia, the capital of Washington, we headed toward the Pacific Ocean. Washington is God's country with vast open areas of wilderness and the breathtaking mountains such as Mt. Rainier and Mount St. Helen (which erupted in 1980).

This sparsely populated land, the twentieth largest state in the Union, has less than 4 million people living in it. The largest congregation of Indian tribes live along the Pacific like the Makah, Quileute, Quinault, Skokomish, and Chehalis who always regard the ocean with reverence. It is a great source of food and beauty, as we were finding out first hand. This is a land of plenty; streams are filled with salmon and the forests are abundant with wildlife. There are tribes living in the interior such as the Nisqually, Puyallup, Swinomish, Lummi, Yakima, Spokan, Colville, and Kalispel to name a few. The Chinook live along the Columbia River.

The viable Indian population existing here in the Northwest were the famous totem pole carvers. These tall poles consisted of numerous figures

Vancouver, Washington Indian Monument, located in Esther Short Park, 3 blocks from I-5. 25 ft. high; 8 ft. across; 40,000 pound white fir.

of mythical animals and heraldic devices that proclaimed the owner's legendary descent from animals. It's beyond me how someone could think my sculpture of an Indian head could in anyway look even remotely similar. Some of these masterpiece totem poles are in museums. Now it's virtually a lost art. Most that are made today are imitations that have lost cultural significance.

Many of the Washington Indians were fishermen and hunters of game. Some of the northern Indians were unique in having Oriental and Asiatic appearances; facial hair was more common here.

My search continued for the best location to place my monument. Olympia or Kelso had possibilities. I hoped to sculpt it on the Pacific Coast, but no suitable place was found. We swung southeast toward Vancouver and when we arrived, stopped in at City Hall. I had a meaningful talk with Ted Brown, head of the Parks Department. He assured me they were very interested in my gift offer of the giant sculpture.

The next day we moved into Esther Short Park with permission to use electricity for the Ghost Ship, or to stay in the historic Esther Short Mansion that was situated in the park. Becki was happy that we had a tub to take a hot bath in, as well as the use of a large refrigerator and gas range in the house.

It took most of September before the giant 8 foot diameter, 21 foot long, white fir arrived. Thanks to Mr. George A. Weidman, United Pacific Plywood & Lumber, Weyerhaeuser donated the log and the National Guard came out to take the 40,000 pound log off the truck with their huge crane. The military (National Guard) was providing services for the cause of the American Indian. In the past, the military cavalry tried to destroy the Indian.

Earlier I had made several small models of the Indian that was hidden in this big log. With a little sizing up, the chipping began.

The next few weeks brought a lot of progress. The big log needed a base to erect it upright. The Parks Department came up with the suggestion to bury several feet of the log in the ground and pour cement around it for support. The last thing I wanted to do was bury it in the ground, exposing it to potential termites and rot damage. My monuments in Pennsylvania, New York, and West Virginia were done this way after my departure, against my best wishes. With the help of the city engineer, we devised a plan where a 3 foot high, 25 foot circumference cement base would be used. A large culvert was used for a form. Eight 1½ inch threaded steel rods were embedded in the cement and protruded 2 feet in the air. These steel rods were lined up with holes drilled on the base of the log. Bolts held the monument 2 inches above the base on the steel rods. This permanent foundation promoted 24 hour a day air circulation.

A few days later a crane raised the half-finished sculpture onto the cement base. The sculpture looked enormous standing. This was to date, the largest monument that I had ever made (even bigger than the one in Punta Gorda, Florida).

The work continued in full speed on the Indian now that I was able to stand back 100 feet and keep it in perspective. Long ladders enabled me to reach the top and all sides of the monument.

Vancouver, Washington and Portland, Oregon are neighboring cities separated by the Columbia River. Becki and I did our grocery shopping in Portland. We strapped a large box on the back of my Kawasaki 175 motorcycle and placed two to four bags of groceries in it. Then we'd cross back into the state of Washington with the large load. By using my motorcycle we were able to save gasoline and also the taxes on the food (Oregon charged no food tax) and besides, the Washington stores weren't any closer to us.

Food was expensive for the two of us, though we made some good buys on potatoes and other fresh foods. Becki liked frozen TV dinners (chicken), so when there was a sale on and providing we had the money, the icebox would be filled with them.

Since Becki and I were the sole legal residents in Esther Short Park, we noticed a lot of strange activities. On some mornings a lone transient with ragged clothes made the rounds on the garbage cans. He would eat half-eaten sandwiches and other bits of leftovers. We felt sorry for him, so Becki heated up a chicken dinner and the wino, or whatever he was, ate it without uttering a word. When he was through with his meal I tried to talk to him, but he seemed hard of hearing or deaf. From that day on he always sat on a bench close to the Ghost Ship waiting for a handout. We fed him for awhile, but our money hardly fed us, yet alone a stranger. Some friends advised us to send him four blocks to the Salvation Army where hot lunches were served daily. For a couple of days he went there, but then just drifted back to his old haunt—the garbage cans. As the weather grew colder he moved out of the bushes where he slept and into a locomotive that was on display in the park. Other winos came and hung around, but with the colder weather of December, they moved South.

On one occasion when we left a two-foot sculpture outside the door of the Ghost Ship for a few minutes, someone carried it away. We searched the park hoping to catch the thief, then Becki uncovered it behind some bushes halfway across the park. The thief must have realized he would be caught carrying the sculpture away from the park, so hid it and decided to return for it in the silent cover of darkness. Unfortunately this would happen again throughout my travels.

An inebriated man stopped by one day cussing me.

"Do you know what the hell you're doing?" he demanded to know. "I've seen totem poles in Alaska and Canada, and you don't know the first *&$?! thing about totem poles."

As he continued to curse me, I started down the ladder with my big hammer in hand. My intent was to explain to him that he was right. I don't know a thing about carving totem poles, never made one nor expect to. My monument depicts an Indian, not copies of Indian art.

As I stepped off the ladder, to my surprise he was gone. Apparently he must have figured that I was going to use the 5-pound hammer on his head.

When the news came out on TV, newspapers, and in "Ripley's Believe It or Not" that this was my 11th monument to honor the Indians, many people came to visit. It was a great feeling when a few people told me that they'd seen some of my monuments in other states. One trucker gave me $10 to buy a steak dinner. Even after explaining that I didn't accept money because my monument wouldn't be much of a gift then, he still stuck the money in my pocket and walked off. How could one argue with a man that was 6 feet 5 inches and 250 pounds, with a big heart to match.

"Thanks!" I yelled after him.

One friend of ours was an older man who walked by every day with his little chihuahua and frequently commented on the progress of the Indian. He didn't have much money, but still gave us a used waffle iron. It was really touching that he wanted to help us.

Becki was having a hard time adjusting to my life style in the cramped Ghost Ship. She was moody, missed her family, and fought with me a lot. To try and patch things up between us, we visited the local Humane Society/Dog Pound to possibly get a puppy. Becki started crying when she saw all the dogs penned up in crowded cages.

Monument builder leaving

After three months of carving a monument to the American Indian, artist Peter Toth is leaving Vancouver.

Monday was his last full day in the city. He says he's going to New Orleans, La., to begin work on another Indian monument — the 12th in as many states.

The Hungarian-born artist said the monument he carved in Esther Short Park should last "a heckuva lot longer than 100 years." He has applied preservative to the face of the 20-foot statue, and has left instructions its care.

The monument, he said, "belongs to the people. Everybody. It's my gift to the people."

When he first began work on the statue, in October, Toth described himself as "a protester trying to let the public know about the suffering of the Indian. But instead of destroying or shouting in the streets, I'm producing these monuments."

He says American Indians are "the most abused race in the world."

Toth, 27, said the people of Vancouver "have been very nice to me. A number have invited me to dinner."

The Vancouver Parks and Recreation Department has paid the cost of materials. Toth, who says he is financially independent, has "utilized my God-given talents" to create the statue.

Working from his hometown of Akron, Ohio, Toth has spent the last four years carving monuments to the Indians. It may take another 10 years to create and place them in the other 38 states of the union.

His goal, he says, is "to erect a monument for peace in every country in the world. This is my dream."

Toth: putting the finishing touches on his monument.

Staff photos by
Jerry Coughlan

A gift — and a memorial — from artist Peter Toth.

Base of large log rests on a cement foundation built by the city (Indian Monument)

The COLUMBIAN

Tuesday, Dec. 31, 1974

Washington
(photo by Greg Johnson)

"Peter, they're all going to be put to sleep!"

A cuddly, little, gray puppy sat in the corner. His long shaggy hair hung over his eyes and a white star stood out on his chest.

"Please Peter, let's get that puppy!"

Becki's pleading eyes and the cute puppy just couldn't be resisted. We paid a small fee and took him home, happy that we could save at least one of them. Becki named our new puppy "Smokey." Surprisingly, he was tolerated by both the seagull and the crow, though when he got out of line, a good peck on the nose put him in his place. All five of us got along as one big happy family.

The monument was nearly finished by Christmas. Washington was still sunny with 50-degree weather and not a snowflake in sight. Several people invited us for Christmas dinner, but we spent the day alone in the park. A tasty chicken dinner and a gallon of eggnog was our holiday cheer.

Like so many times before, I was wondering how and when the money would come to pay for traveling expenses to the next state, over 2,000 miles away. Somehow, my luck with bartering and selling a few small carvings created enough money for most of the traveling expenses.

More wood preservative and sealer was applied on the Indian statue and a little touch up, here and there, was needed before I was finished. After a short dedication and a certificate of appreciation from Vancouver, we packed and prepared to depart.

It was with sad hearts that we crossed the Columbia River for the last time. The state of Washington, our home for the last three months, would be missed.

We had a long and pleasant drive through the enchanting state of Oregon, following the endless Pacific Ocean to the giant redwood forest. In the shadows of the huge trees we walked in silence. This was the land of the giant redwoods where man stands humble and nature is supreme.

We stopped in to see my family in southern California, then continued to Louisiana.

NO. 12 MONUMENT
NEW ORLEANS, LOUISIANA—FEB. 1975

New Orleans was as big of a city as I remembered it from my Mardi Gras days. Mayor Moon Landrew invited me to sculpt the Indian for his city, but it was another thing to get a personal audience with him. The Mayor's office referred me to the Parks Department and the next few days the city crew and I scoured the city and outlying area looking for a suitable tree. Finally, a dying oak was found and in shrouded secrecy, the Parks Department cut it down. They feared retribution from the public since there was still a couple of green leaves left on the dying centurion tree. New Orleans has a most stringent law on cutting trees. One has to get a permit to cut a tree on public or private property.

New Orleans, La.
March 1975

New Orleans, Louisiana Indian Monument, using a 5 pound metal hammer and chisel. Oak.

Two weeks were spent awaiting the arrival of the big log. We camped beside the Park Department building, hooked up to electricy. My wait was well utilized in sculpting small carvings until I was ready to start on my twelfth monument.

For some reason, the lady in charge of the Parkway Commission seemed to have a grudge against me. I am a demanding and challenging person, as she was, so our personalities clashed. She decided to drop the log in an isolated, undeveloped park. I had to put my foot down and insisted that the monument be placed on the corner of Gentilly Blvd., or an equally visible spot.

A notice was given to me that the log was going to stay in the first selected spot and that was that! I started packing and made it clear that the news media, Mayor, and the entire city was going to hear why the monument was lost to New Orleans.

My threat must have been taken seriously because the next morning the log was moved to the Parkway Commission on Gentilly Blvd. and my work began in earnest. Problems such as this run-in in New Orleans were rare, but I usually won out.

Over 90% of my work is done with a 5-pound hammer and chisel, but when needed, I will use a chain saw to square off the base of the log, make a few lines, or cut through impenetrable knots.

Often when I would crank up a saw for 5 minutes to cut off a knot or make a line, invariably someone would ask me, "You carve it all with a saw?" This was always a source of irritation to me because though I have indeed used a saw to make a few cuts, the hammer and chisel were my tools for scuplting. However, it is my contention that an artist should use any tool of his choosing, providing it gets the job done.

The sun warmed the late February days when Becki decided to go home. She wanted to get a job before the college and high school kids had a jump on her. We parted sadly at the bus station, never realizing that New Orleans was to be the last happy memory for us.

The chips piled up around the big horizontal log and it started to look more like an Indian. As in Washington, we poured a cement base for the monument and embedded a heavy-duty steel pipe which protruded from the cement. An oversize front-end-loader came to raise the Indian monument upright and for the first time I worked on scaffolds which made the work less dangerous than on a ladder and proved more productive.

It was now March 1975 and newspaper, radio, and TV news people came to interview me. Many people were stopping; most seemed amazed at the large unique looking sculpture of an Indian.

People's attitude about my work has never ceased to amaze me. On several occasions religious fanatics have referred to my work as idols. One such fanatic walked up to my monument.

"How's the idol taking shape?" he asked sarcastically.

I snapped at him in frustration. "If you think it's an idol, get on your knees and pray!"

He just left quietly without further words.

Near life-size walnut maiden, created in 1973.

Later that afternoon, a young Negro man demanded to know why a Hungarian sculptor would make an Indian. He felt that because of my mission, I should be an Indian.

"Do you think that since you're a Negro, you can't sculpt anyone but a Negro?" I questioned him.

"What!" he yelled angrily. "I'm an Indian! My grandmother was a full-blooded Cherokee."

It was strange that a man looking every bit a Negro could claim to be an Indian and yet try to deny me the privilege to sculpt an Indian. In my youth, after attaining a dark tan from the summer sun, people often mistook me for a Native American.

Before the frustrated young man left, I told him that no matter what a person is, above all, he is a human being and I am sculpting just that. He left with a chip on his shoulder. Whenever people, such as this man, frustrate me, I just work it out of my system by swinging my 5-pound hammer harder, really making the chips fly.

One afternoon a young girl brought me a plate of food. "Compliments of Leona's Il Restorante," she said and walked off. Every day at noon Leona's sent me her special of the day, all great Italian food. Leona was an attractive generous lady who must have had a soft spot in her heart for me. I gave her one of my favorite carvings to show my appreciation and we became good friends. Before I left New Orleans, she bought three or four of my small carvings for her kids.

Besides good people like Leona and a few religious fanatics, I met several girls. A sweet young girl named Lisa thought she was madly in love with me after only knowing me for a week. An attractive black girl and many other people invited me over for dinner. The black family, as so many people, were very hospitable to me.

The historic French Quarter was really, at times, a place of violence. One or two homicides occurred there almost every day.

In February I walked down to the Quarter to see the Mardi Gras, homosexuals were everywhere. Their kissing and making out in the streets spoiled the festivities for me.

My stay in New Orleans was in a racially mixed neighborhood at the edge of the city. No one ever threatened or bothered me.

New Orleans is a town of over half-a-million and the surrounding metro area is nearly one-and-a-quarter million. More than one-quarter of Louisiana's people live here. Many of them are Creoles, a mixed descent of the original French settlers and are a friendly, good natured folk with a unique trace of accent and food that's out of this world.

Louisiana was discovered by Cabeza de Vaca and Panfilo de Narvaez. The Pelican State now has nearly four million people living here.

The two major Indian tribes that lived in Louisiana were the Natchitoches and the Chitimacha. Several other tribes crossed into this area, such as the powerful Choctaws, Natchez, and some lesser tribes. Today there are small Indian communities throughout the state. Though the old ways are gone, many Indians are trying hard to cling to their heritage.

By the latter part of March the temperature was in the 70's, sunny and beautiful. Each day Smokey and the seagull went for a swim in a nearby pond, as my pet crow watched from shore. I was putting the finishing touches on the Indian and packing for my trip to Arkansas.

Pretty Lisa cried that last night and made me a little misty too. She kissed me goodby and in the quiet tranquility of the early morning haze, the Ghost Ship disappeared from view.

NO. 13 MONUMENT
LITTLE ROCK, ARKANSAS—APRIL, 1975

On my journey toward Arkansas, my thoughts were on Lisa and the plans we made to meet in the near future. Lisa said she loved me and couldn't bear to be apart from me. At first I just wrote it off as infatuation and even told her that in a short time she'd forget about me. Her insistence seemed sincere. She made me feel that I was special—one in a million. Now that New Orleans was left behind, I was beginning to take her words seriously.

It was after midnight when I drove into Little Rock, Arkansas and decided to drive the last fifty miles to Hendrix College. That way I could sleep on the campus and check out the tree they had written me about. In the morning, I found the college pleased at my presence, but the tree they selected was deteriorated beyond use.

It was a tossup to go north toward the Ozark, or south back to Little Rock. The choice was Little Rock, which had a small town flavor despite the 145,000 population (380,500 metro—the biggest city in Arkansas). The perpetual green and beautiful country of Arkansas must have been some place to explore in the early frontier days. In 1541 de Soto and in 1673 Jolliet came to find the peaceful Quapaw Indians living in harmony with nature.

Now over 400 years later, the Indian's homeland is called Arkansas (a Sioux Indian name for "South Wind People"). Over two million people live here. Eighty-one percent are white, sixteen percent are black and hispanic with little trace of Indian.

After stopping in at the city hall and talking to the Parks Department supervisor, we immediately went to check on a large dead oak in Mac Arthur Park. It was perfect! All that was needed was to have the top cut off. So as not to waste much time, my work began immediately.

March was over and April 1975 was here. The tree cutting crew lopped the top off and left me with a near 20 foot high, 60 inch in diameter stump to create the Indian sculpture from.

All day long the chips were flying as the monument started taking form. I was dressed in my hot weather clothes—a pair of well-worn shorts.

The local newspaper was following my progress weekly. One front page headline read, "Immigrant to Make Indian for Little Rock." People came out looking for the Immigrant. I suppose they were looking for a guy with a

Little Rock, Arkansas Indian Monument. Putting on the finishing touches.
Oak. (photo by Gene Prescot, Arkansas Gazette—also cover photo)

long trench coat because I overheard some frustrated person remark, "I see a damn hippie, but where is the Immigrant?"

The sculpture was adjacent to the Art Center—a perfect place to have my thirteenth monument. The Art Center had many elaborate shows, from painting to sculpture, as well as all conceivable art forms. A great many people also visited Mac Arthur Park for picnics and walks.

Camped in my Ghost Ship about 30 feet from the monument gave me a clear view of the procession of people coming and going. This gave me a chance to meet some interesting people. One was an attractive, shapely, black girl who modeled nude for the Art Center and offered to pose for a nude sculpture.

At noon each day, a nice looking blonde girl came by and sat close to my Indian and meditated. After we got to know each other, she convinced me to join her at a yoga meditation class. The class was 10% yoga meditation and 90% religion. It turned out to be some kind of moonie group trying to recruit unsuspecting confused kids who were lost, lonely, and unsure of themselves. Their aim was to bring in suckers on the pretense of teaching them yoga and the poor naive kids were peddling flowers and giving up their worldly possessions to their God and Master Rev. Moon. It was a total failure with me, though, because I didn't swallow all their brotherly love crap, or perhaps the reason was that I have a mind of my own.

An attractive dark haired girl had Smokey and me over one evening for supper. It was nice meeting her family. Her younger brother excitedly told me he saw a picture of the Ohio and Florida monuments in his Weekly Reader and was studying about my work. During the evening Smokey had a great time with their female dog who was in heat. Months later, the bitch gave birth to several of his puppies.

Little Rock, Arkansas, like so many other states that I'd lived in, started out lonely during the first week or two. Lisa wrote me several letters expressing her continuous love for me and explained that, when she went out with other guys, her thoughts were only on me. Because of these letters I became caught up in this culminating infatuation.

Then suddenly (even before there was any publicity on my work), several girls started coming by to visit. I don't know if it was my cause they were interested in or my art, but several meaningful friendships were made with these delightful Arkansas girls.

It was during this time in 1975 that streaking was a popular fad. Streakers were commonplace on any given day on college campuses. One hot muggy evening, in the cover of Mac Arthur Park's darkness, I tried my hand at streaking. On my last sprint home the high beams of a police searchlight just missed me as I dashed through the door of the Ghost Ship.

All the work and fun came to an end in early May; the Indian was finished. We had a dedication attended by the Mayor, a senator, and media people. I hated to leave beautiful, memorable, Little Rock behind, but the Indian was now finished and I wanted to get home for the 17th of May—Becki's birthday.

While packing the Ghost Ship, a Choctaw Indian friend stopped to say

Sculptor Toth assisted with ideas on where and how to begin.

116

goodby. Unfortunately he had a drinking problem and seemed kind of down and out. Since some of my carvings were sold earlier, I was able to give him a few dollars for helping to load my motorcycle on the back bumper. Sadly I watched him walk toward a liquor store smiling.

TRAVELS

On my way to Ohio, a slight detour was made to the Smoky Mountains for a clandestine meeting with Lisa, the blonde from New Orleans. It was as if I relived the exciting time in 1961 when the big Toth family traveled to these same mountains. What fun we had on our first real vacation in America.

It was good to see Lisa again. In her previous letters she told of her great love for me and I was just carried away. After a memorable day in the shadows of the cool Smoky Mountains, I gave her an 8 x 10 picture of Smokey and me with the thought she would cherish it. There was something strange or different about Lisa. I couldn't put my finger on it at the time, but in a future letter she confessed that it was over. What a fool I was to think that she would really care. As I predicted earlier her infatuation wore off, now I felt foolish that I gave her my picture. Not only my pride, but my ego was hurt. Some girls were carried away with me, perhaps because of my recognition from the newspapers, television, and radio. More often than not, this short lived infatuation would soon wear off.

Anxiously I pushed the Ghost Ship toward Ohio, not at all aware of the sadness and potential danger that would face me.

The Ghost Ship pulled up to my parent's house, who had moved back from California, to unload my supplies. Later that evening I called Becki and she sounded happy to hear of my return. She came over and Smokey barked at her. Since Smokey was really her dog, I laughed and thought it was a joke, not realizing how cruel it was and how much it must have hurt her.

The next few days we spent together, but I knew that something was definitely wrong. It turned out that Becki was serious about some other guy. I was the one that wanted to break up with her, but now it was hard to see her going out on me—something I'd been doing to her for years. Now I was getting a taste of my own medicine and it was painful.

During the next few days I waited anxiously for a positive reply from Indiana. Ohio was a sad place to be. Somehow deep down inside I had hoped to patch things up with Becki. To keep busy I tried to work on small carvings, but found my tools were drawn toward a larger 3 foot high walnut log. This carving turned out to be an abstract with a special meaning behind it. My twisted emotion of sadness was in this piece and it was ultimately named "Aching Heart".

Several days later I was moved to call Becki and some guy picked up the phone. I demanded to know who he was and names were exchanged in anger. Obviously the guy's intent was to intimidate, when he informed me that he was a member of a motorcycle gang. My anger and hurt at Becki was redirected at this guy and he was quickly challenged to a fight.

Heartbroken and in a real quandary about Becki, I wondered how she could get messed up with some motorcycle gang member. Later that afternoon a car came to a screeching halt in front of my parent's house. Five people came piling out—one big heavyset guy, three girls, and Becki's new boyfriend. They were all dressed in their motorcycle gang colors and may have carried knives or guns.

Most of the time I am quite brave, but to run out of the house and meet them might have been stupid. Had there been only one or two guys, perhaps I could have handled them, but five against one didn't seem right. Just because three were girls made little difference. These chicks looked tougher than the guys.

The ways of motorcycle gangs were familiar to me. Since at one time, I used to ride a big bike and appear tough. Two gangs invited me to join their clubs. Even religious men when in a mob can be unthinking and ugly. The last thing I needed was a bunch of idiots doing my thinking.

At first I hesitated to come out and face the motorcycle gang, but what other choice was there? Perhaps this would have been a good time to have a gun for protection (but taking a life was against my moral belief). My hands were shaking a little, but I tried hard not to show fear and flung the door open, carefully keeping my back toward a safe exit in case weapons might be brandished.

My mind raced 100 mph to devise a way to get out of this self-imposed potentially dangerous predicament. Brawn and brute strength was not the answer. Even if by some miracle I could beat them off momentarily, my parent's home may face backlash of the gang after my departure for Indiana. Without showing much fear, I managed to talk my way out of a direct confrontation. Later I called Becki to see if she sent them.

"No, Peter!" she assured me. "I tried to stop them."

"How can you even be seen with these people?"

"I've been alone for so long Peter and he is good to me. He wants to marry me."

"You've got to be crazy, Becki! Please don't get involved with this guy!"

With cracking voice Becki told me that she didn't love me anymore, but still agreed to meet me in downtown Akron on her lunch hour.

The next day I was determined not to drive the Ghost Ship through the heavy downtown traffic. My motorcycle had developed a flat. In my stubbornness I tried to repair it and lost valuable time. In disgust I gave up and asked my mom to drive me to Becki's place of employment. By the time we arrived her lunch break was over. Our last meeting was brief and very impersonal over a public counter.

That evening I called Becki and talked to her for the last time. Short of offering her marriage, in a last ditch effort, I suggested that she move to Indiana with me; if nothing else, at least to get a new start somewhere else. All I wanted was her happiness.

Indiana was waiting for me, so in a sad quandary my last packing was done. That last night in Ohio was one of the saddest nights of my life. It was just a few days ago that I was so carefree and happy seeing so many different girls. Some of these girls were just as beautiful as Becki, but somehow it didn't seem to matter anymore. No two ways about it, I caused Becki a lot of heartaches. It was hard for me to forget girls that wrote me from all around the country saying that they loved me. Now all this was past history and seemed trivial. This last night in Ohio the sleep didn't come, only the sharp pain in my heart was real.

NO. 14 MONUMENT
FORT WAYNE, INDIANA—JUNE, 1975

Before dawn was breaking, the Ghost Ship headed west. That same afternoon I drove into Fort Wayne, Indiana. The Parks Department was most helpful. They had already found a large tree, 25 feet high and 50 inches in diameter, with all branches removed, in a peaceful residential neighborhood. I parked the Ghost Ship beside the stump and went to work. The friendly neighbor allowed me to plug into his electricity and park the van in the shade of his big maple tree.

The fourteenth monument was taking shape. It was a good feeling to bury my broken heart in this work, it was helpful to keep my mind off of Becki and the past troubles in Ohio. The chipping was moving forward steadily and in two weeks the Indian was slowly taking shape.

It was June and the heat was intense, so Smokey and I went searching for a lake to cool off in.

The month was nearly over and although the Indian was only roughed out, some people already thought it was finished. People seemed interested in my work and when the local TV and newspaper came out to interview me, many more people took notice. More dinner invitations came my way. As in other states, people invited me over because they thought of me as a VIP, or because they assumed I was a poor hungry bum.

In the last few weeks the city crew prepared the cement base near the zoo entrance in Franke Park. Now the cement was cured and they came with a big saw, crane, and a flatbed truck to haul and erect the three fourths finished monument on its pedestal. The work took most of the day, but before dark the base of the Indian was drilled and mounted with a crane on the cement foundation. Though the statue was in need of work, it already commanded respect overlooking his new domain in the park.

A girl with long blonde hair came by one day.

"How can you keep working uninterrupted and not even notice me standing here, or the people that come by staring at you?"

Boy was she wrong! I noticed many people, especially a pretty girl. Sometimes, though, I get so wrapped up in my work that time slips away.

"You look like a captain," the pretty girl blurted out.

Well, I was the captain of my Ghost Ship. The girl came back a couple days later and we went swimming. One evening she drove me to a park where Johnny Appleseed's grave was. What a romantic night it was as the sun went down and the shadows fell.

Fort Wayne, Indiana Indian Monument is moved to its permanent location in Franke Park. Oak

120

Several of the neighborhood girls were young and pretty. Many of the older generation get the idea that young people of the 70's jumped in the sack at the drop of a hat. Some older men have indicated to me how lucky I was to be young in a time when most girls think nothing of having sex. The truth that I have found throughout my travels is that girls are basically the same as they were ten to twenty years ago. Today sex is not considered evil or dirty and it's true, there are more relaxed morals in the country, but most young American girls still have high morals and will not sleep with a guy unless they feel love or deep affection and respect for him.

At night it was so quiet and eerie living by myself in Franke Park that I could almost see the ghosts of Indians peering at me from the darkness. Although the only Indian was the giant wooden statue, I somehow felt that he perhaps had bridged the span of time, bringing an awareness to the first Americans of this state.

Indiana means "Land of the Indian." The state was lightly populated by Indians at the time of the white man's arrival. Little did La Salle, the first white man to visit this area in 1679, realize the chain of events to follow. France ceded this fertile land to Britain, who in turn ceded it to the United States. Now there is over 5 million people living here, but few are Indians. The Mascoutens, Potawatomi, Piankeshaw, Wea, and Wyandot lived in and around Indiana; often Wisconsin, Illinois, Michigan, and other states were also their homes. The Miami were the major power base in Indiana. Miami braves were fierce fighters defeating the U.S. troops in 1790, but then they were defeated in 1794 at Fallen Timber. In 1840 the Miami were induced to part with all their remaining holdings in Indiana. Tecumseh united several tribes and with his confederation fought desperately for his country, but lost to General William Henry Harrison at the famous Tippecanoe battleground near present day Lafayette, Indiana.

Indiana is mostly fertile rolling plains; a wide open state with a lot of farm country, as well as big cities like Indianapolis. It seems when I really start to like an area, it's almost always time to go.

While putting the final touch on the monument, a car drove up and a lady yelled up to me.

"Hey, we're tourists from out-of-state, do you know some interesting things to visit around here?"

These people puzzled me. In the past some families have driven over 100 miles to see my monument and this lady didn't even notice it.

Before leaving Indiana, an attractive dark haired girl who looked like an Indian, stopped by with her mother to view the monument. Allison Walters soon became a friend and in the future she and her parents would visit me in Michigan, Illinois, and New Jersey. The next day while walking in the park, my pet crow and seagull disappeared. For 3 days Allison helped to search the area for my pets, but to no avail. Michigan was awaiting my arrival, so with faithful Smokey by my side, I packed the Ghost Ship and disappeared into the emptiness of the night.

Peter talking to Lovefree, his pet crow. (photo by Harold Haven, The Chattanooga Times)

Lansing, Michigan Indian Monument in Potter's Park. Two Ottawa maidens (the Brunk sisters) pose with artist in front of sculpture. Elm.

NO. 15 MONUMENT
LANSING, MICHIGAN—AUG., 1975

The Great Lakes are like inland seas; many people refer to them as such and now I was again heading toward them. It had been two years since I'd lived on the shores of Lake Erie in Dunkirk, New York.

My decision to make the monument in Lansing was based on the very rich Indian history of the area. Many Indian wars were staged in this region. Lansing is Michigan's capital sandwiched between Chicago and Detroit.

After corresponding with the Mayor of Lansing, he wrote back and indicated a positive response to the gift of my sculpture. However, after arriving at Lansing's Park Department, they seemed unaware of this project and told me they'd look into it.

My assumption was that they'd have several logs and trees already located, but virtually nothing had been done. After the first day I wasn't about to waste my time waiting, so drove around Lansing looking for a large tree myself. In no time at all I found a huge dead elm tree on a small vacant lot hidden between two buildings.

The visual image of the Indian was evident in the 60 inch diameter, 30 foot main trunk of the old elm. The owners gave me permission to use the dead tree. Without any help from the Parks Department, my fifteenth monument was well on its way as chips started piling up.

One of my neighbors was a little old lady whom I met during the first week of my stay. When she found out about my endeavors, creating monuments with no charge, she demanded to know where I hid my gold mine. It was hard for her to understand how I could do it for nothing.

"I don't do it for nothing," was my answer. "It's to help the Indians. This cause is more important than money."

She let me use her electricity and later was compensated for it.

Directly across the street was a church and after some contemplation, I decided there was no possible excuse for me not going to the morning services. The next Sunday I tried to derive some spiritual benefit for my (as religious people call it) sinful soul. Just before the services were over, I left, changed into cool shorts, and rode my motorcycle to get some groceries.

On my way back an 80-year old lady pulled out from a hospital parking lot directly in front of me. Even before I could hit the brakes, there was a sickening thud as metal crushed metal. The bike went one way as I tumbled and scraped the asphalt with my bare knees. It all happened so quickly! Sprawled helplessly on the busy street, I worried that a car might run over me. As the ambulance crew gently picked me up and carried me away, I could still hear the old woman giving the cops hell!

"Why didn't he get out of my way?" she squawked.

The nurse used sandpaper on my knees to clean the embedded gravel and dirt from my skin. After many X-rays and tests were taken, I came out of the hospital with crutches and a cast on my left leg. The first thing I tried was to ride the bike home with the cast. It was impossible, so a kind police officer helped me take it home.

I hobbled back to the Ghost Ship a little bruised and broken, but thanked God that I was alive. It was odd that this happened—of all days—the day I went to church. Second thoughts were given before going to church again. Anyway my thoughts are, that the best church is God's own temple—the tranquil forest and mountains, away from the maddening crowds. That is where God's presence can be felt.

The next day I laid in pain, suffered under the burning roof of my van, and prayed for rain or at least some shade from the near 100 degree temperature and humidity. In the next few days I slowly hopped back to work on one leg.

In two weeks I broke the cast off and fortunately the doctor said it was healed. A small carving was his pay and before long I was almost as good as new.

In each state some Hungarians, Austrians, or German people looked me up. In Michigan a fine Hungarian family invited me and the smallest man in the world for goulash dinner. The man introduced me to one of his friends as the Hungarian that is giving Indian sculptures to America, unlike the other Hungarian who gave the atomic bomb to America.

How many Americans have ever thought of the Hungarians that contributed to America? Some of the top-notch football players in the nation are Hungarians like Larry Czonka and Joe Namath. Zsa Zsa and Eva Gabor are pretty well-known celebrities. The point this author is trying to make is, if a little-known country like Hungary gave so much to America, then how much more the Indians, English, French, Polish, Spanish, Negro, Mexicans, Germans, and all other nationalities gave? No matter what part of the world we're from, we should be proud of what we are because above and beyond all things we're all human beings, equally endowed by God, the creator, to accomplish great things. Be proud of who you are!

The smallest man in the world arrived for goulash at my friend's house. We feared for his safety from the big family dog. Mihaly Meszaros instantly made himself comfortable in the highcair (baby chair), drank whiskey, smoked a big cigar and challenged me to hand wrestle. He was the most arrogant, foul mouthed man I ever met. His usage of dirty words almost embarrassed me. Then he started in on the virtues of communism. His foul mouth never got him into fights because he was too small. We may have disagreed on ideology, but Mihaly was one of the most colorful and interesting persons that I ever met.

The waiting continued for the Parks Department to move the partially finished sculpture. The present location, between two houses, was a most unnatural setting for it. Surprisingly, people started noticing the sculpture and a few would occasionally stop to ask what was going on. The answer was always simple.

"This is the land of the Potawatomi, Piankeshaw, Ottawa, Menominee, and Chippewa. These are the first settlers. Many Native Americans have lived here, hundreds, perhaps thousands of years before the white man's arrival, and we have the gall to claim that Columbus discovered America?

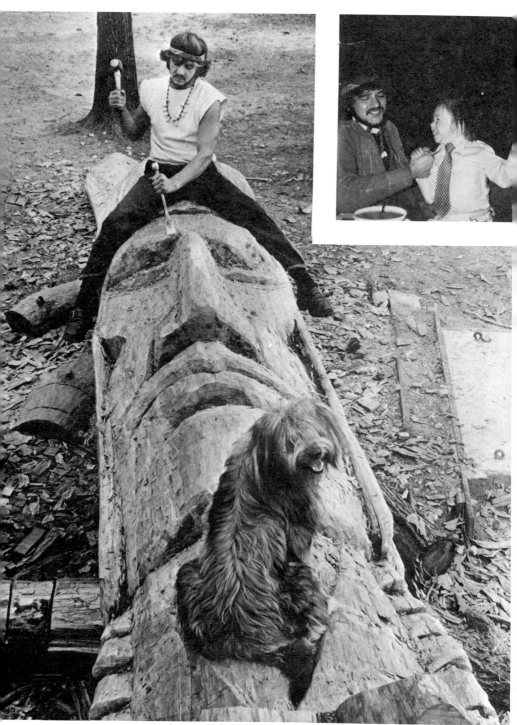

At work in Potter's Park with faithful companion, Smokey. (insert) Hand wrestling with the smallest man in the world.

How ridiculous! These noble people have suffered great defeats trying desperately to cling to their homeland, heritage, pride, and dignity.''

Such was the way Pontiac was brought up by his father, to respect the ways of his people. Because of his hate for the English, and love for his people and the French, Pontiac had a plan to unite the lake tribes and destroy the invading English. He had a brilliant military strategy and lived to see the day that most English forts, except Detroit and Fort Pitt, fell to Pontiac's War.

Although Pontiac was unsuccessful, he brought on the longest siege of Detroit in American military history. As the siege dragged on nearly one year, the promised help never came from the French. The Indians felt discouraged and wanted to return home for the seasonal hunting and made their own peace with the English. With his warriors abandoning him, Pontiac withdrew his remaining forces from Detroit and went to live a peaceful existence in Ohio. While on his way home from visiting French friends in St. Louis, Pontiac was assassinated by an English serogate as he stayed in a Cahokia village. Because of the lake tribe's love for Pontiac, they declared war on the Illini tribes and exterminated most of them.

Visiting with Native Americans. (photo by Jerry Skuse)

Most Indians seem to nave inherited difficulty conforming to our culture. It's understandable since they were used to a differnt way of life that was practiced for hundreds of years.

One Indian family that I became close friends with in Lansing were the Brunks, a successful example of harmony and unity between the two cultures. Jim and Alice Brunk, and their handsome family, lived in a quiet average neighborhood in Lansing. It was a treat and honor for me to be invited to a real Indian supper. Mrs. Brunk prepared the meal much the same way that her ancestors had done in the past. It was quite an honor to be among these people. Alice went to a lot of work preparing this delicious meal, the only one of its kind I've eaten. Before my departure, Alice gave me a gift of a hand-crafted necklace that she made from bear claws.

Peter wearing bear claw necklace, a gift from Indian friend, Alice Brunk. (photo by Bruce Colwell)

The Lansing Parks Department was not only unhelpful, but to make matters worse, one morning they stopped out with a letter that read, "All work must cease immediately."

"What the hell is the meaning of this insulting letter?" I demanded to know from the messenger who was none other than the Director of the Parks.

"If you remember, Peter, I told you to wait for our approval to start this project. For three weeks now you've been working on it."

"Your approval? Hell! I don't need your permission! This is not city property and as far as I'm concerned, you can all just go to hell!"

Angered at the shabby treatment from the Lansing Park Department, I threw my tools in the Ghost Ship and contemplated leaving. After all, some of my previous monuments had been assessed at over $25,000 in value and I was giving it as a gift to the city.

About this time a young black man stopped from the newspaper and interviewed me. He promised that the media would come to my rescue. The newspaper blasted the city for not doing their part since I was giving this monument to the people, especially since the city recently bought an $80,000 "metal monstrosity sculpture" as people called it. The local TV talk show interviewed me in length. Several outlying cities offered to move the partially finished sculpture and erect it in a desirable location in their communities. People thronged out assuring me of their support for the Indian's monument. Native Americans from the Lansing Indian Center came to offer their help. All of a sudden, the City and Parks Department did a complete turnabout and promised their complete cooperation. It was a good feeling to have such support from the community.

We selected the best available spot for the Indian in the interior of Potter's Park. The cement base was poured and finally the Indian sculpture was at its new location.

Many people came to enjoy the park, zoo, and my sculpting. Some stood around watching me chip lifelike features into the big 30 foot high, 15,000 pound log.

"How can you stand people staring at you like some animal in a cage?" a young college student asked me one day.

For some reason I felt a little offended by that remark. Many people are curious and ask questions, others just stare because they may be too bashful to speak up.

"Yes, at times it does bother me when people stare, even to the point of a fast retreat into the privacy of the Ghost Ship. But what about a celebrity, politician, or attractive people? All are stared at. Staring can be interpreted many ways, some negative, but mostly it's a positive, well-meaning gesture and usually I am not offended, but flattered by it."

The August heat was tempered by the shade of an oak tree grove that towered above the monument as it was taking shape. A couple times a day, I'd run Smokey down to the river that was only 300 yards away for a swim.

Now the monument was not too far from being finished. People came by to shake my hand. A distinctive middle-aged man stood around a long time admiring my monument and seemed especially interested in the sculptures I made for other states. He introduced himself as Ralph Brown. He praised my work and asked me if I had plans for Illinois.

"No, I haven't. Not yet anyway."

"Then how'd you like to sculpt it between Peoria and Chicago, Ill., in a mini-park beside some Hopewell burial mounds?" He paused for a moment.

"Don't say yes or no, think about it and call me. By the way, we'll get the log and materials for you and work with you all the way."

Summer was over and it was almost September, and so far I hadn't received a positive response from the state of Kentucky. It was too late in the season to head north, so the news that Illinois wanted me was welcomed.

The next few days were spent putting the near 100 coats of wood preservative and sealer on the finished sculpture. To make a few dollars for gas and barterings, I worked on some small carvings. Besides a small eagle and a female nude, I finished a plaque for the elderly lady that let me use her electricity. Alice Brunk and her family, as well as a couple other special friends, received one of my carvings as gifts.

On my last day as I packed the Ghost Ship, the Lansing newspaper came to bid me farewell and take several pictures of the finished Indian sculpture. At about the same time, my friend Alice Brunk and her two daughters, Barb and Shirley, stopped to say goodby. Her daughters were in native costumes, so I persuaded them to pose with me in front of the monument for the newspaper photographer. These Ottawa Indian maidens really enhanced the picture. Their mother, Alice, was sure proud of them. She also took much pride in their culture and her native arts and crafts. Even to this day, we have remained good friends and keep in touch through letters.

NO. 16 MONUMENT
HOPEWELL ESTATES
SPARLAND, ILLINOIS—OCT. 1975

Driving southwest toward Illinois with the western sun burning my eyes, I was completely lost in thought about this flat prairie state. Smokey panted from the heat; his long red tongue dripped saliva as we pushed forward.

Ohio's Becki was now just a memory, but leaving two girls that I dated behind in Michigan made me feel a little sad. At the same time it was a feeling of relief to be free like the wind, not fettered by women, house, or by any place or thing.

As we moved down the quiet country highway my thoughts were focused on my freedom. Sometimes I dreamed of finding someone special to share my life with. My thoughts drifted back to all the girls I knew and loved. At this period of my life, I was greedy and never satisfied with the attentions of only one young lady. Due to the loneliness of the road, I turned to the affec-

Illinois Indian Monument located on Highway 29, Hopewell Estates, Sparland, Illinois (30 miles north of Peoria). Oak

tions of attractive young women I met. Ann was a beautiful blue-eyed blonde with a perfect smile, and Jan was appealing with her soft brown eyes and short brown hair. Though I was in love with only one, however strange this may sound, I cared deeply for others at the same time. It was an enriching experience to have the opportunity to know and care for so many different individuals. I learned a lot about people and grew from this experience, even from those who cursed me and this happened more times than I care to admit.

It always seems easier to remember the good things of my life, the many kind things done and it's so easy to erase all the unkindness and tears I have caused. If only the hands of time could be turned back, allowing me to be more forgiving, understanding, and above all, kinder to everyone. It's impossible to go back and undo all the wrong done, but perhaps now would be a start to resolve and improve over my past errors.

I drove across the Illinois River into the congested traffic of Peoria and turned north onto a pot hole filled Highway 29. We were now close to Hopewell Estates, a distance of less than thirty miles away. The road widened and seemed to improve as I left Peoria.

Four miles from Chillicothe, on the west side of the highway, the big sign read HOPEWELL ESTATES. The gravel entrance road wound its way up a steep embankment, even Smokey seemed disturbed by the sudden incline. He looked around nervously as if he was going to slide off the seat.

From the top of these bluffs one could see the winding Illinois River cut through the heavily forested lowlands. This created a breathtaking view, especially as white clouds rolled in. These bluffs were the home of the Hopewell Indians—the mound builders. I could just see them looking over this same scenery, thanking the Great Spirit for the beauties of his creation.

At the top of the bluff was an attractive cedar model home under construction. The front of the building had many glass windows for visibility. Across the gravel road stood a used trailer.

While sizing up the place, looking for the best location to erect the monument, I heard a familiar voice.

"Glad to see you made it, Pete," came the voice of Ralph Brown as he walked up to me.

Ralph was my first contact in Lansing, Michigan who invited me to come and make the monument at Hopewell Estates for Illinois.

"Well, what do you think of this place?"

"It's beautiful here," I said.

"I thought you might like this high bluff for your monument. There is clear visibility up here from Highway 29. Later, I'll show you the Indian mounds I told you about, but for now, let me introduce you to the owner, Bob Dose, and the boys."

We crossed a ditch and climbed the stairs up to the trailer and met everybody. I discovered Hopewell Estates was being formed by a land development company and Bob, being the owner, had five men working for him. Ralph was his right-hand man who managed the place. The development was just opening and was bustling with activity. Roads were being opened, water lines laid, and lots were being staked for prospective buyers. It was true, I was taken with the impressive view, but I was having second thoughts about placing the monument in a likely position for exploitation by advertising.

Ralph, Bob, and I sat and discussed the large log and other materials needed for the monument. Bob was ready to get started and said he would take care of all materials. He understood that the Indian monument was my gift to the people of Illinois, so he would dedicate a mini-park at the entrance of the bluff specifically for it. After giving it much thought, I decided that even if the monument should be used for promotion, it would still serve the purpose of my cause, to bring awareness to the difficulties of the American Indian.

Our meeting concluded and my commitment was established. I sat in the trailer drinking a cold glass of water when a young attractive girl entered. What struck me immediately was her pretty face. She was light complected with blonde hair and blue eyes, and her full lower lip protruded slightly. She wore rust colored slacks and a matching shirt over her small frame and flashed a beautiful smile that was warm. I felt immediately drawn to her.

After a brief introduction she exclaimed, "I thought the man that was making the totem pole was much older."

"But I don't make totem poles," was my patient reply, and after showing her pictures of some of the other monuments, she understood that it was to be an Indian head. We chatted about the reason for my monuments, little did I realize that this girl, Kathy Jensen, would someday play a most important role in my life.

Kathy lived at home with her parents and younger sister on a farm close to Toluca. She commuted an 80 mile round trip to an office job in Peoria. The visit to the trailer was to see about working for her Uncle Bob as his receptionist/bookkeeper.

The prospect of having her work here was inviting. I wanted to get to know her better. She wasn't married, but as pretty as she was, I was afraid she would have a steady guy.

That week a huge burr oak log was hauled in and my work began. By the weekend the oak was stripped of bark and ever so slowly I was making progress. Saturday morning the place came alive with visitors. The weekend consisted of promoting lot sales by inviting people out for free barbecue sandwiches and cider. I saw Kathy waving to me as she walked up to the cedar building which was used as the office and disappeared inside.

The following week a crane was scheduled to raise the Indian onto the cement base. It was a hectic day, but in less than an hour we had the Indian standing, as well as the feather secured in position.

*I watched Kathy's car disappear in the enfolding darkness. She was the last to leave and the bluff was quiet and empty without her. Since she had started working here, I had grown accustomed to her pretty smile each morning as she arrived for work.

Fall brought with it more than colorful leaves and pumpkins. A mutual bond of love developed between Kathy and me. Time passed quickly at Hopewell; days became weeks. Often we'd drive my motorcycle up to the tallest Hopewell mound and sit around enjoying the fabulous view with clear visibility for miles around. We would contemplate the lives of these ancient people. A short time back, three skeletal remains of a man, woman, and child were uncovered by an archaeologist here. It was a tempting thought to dig into the mound and perhaps uncover valuable ancient artifacts, but the thought of desecrating this link to the past was abhorrent. We just gazed and dreamed of a different world.

In our minds we could hear the beating of the Hopewell drums and below us the Illinois River came to life with Indian trade canoes. Women with long black hair washed their clothes as children giggled and played along the muddy shores of the big river.

While the life of the Hopewell Indians was at times filled with sudden storms of terror and violence, it was by no means one of constant strife. Above all, it had a magical sense of rightness that enveloped the people with a certain serenity. Among the Hopewell, as with more modern tribes, there is little indication of whole nations overrun by war. Strangers were often treated with hospitality. The raids that were called wars by historians often involved only a fraction of the available fighting men and then only briefly. When a tribe was completely defeated they were assimilated rather than annihilated.

Nearly two thousand years later the Hopewell Empire was gone, but most Indians lived on in much the same way. At the white man's arrival in the 1600's, the main Indians in Illinois were the Kaskaskia, Peoria, Kickapoo, and Cahokia.

The recognized Indian village of Saukenuk was located near present day Rockford. It was one of the larger settlements in this country and in the early 1820's consisted of 4,000 Sauk Indians. Several families were housed in a lodge and in all there were about 100 lodges. This was a land of plenty with fish in the river, fine springs, and 800 acres of cultivated fields.

The last resistance of the northwestern tribes came by way of Black Hawk's War of 1832. The Sauk Chief attempted to rally support among other Indian tribes and hold out against the order of the government to move his village of Saukenuk west of the Mississippi River. Black Hawk fought hard against the military, but it was a futile war. The village of Saukenuk was attacked and the military shot up Black Hawk's fleeing people. Before his defeat, he waged terror over the settlers up and down the Mississippi River. This was one of the last sad wars of the Old Northwest, where young Abe Lincoln was called out for possible action.

In the daytime my sculpting continued on the high scaffolds. The Indian looked over his valley at his long lost domain with a silent stoical gaze of a sentry warrior.

October and November were months of bright Indian summer days. The sun draped the land in hues of yellow, red, and orange. It was as if the Great Spirit painted the leaves and earth before our feet and enhanced my time with Kathy. In the late afternoons, we'd go for bike rides and long walks under the trees.

Pete and Kathy at Illinois dedication with Indian dancers in background.

On occasion Kathy would invite me over to her parent's farm by Toluca to spend time with her parents, Lowell and Rosemary Jensen; sister, Carol; and brother Bruce and his wife, Linda. We'd all sit around and talk of Indians, Europe, and farming while dining on a fine supper made by Kathy's mother, Rosemary.

In the chill of the autumn night the harvest moon lit up the freshly plowed and disked fields. We saddled the horses and galloped across the open fields. I loved Kathy and it was hard to think of leaving her behind, but my days were numbered and Mississippi was awaiting my arrival.

Many nights I slept on the couch in the living room of the Jensens and thought of how they treated me like family. Marriage was on my mind and Kathy's too.

The festivities for the dedication at Hopewell were well planned in advance. The day before the big event a catering service from Peoria prepared a pig roast. A huge tent was put up where food was served.

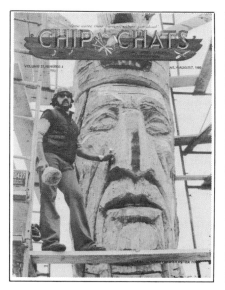

Some of the national and local magazine covers that carried the "Trail Of The Whispering Giants."

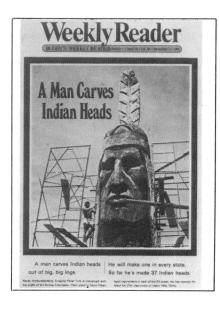

Jimmy Mustache (Running Elk), a Chippewa medicine man flew in from Hayward, Wisconsin to appear at the ceremony in full headdress and Chippewa attire. Boy Ladd, a friend of Jimmy Mustache's, and several Chippewa tribal dancers entertained and spoke to the people of their Indian heritage.

The weather was beautiful for the middle of November, it reached near 70 degrees. Boy Ladd presented to me, as a gift of thanks, his colorful beaded neck broach that he was wearing made by his Indian wife; in turn I gave him a small sculpture. In the final dance of the Circle of Friendship, a few people from the crowd participated in keeping step with the drums. The day ended successfully.

The Indian monument was finished and the late November winds told me that I had to go. I drove the Ghost Ship to the Jensen's house and left Kathy with a promise that we'd see each other soon.

Many states were left with an empty feeling inside, but in Toluca Kathy stole my heart. She was the girl for me, but our love needed the test of time. In my heart I knew Kathy loved me, but I remembered girls in the past that told me that they loved me, but it turned out to be mere infatuation, here one day and gone the next. In this age and time, fools marry over and over again not thinking that their vows of love and respect are suppose to be forever, but instead are meaningless words to them. My marriage must be an example of trust based on respect, not some feeble promise of religion or other excuse to keep me true. When my time for marriage to Kathy came I would know and accept it with a true heart.

NO. 17 MONUMENT
OCEAN SPRINGS, MISSISSIPPI—DECEMBER, 1975

The long trip to the Gulf of Mexico was made even longer by the snowstorm I encountered. The main roads were quickly cleared off and soon the warmer climate of the South was upon me. Mississippi was in the midst of a heat wave and the Gulf of Mexico was nearly warm enough to swim in.

Ocean Springs Chamber of Commerce and Percy Miller prepared a roadside park along Highway 90 to be the site of my monument. The Gulf was only a couple of blocks away and my fishing pole was ready for action.

The next morning Percy Miller drove me out to the Cumbest Sawmill to check out a large cypress log that was available for the sculpture. The ancient, approximately 1800 year old log was drug out of the Pascagoula River Swamp many years ago by the father of Lum, Elvis, and Hilliari Cumbest. They now donated it to my cause. The following day the over five-foot diameter red cypress, along with a smaller two-foot log for a feather, was trucked out to the roadside park rest area and my work began.

Up until now cypress was never available for my large monuments. The wood was fairly soft and cream in color; when exposed to the sun it soon turned silver.

Ocean Springs, Mississippi Indian Monument. Toth speaks on plight of the American Indian at the dedication as Governor Cliff Finch looks on. Cypress. (photo by George Ziz, The Sun-Herald)

After a couple of weeks the chips were piled high and the cement base was poured. Passers-by started taking notice and the friendly people of Ocean Springs invited me over to their homes.

My neighbors, Hurley and Edna Mathieu, offered to let me use their bathtub for washing up and frequently they came to see how the log changed.

They told me about the time that a man was found murdered in the park just a couple of years back and the killer was never found. It didn't worry me much because the Ghost Ship was never bothered before, besides, good old Smokey kept an all-night vigil outside my door. If someone wanted to harm me, Smokey would give me a signal and I'd come out fighting like a wildcat. My adversary should be real careful trying to attack me, lest he gets hurt. My rifle gathered dust because it was never used. Should a maniac attack me, a well placed bullet in the legs might scare him off. The belief of not taking a life has always stayed with me, even in war, killing is nothing short of murder. Besides a few wild women that came to my door, no one gave me any problem.

It would be a terrible boring world where a person would not have any strife and everything would be hunky-dory with no uncertainty. My mom has often described heaven as such a place. We will sing and pray all day, she would say.

The American Indian lived in a world of uncertainty, a world full of ghosts, goblins, Gods, and incredible beasts lying under lakes, rivers, and oceans. Their life was much more full of uncertainty than ours. Sometimes much is lost because we know for a fact that beyond a giant forest of pine is just more pine. How much more exciting would it be not to know what mystery lies beyond swamps or lakes. Those old days are gone forever.

The Biloxi and Mobile Indians made their homes along the Gulf in this state.

The Natchez were one of the most interesting and unique tribes of people in the 17th century. They numbered approximately 4,000; an example of a Temple Mound state surviving into modern times; perhaps the Natchez were a link to the ancient Hopewells.

They were ruled by a king who was a descendant of the Sun, called the Great Sun. Their complicated, yet precisely defined hierarchy, was controlled with such accurate rank, that the king had absolute and despotic control over everyone's lives. In affairs concerning the nation as a whole, the Sun was controlled by a council of respected old men. Below the Suns in importance was a class of Nobles, and below the Nobles a class called the Honored Men. (This was a rank anyone could aspire to by a great deed in war or piety.) Below all these titled aristocrats were the Stinkards. These commoners were treated like dirt and justly hated their title.

The Suns could not intermarry, but had to find spouses from among the Stinkards. Descent was held in the female line. The children of female Suns remained Suns, but the children of male Suns were reduced to Nobles. It was the same with the Nobles. The children of female Nobles remained Nobles, but the children of male Nobles were reduced to Honored Men or

Women. Likewise, the children of an Honored Woman remained an Honored Man or Woman, but the children of an Honored Man were reduced to Stinkards. And of course the children of two Stinkards were absolute Stinkards.

The female Suns had great power. Her Stinkard husband had to stand in her presence as a servant, shout his praise of her every remark, could not eat with her, and for any minor reason she could have his head cut off. She could have as many and any lover she chose, or replace her Stinkard husband at a snap of her little finger. And yet all this was going on in a warrior state where a husband alone commanded.

De Soto, the first white explorer in the Mississippi area, was believed to have encountered the Natchez worshipers of the sun. He sent word that he was the Sun's younger brother. They told him that if he could dry up the Mississippi River, they would accept his credentials. The Natchez joined other Mississippi tribes in merrily chasing de Soto and his group down the river.

One French observer recalls seeing transvestites among the Natchez. They wore their hair in female fashion, long and braided, wore skirts, and worked with the women. Some homosexuals among the numerous Indian tribes were severely punished, while others were looked on as deities, but most were treated with embarrassed tolerance.

The Chickasaw tribe of northern Mississippi were one of the most feared, aggressive, and far-ranging war-like people. Since Chickasaw country was by the Mississippi River, they were a constant menace to the French trading canoes. From 1736 to 1753 the French waged five wars against the Chickasaw and were beaten each time. The feared Chickasaws handed thundering defeats to the Creeks and Cherokee at different times in major wars, although both of these nations outnumbered the Chickasaws terribly. The Chickasaws never lost a major battle though they were by far the smallest of four Civilized Tribes of the Choctaw, Cherokee, Chickasaw, and Creek.

During the eighteenth century, the intact nations of the Southeast prospered. Livestock was acquired and improved farming methods practiced. Many Indians took to European clothes and houses. The Chickasaw developed the locally famous Chickasaw horse which was a breedy and nervy strain supposedly based on imported stock from New Mexico. The Choctaw developed the Choctaw pony. It was admired by many and claimed to have more bottom to the hand of height than any other horse in existence.

*Because of the French tyranny against the Natchez in the year 1729, a full-scale war was raging in Mississippi. Natchez warriors attacked the French, killing 200 and making prisoners of hundreds of women, children, and black slaves. The Choctaws agreed to fight against the French, but then double-crossed the Natchez. Their defection to the French had been a decisive factor in the war, even if only the western village of the collosal Choctaw nation was involved in the conspiracy and double-cross. They were divided into two parties, pro-English in the east and pro-French in the west.

The Natchez were defeated and many were tricked by the French to surrender. Some were burned at the stake, but most were shipped and sold as slaves in Santo Domingo. Remaining groups of Natchez went into exile among the Chickasaw, Creeks, and Cherokee. As the three great Christian nations collided in their power struggle, determined to fight to the last Indian, the Natchez went the way of the Southeast Indians, into oblivion. Now, only a town in Mississippi bears witness to their existence by name only.

The first month in Mississippi my thoughts drifted to my pretty girlfriend in Illinois. Many letters and poems were written to her. Dating other girls was of little interest. Somehow the lonely mood, at the time was right for me. Kathy wrote that she missed me and decided to take up my invitation to come and visit for Christmas.

With a chain saw, I split the 2 foot diameter log in half and proceeded to chisel a 15-foot feather from it. We raised the Indian with a crane to its cement base and fit the feather on top which sure made a great difference. Already it was better than halfway done, but the real shaping was yet to begin. The scaffolds were secured in place and with hammer and chisel I really started working to improve the Indian's proportion.

The historical town of Ocean Springs is nestled on the Gulf of Mexico with Biloxi to the west and Pascagoula to the east. It is known for its enchanting environment, tall oaks are laced with Spanish moss. Magnolia and tall pines landscape historic old homes. The town's population is about 15,000. The French Fort Maurepas, built here in 1699, was the first permanent settlement in the southern Gulf region. The area has been continually occupied since. The Gulf breezes make it a year-round haven, especially from the cold winds, ice, and snow of Northern winters.

One day as I worked on the monument a man walking along the road caught my attention. He was a little old man whose raggedy white beard and old worn clothes gave him an artistic appearance. Over his left shoulder hung a bundle. He favored his right leg and limped from the rigors of the road. Since the old man looked like he could use some food and perhaps a little kindness, my arm raised in a friendly gesture to say "hello".

One traveler could only understand the pain of another—loneliness, hard times, and sadness. All this is many times compounded when you're penniless and on in years with deteriorating health. The little old man didn't need a formal invitation to stop and approach the monument. He praised my work lavishly and as he came closer, the yellow eyes and strong urine smell gave him away as a man whose troubles are washed away by a bottle of wine. I had some extra food, some kind words, and a dollar to give him that hopefully helped him escape from the harsh realities of life. Before the old man slowly wobbled away, he exchanged a few words about his travels as his image was captured in my camera. Even an old sober wino has his song.

Old traveler stops to exchange a few words.

Some days later another wino came by, not asking for a handout, but selling slingshots and pea-shooters that he made for $1 each. He impressed me so much that I bought five of them.

Two young fellows came to live in my Davidson Roadside Park—they just drifted in one morning and stayed for many days. On cool nights they kept warm by building a bonfire. They worked for a few days for the city, but when their money ran out, one walked five miles to sell his blood.

Most people that stopped to visit were very cordial and kind, but on a few occasions some would get smart with me. A couple of guys once asked me if my membership dues in the Woodcarvers Union was paid up. They seemed angry at me after I informed them that woodcarving was only part of my work. My media was also stone. Some people really tried to unnerve me.

Most of the month of December was now gone and the Indian continued taking shape. Kathy was flying in to the Biloxi airport, some 10 miles away, so a friend drove me there to pick her up. Her flight was delayed in New Orleans, but when she finally arrived it was a joyous reunion. Kathy looked pretty as she flashed a happy smile. I couldn't wait to show her the vast blue Gulf, the Indian monument, and Ocean Springs, but it would have to wait another day because darkness settled by the time we arrived home.

In the next several days there was little time for sculpting, most of my time was spent showing Kathy around. The scenery around Ocean Springs was spectacular. We went motorbike riding and on a sailboat ride with a friend on the Gulf—we had a grand time.

142

My neighbors, the Mathieus, opened their house and hearts to us. They had us over for a wonderful Christmas dinner and treated us just like family. A few days before Christmas, several people stopped by with food and treats for the holiday. Several times we visited the Raymond McKeny family and had dinner with them. We had the pleasure of meeting so many good people who were concerned about our welfare. Kathy met my Choctaw friend, Jim Bell, who came by to take lessons from me in sculpting. One morning we all went out to breakfast and talked of the problems of his people and decided on a name for the monument. After two weeks Kathy flew back to Illinois and the comforts of home. My tough way of life was very difficult for her as it had been for my ex-girlfriend, Becki.

After Kathy's departure, I felt sad and despondent. Contemplating the good times we had, I took out some of the many memorable photos. Kathy often told me of her hard years of growing up in Toluca, a small town of 1300. A boy from school would pick on her until she was in tears. This particular boy teased and embarrassed her in front of the other children—up to the eighth grade. Children can be so cruel, as much blame can be placed on some teachers who allow this to go on in the classroom. In my youth I was much like Kathy, only in my case, my European teachers would insult me and once in a while beat me. The bullies and kids much older and bigger than me often chased and sometimes even beat me up too. Growing up is tough for almost all kids everywhere in the world.

Since the loss of Kathy's company I worked harder than ever on the monument. Several newspaper and TV reporters came to interview me, some from as far away as Jackson. Each was accepted with gracious courtesy. I went out of my way to explain in detail my dream of the whispering giants and how they would help the Indians.

A few days before my departure, a nearby TV station finally took notice of my work and sent a young man to inform me they wanted an interview with me on their morning talk show. They didn't take an interest in the sculpture for all the months of my stay, now it was my turn to refuse to appear on their show.

The day of the dedication finally came on February 13, 1976. Representatives from several Indian tribes and the Governor of the 2½ million Mississippians arrived. The crowd of near 2,000 people seemed pleased with my monument. The high school band played the national anthem as Governor Cliff Finch autographed for me a newspaper clipping of the sculpture. He wrote, "To A Great American." The people of Ocean Springs and the state of Mississippi made me feel like a V.I.P. that day.

It was with some sadness, but much pride that I drove the Ghost Ship east toward my next state.

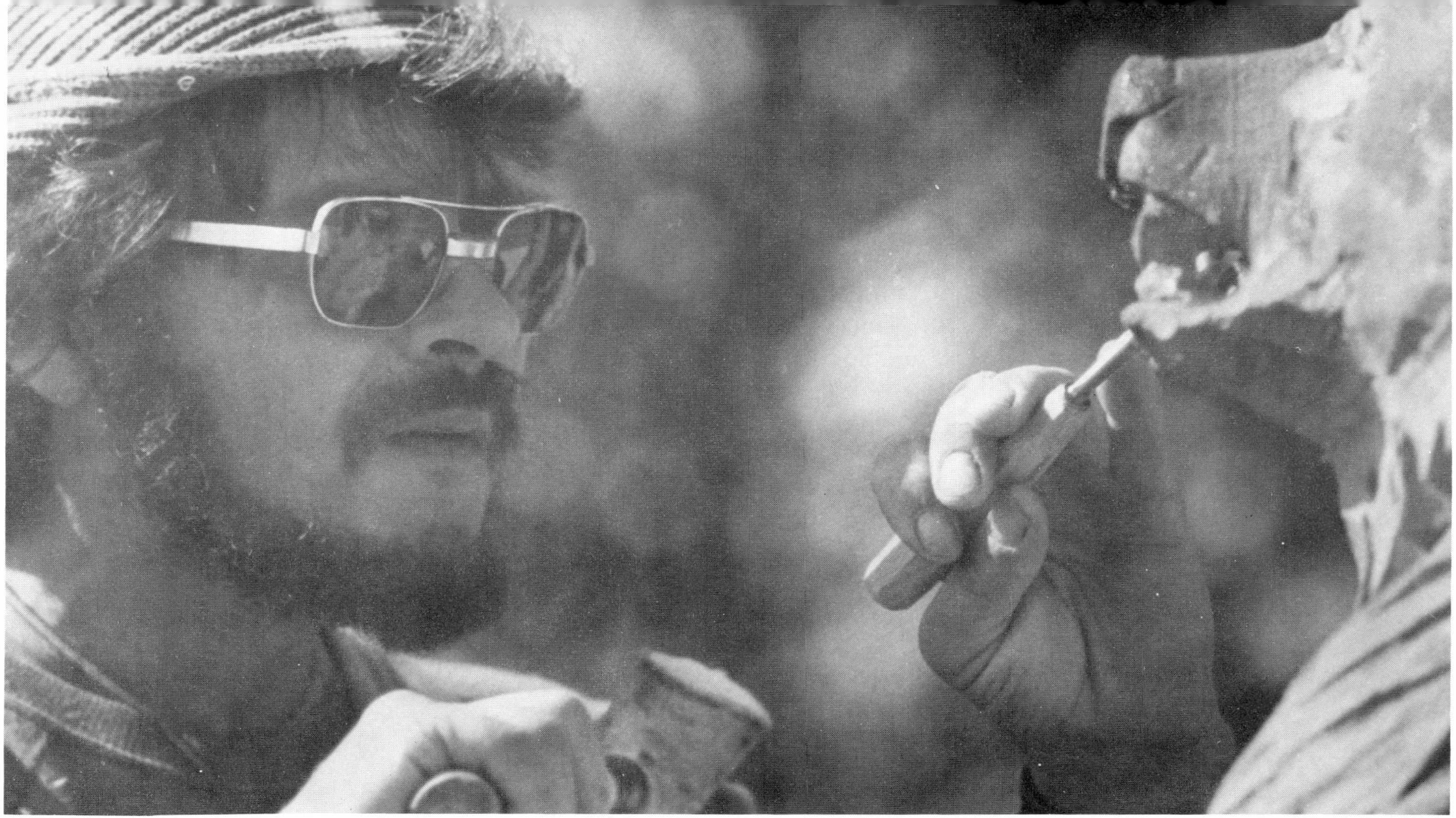

(Photo By Debbie Beckwith)

Mississippi
(Photo by Linda Skupien)
Mississippi Press

Statue dedicated
A crowd estimated at 1,500 turned out Saturday in Ocean Springs for the dedication of a wooden statue of an Indian. Sculptor Peter Toth (top left and right picture) signs his autograph and talks to the crowd attending. Gov. Cliff Finch spoke at the dedication (center left) along with Princess Neoima Whitecloud of Biloxi (center picture). The bottom photo shows the crowd along with members of the Ocean Springs High School band. (Mississippi Press Photos by Linda Skupien)

TRAVELS

It was a long drive toward North Carolina and my slow leisure pace allowed me to stop in Dothan, Alabama to see a couple of friends, including a Sioux Indian lady and her family. The Indian monument looked very good in front of the Houston Memorial Library. Before leaving Dothan, I stopped at a record shop and bartered my two foot-high sculptures for an eight-track tape player, tapes, and a CB radio. It was a good feeling to be able to use my carvings for payment.

Next stop was in Colquitt, Georgia to see some of my friends there. Smokey was in good spirits as we then made our way across the southern part of Georgia and drove well outside of Savannah's crazy traffic.

Triumphantly we made it to the East coast because to this date, I had no monument here. Almost a year ago, a Michigan girlfriend typed several letters that stated I would be hitting the East coast in 1976, and would possibly make an Indian monument for their state at no charge, but their assistance would be needed for materials and support. So far, only six towns and cities answered from the near twenty letters written. Still optimism was with me because three states wrote very positive letters with a promise to assist me should they be chosen. So now was my chance to follow up on other letters and drum up support from the uncommitted states.

Rubbing elbows with high ranking Indian chiefs, governors, senators, and influential, wealthy people gave me a fired-up zeal—nothing and no one could stop me now.

The Ghost Ship crossed into South Carolina. With literature in hand on my monuments, my first stop was in Charleston to talk to the Mayor and city officials about placing the monument in their area. Wilmington, North Carolina was awaiting my arrival, but my push was to find a location in South Carolina for the following winter. Many times it took months to get everything worked out—log found, hauled, cement poured, et cetera.

It took exhaustive days of driving through South Carolina towns and meeting with city officials before Myrtle Beach came into view. Frustration set in because of the seemingly low interest in my cause. The city hall in Myrtle Beach closed its doors for the weekend, so my decision was to stay there till Monday.

My thoughts were with Kathy and wished we could share and enjoy this beautiful place together, so I called her. We talked in length on the phone and decided that being together was more important than anything else. Kathy walked out on her job and despite her parent's disapproval, flew out on the first flight to Myrtle Beach. It was a happy reunion to have her in my arms again.

Within an hour we were on the beach collecting shells and soaking up the sun. That evening I went to a nearby motel and registered. After I paid the cashier for the room, the motel owner self-righteously handed me back my money and sent me off with insulting words.

"Beach bums give my motel a bad name. We don't want your kind staying in our motel. You've hung around the beach now for days."

My first notion was to slug the *@ + &, but fully under control I just walked away. I was glad Kathy didn't see me in this degrading light, especially since she thought of me as an important person. This was some drop in prestige from a few days back when Governor Finch of Mississippi called me a "Great American." I registered at another motel with a more friendly owner.

The next morning we made some friends with whom we went scuba diving. Later that evening they also invited us to park in front of their house for safety. We pulled off the road onto the sandy shoulders. Early the next morning there was a loud knocking on the door. Kathy was scared and before she had a chance to ask who it was, a gruff voice yelled.

"Open up, this is the police!"

"Stay here, Kathy, and don't make a sound," I said quietly. "Let me handle this." Slowly I made my way to the door and listened.

"Maybe no one is in there," said a voice. "Let's get a towtruck out here."

After awhile they left and I quickly fired up the motor to make a quick exit to avoid the towtruck, but the van's tires were bogged down in the sand. It just so happened that our friends were renting this house and the owner drove by early that morning and saw the van and immediately called the police. The cops came by again and told us that if we didn't leave in five minutes, they'd haul us to jail for violating the city ordinance against camping in the street. The van was hopelessly stuck in the sand and I nearly burned out the clutch desperately trying to get the hell out of there.

By now the word Myrtle Beach was a curse word for me; it seemed like almost everyone here was down on us. Then came our salvation, a big stinking beautiful garbage truck. For a couple of dollars he pulled the van out of the sand and we left our nightmare of Myrtle Beach behind.

NO. 18 MONUMENT
WILMINGTON, NORTH CAROLINA—MARCH 1976

We crossed into North Carolina where the seacoast in this part of the country was sparcely populated and the area was thick with timber.

Upon arriving in Wilmington we met with the Parks Department in Greenfield Park. Soon we had an understanding worked out; they agreed to let us stay in the park till the completion of my monument. We waited for the arrival of the big oak log.

The early March days in Wilmington were sunny and warm, but the nights were cold. It wouldn't be long before the park would blossom with millions of flowers. Every year the town holds an Azalea Festival.

In a few days the log was shipped in on a flatbed truck and my work began. Many people came to watch the oak log slowly taking shape.

We searched for an apartment, but they were all too expensive or the ones in our price range were in dangerous neighborhoods. I couldn't even think

Wilmington, North Carolina Indian Monument, located in Greenfield Park. Oak.

of leaving Kathy there alone. Part of the area surrounding Greenfield Park was a rough neighborhood, scattered with low-income housing projects. Bums and winos frequented the park and on pleasant sunny afternoons they'd sit around on the park benches. On one occasion, while I was away, Kathy sat reading a book on the passenger side of the van with her legs dangling out the open door. A young wino accosted her and kept repeating that she was beautiful and wanted to know if she was alone. Kathy was terrified and afraid to make any sudden moves that might bring on an attack. She tried to remain calm and spoke quietly to him. Upon my return the wino took off. The naive way Kathy handled the situation infuriated me. After understanding Kathy's fears and her sheltered upbringing, I sympathized with her dilemma and advised her next time to just tell the bums to get lost.

Greenfield Park was quiet and serene during the week, but after dark on weekends, it was a gathering spot for undesirables. Any items, such as my radio or hammer, that were left out at night were found missing by morning. One morning a four foot sculpture was drug halfway through the park. The person dragging it must have abandoned it after finding it too heavy to proceed with.

Each day Kathy grew more despondent with the hard conditions. She was self-conscious of people gawking at her. I explained to her that it was not her, but rather the Ghost Ship decorated with a small figurehead of a nude woman and other carvings and paintings that caught people's curiosity. Still she missed her family terribly and thought of going home.

Pressures weighed heavy on my shoulders. The Parks Department was slowing me down on the monument because they were holding back the cement for the base. To hurry things along, I paid for the cement myself, which was later reimbursed.

We became friends with a newly married couple who had a three month old daughter. When the young wife came to visit one day, Kathy noticed a bruise on her. She confided that her husband had an uncontrollable temper and would beat her and was surprised to learn that Kathy was never beaten. She assumed that all women are beaten occasionally—how sad!

A local crane company offered their services free of charge and we triumphantly raised my 18th monument. The feather was attached separately.

Early one morning with a stretch and a yawn, I stepped out of the Ghost Ship to begin my work when a sudden loud voice broke the morning silence.

"In the name of God, Lord Jesus, I command you to cover up the nude carving on your van or you will go straight to hell!" came the thundering voice of a short-statured man.

"What the hell is this?" My mouth fell open at the wild outburst of this religious fanatic at such an early hour.

"If you don't heed my warnings, I'll write the newspapers and boot you out of this park and the state of North Carolina!"

A bit shook up I tried to come back quickly, fighting fire with fire.

"Judge not, lest ye be judged!" was my retort.

For a minute the little man seemed puzzled. After he caught his breath he went on ranting and raving, quoting his favorite scriptures. The thought of arguing with this fanatic and acting as ignorant as him would make me feel foolish. Ignoring him, I climbed the scaffolds to get back to work on the sculpture and told him that religious fanatics made me sick. He did in fact write letters to the paper, but unfortunately for him, no one kicked me out of anywhere.

Kathy wondered if the Indians of North Carolina faced as much antagonism and nerve-wrecking situations as we did. The numerous tribes in this state were chased out, subjugated, or destroyed by the white settlers. The Tuscarora, Weapemeoc, Secotan, Pamlico, and Coree were some of the regional coastal tribes. Some may have lived on the very spot that the monument was now sculpted on in their honor.

The Waccamaw and Lumbee Indians still live in this state in small numbers. The Tuscarora once called this beautiful land their home. They and many other smaller tribes were pushed out by the onslaught of white expansion. Most refugee tribes joined up with the larger, more powerful nations like the Cherokees that lived and still live in the Smoky Mountains of

North Carolina. Most of their sacred mountains and homeland fell victim
to the greedy white demands upon their removal.

Much mystery still surrounds the "Lost Colony" of the North Carolina
Coast. It was established on Roanoke Island in 1587 by Sir Walter Raleigh.
The colony just disappeared, never to be heard from again. Rumors had it
for many years thereafter that some of the North Carolina Indian tribes
were found to have blue eyes which would have meant that the Indians accepted the second group of the English colony in America. Other reports
had it that they were all tortured and killed by their captors. It is my guess
that the hardships of the island forced the colonists to make their way to the
mainland and there they were assimilated by the often friendly Indians.

In 1975 when I spent time among the Cherokees of the Smoky Mountains, I met and conversed with a blue-eyed Cherokee who told me that blue
eyes were in his family for generations. This got me thinking, could this Indian be a direct descendant of the "Lost Colony?"

Kathy struggled to make the best of an unpleasant situation, but decided
to go back to Illinois for awhile. To prove my love for her, I bought an
engagement ring from a pawn shop and gave it to her at the airport before
she boarded the big jet. After all our differences Kathy still loved me, but
felt that she just had to go home.

An enormous burden seemed to be lifted from my shoulders, but the feeling of relief and freedom soon turned back to loneliness. Strange how a person can be lonely with dozens of people milling around. The opportunity to
date several girls arose, but my thoughts were only of Kathy.

In the evening the noisy winos around the park laughed and carried on.
This was a great time for me to compile notes for my future book, as well as
continue my study on Indians, and write poems.

My sculpting went on from dawn to dusk which helped keep me occupied.

During this time away from Kathy, I thought of changing my life style so
it would be possible for us to be together. After living in the Ghost Ship for
five years, it had become a part of me and I was reluctant to let it go. Life in
the van was too rough for Kathy to handle, though, so my thoughts drifted
to purchasing a Winnebago Motor Home, but this was something only rich
retired people could afford. Still the thought was on my mind for our
future. Due to my stubborn refusal to tow anything behind the Ghost Ship,
a trailer was out of the question. Our vehicle had to be one complete unit.

Time slipped away and in May the Indian monument was finished. The
dedication was continuously delayed because the governor was unavailable.

"He is an important, busy man, as is the Mayor of Wilmington," was the
Park Departments reply. "You'll just have to have patience."

But I couldn't wait! My time was important too and Virginia was waiting
for me. . .

Virginia Beach, Virginia Indian Monument. Located in Mt. Trashmore Park. Cypress. Small unfinished oak sculpture in foreground. (photo by Bruce Colwell)

NO. 19 MONUMENT
VIRGINIA BEACH, VIRGINIA—MAY, 1976

The Bicentennial Commission was in charge of the Indian monument project and made my monument a bicentennial theme for the city of Virginia Beach. I didn't mind, my mission had been going on for four years before the bicentennial and would be ongoing for many years after it.

It was a sunny warm day when I drove into Virginia Beach. A search was made around town for a visible spot where the Indian monument could be easily seen, where thousands, or perhaps millions, of visitors and local residents could understand the meaning behind it.

My original plan was to place the sculpture on the ocean front, but no protected site was available. Finally after two days of searching, it was agreed to place it in the nationally famous Mt. Trashmore Park, along busy Highway 44. The mountain was made from solid waste and was beautifully landscaped—one of the most picturesque parks I've seen. The park's corner, where the monument was to be placed, had millions of people driving by on their way to the beaches.

The log was to be hauled in from the other side of the state and since it was going to take at least a week, I decided to visit Kathy and also haul back some accumulated sculptures and wood to Ohio.

The following morning Smokey and I were on the long and lonesome road again as we headed northwest toward the Allegheny Mountains. The curvy steep mountainous roads of West Virginia were slow and grueling, but in two days we made it to Akron, Ohio.

My parents were real pleased to see me, and Smokey was also happy to be back in familiar surroundings. It was nice to be home, but kind of sad due to the unhappy memory of what transpired between Becki and me a year ago.

That evening I called Kathy and talked to her in length and she decided to fly to Akron to see me, which also gave me more time with my family.

My parents drove me out to meet her at the Akron-Canton Airport—I introduced Kathy as my fiancee to them.

Kathy did not get along well with my family, partly because of my parent's religious and old-fashioned European ways. (Kathy was brought up Lutheran.) The language barrier and broken English spoken by my mother made it difficult for Kathy to understand what was being said. To add fuel to the fire, on many occasions they called her Becki (my ex-girlfriend's name) which caused her a lot of emotional anguish.

Our time was spent riding the motorcycle around town as I showed Kathy where I grew up. The weather in Ohio was beautiful in early June.

One afternoon Kathy decided one of the reasons everyone was calling her Becki, was because of all my ex-girlfriends' pictures openly displayed. She decided to take things into her own hands. I came home one afternoon and found her tearing up pictures of Becki. To me, these pictures were irreplaceable because my sculptures that Becki posed with had been sold.

Peter looking for the Indian in the log.

Kathy

Whispering Feathers

Peter's Abe Lincoln—creation out of walnut.

They were the last evidence of my creations. This act enraged me and a terrible verbal fight ensued and Kathy threw her diamond ring at me and left in a cab. I was too angry and stubborn to stop her.

Unknown to me, Kathy called that evening and left her flight schedule with my mom. The morning of her departure, my mom finally brought up this information, but too late for me to do much about it. Deep down inside, my mom, like all moms, didn't like losing her son. She never liked any of the girls I dated and wanted me to marry a girl from a "Christian" family. On occasion I wondered if she subconsciously wished Kathy to be gone.

I respected and loved my mom, but my anger and frustration now turned on her. I yelled at her, an act that was almost unheard of from me. I jumped on my motorbike and took off like a bat out of hell and arrived at the airport just in time to see Kathy's plane boarding. From the flight deck I sadly watched as the plane took off for Illinois.

That same evening there was a message from Virginia that my log was to arrive in several days. As I was packing to go back to Virginia, I felt sorry for myself, but realized that perhaps fate was against Kathy and me. As a last resort to gap the crumbling bridge between us, I wrote and told her how bad I felt that her plane took off before I had a chance to let her know I still loved her.

Upon my return to Virginia Beach the benevolent gift of the 27-foot, 280 year-old cypress log from the Union Camp Corporation of Franklin was recorded with much fanfare by the media.

As before, I immersed myself in my work by hacking away at the log with my 5-lb. hammer and chisel. My mom forwarded a letter from Kathy and we resolved our differences.

Days blended into weeks; the cement base was poured and soon the Indian stood tall in the shadows of the man-made mountain.

Many friends were made during my stay and I grew to love Virginia Beach. My brother Julius, and bride Bonnie, came here for their honeymoon, so they were pleased to find out that my monument was to be here. My work continued at a good steady pace because I was committed to do three more states yet this year and though it was only late June, winter comes early in this part of the country.

The Fourth of July and the great bicentennial celebration was upon us. People were milling around anticipating the fireworks for that evening. Earlier an air force parachute jump went off successfully; not so for a water-ski kite flyer on Mount Trashmore Lake. A young man was attached to a large kite and was being pulled behind a boat. He was high in the air when he crossed over the edge of the lake and was suspended above land when tragedy struck. He fell to his death.

The fireworks were most spectacular that night. That evening on the news they showed films of the tall ships sailing in New York Harbor. What a spectacular memorable event that day was. It made me proud to be an American.

The Indian monument was close enough to completion so that we could

Hard at work.

have dedicated it for the 4th celebration, but the city and the Bicentennial Commission decided to use a three week notice and send out invitations to the state's remaining Nanticoke and other Indian tribes, the governor, and other dignitaries.

The July heat was intense and there was little shade to be found. On the far side of the mountain Smokey and I would swim in Mount Trashmore Lake. Once or twice a week I'd drive down to the ocean beaches and spend a little time there.

Smokey and I were the only residents of the park and at times it was a little lonely at night. On some evenings girls would stop by, but were often chased out by a big lady guard.

A pretty girl named Mary stopped out frequently to see the progress of the monument. We became good friends. Often she would speak of her fiance and the house they were planning to build. We'd discuss our mutual relationships and she would ask my advice on her upcoming marriage. Since Kathy and I were apart, we decided it was ok to date others, so this complication of our lives was also discussed.

Some new changes came between Kathy and me. She wrote me for my approval of any steps of independence she might make. Her happiness was most important to me, so I told her to go ahead with her plans. She paid cash for a car from the $5,000 + savings that she accumulated over the past few years and found an office job in East Peoria. Since Kathy had quit three previous jobs to be with me, she was in need for some permanence in her life. Through her friends, Sharon and Stella, a small apartment was found in East Peoria. With most of her remaining savings she bought new furniture. It must have been quite an accomplishment for Kathy to be out on her own and independent after spending the last several years with her parents.

As the monument was nearing completion, news went out on my nationwide whispering giants. People sent me letters applauding my efforts. Several letters were from different states requesting that I make their city an Indian sculpture.

A young transient, named Bob, that I met in Ocean Springs, Mississippi looked me up here in Virginia Beach. He had been following my progress on the East coast. Before he thumbed his way down the road, I shared my dinner and packed him some food for the road.

Artist's home on wheels, "The Ghost Ship." (photo by Bruce Colwell)

The day of the dedication was here. A crowd gathered to listen to speeches from the distinguished guests. Chief Curtis Custalow of the Mattaponi tribe gave the main speech; he spoke eloquently and with much dignity of his people's problems and accomplishments in modern Virginia.

With the state's population of over five million, the Indian population hardly constitutes a fraction of this figure. Still the Mattaponi and the

Chief Curtis Custalow at dedication

Pamunkey Indians are holding their own in Virginia on a state reservation. Other non-reservation Indian communities in Virginia are the Chickahominy, Rappahannock, Potomac, Accohanoc, Accomac, Nansemonds, and mixed tribes.

At the founding of Jamestown in 1607, many tribes of Indians lived here. The giant Powhatan Confederacy numbered some 200 villages led by King Powhatan (he was named after his village by the English colonists, his real name was Wahunsonacock). This village was located in the area of present day Richmond, Virginia. King Powhatan could have easily wiped out Jamestown during the first few ghastly years when the settlers died in batches in the miasmic Jamestown swamps. Of the 900 colonists that landed, after three years only 150 survived to the year 1610.

The Indians helped the white survive by sending them food and giving them the know-how of survival in the new world. There were flare-ups, but peaceful coexistence was the general rule while Chief Powhatan lived.

Pocahontas, Chief Powhatan's daughter, was the most famous woman of early American history. She was married to an Indian brave and at the age of 17 was kidnapped by the white settlers. She helped to preserve the Jamestown colony from death, famine, and war. She married John Rolfe who learned with the Indian's help how to cultivate the fortune-finding cash crop "tobacco", still the number 1 crop of Virginia. Tobacco had many spiritual facets to most Indian tribes. It was smoked for religious experience to cast out the evil, and brought good luck in wars and good weather in peace.

Pocahontas's marriage brought peace between Indians and whites. She traveled to England with her husband where she was a sensation and met the Queen and many other dignitaries. Mention of her was made in a play by Ben Johnson. Pocahontas (whose real name was Matowaka) was baptised the Lady Rebecca and later bore a son. Many of the illustrious Virginians have claimed extraction from her. At the youthful age of 21, after a short but historical life, she died of smallpox.

Less than 40 years after Jamestown's founding—the once mighty Powhatans were heading for oblivion. Now, 300 years later, it gives me pleasure to say that I can still see strength and hope and pride in Chief Curtis Custalow's eyes; a descendant of a once powerful Indian nation.

NO. 20 MONUMENT
ATLANTIC CITY, NEW JERSEY—JULY, 1976

The Ghost Ship rumbled over the Chesapeake Bay Bridge. It was a spectacular drive over the ocean. Briefly I stopped in Ocean City, Maryland to start the proceedings for the monument that was to be done later that year. Before long I was in the tiny state of Delaware and ferried across Delaware Bay. Soon conjested traffic carried me into Atlantic City, New Jersey, the home of the crowning of Miss America, as well as the host of beautiful beaches and boardwalks.

The large 4-foot diameter tulip poplar log was waiting for me in Historical Gardner's Basin, but it was situated in the middle of urban decay in a predominately black and Puerto Rican neighborhood. My first impression was completely negative of the Gardner's Basin area of Atlantic City, but optimism set in when it was pointed out to me that the city was under reconstruction to regain her former glories. Buildings were torn down and improvement was evident. Gardner's Basin was a small attraction of historical buildings and sailing ships at the old harbor. A tall link fence protected it from undesirables and vandalism. Tourists already started trickling in which convinced me to place my monument there. This will be an important location in the future and my sculpture will bring the Indian history into focus.

After much study, I decided that this Indian would be protected by an abstract, two-headed eagle. The 5 lb. hammer smashed against the chisel handle all day long and the chips piled up. Slowly the form of an Indian and eagle materialized in the state where the memory of the Indian is virtually forgotten.

It wasn't that many hundreds of years ago when this area was the thriving home of the Lenni Lenape Indians, more commonly known by the English as the Delawares because of their numerous villages along the shores of the Delaware River. The Delaware originally occupied the entire basin of the Delaware River in eastern Pennsylvania, southeastern New York, and most of New Jersey and Delaware. They lived mostly in peace with the European colonists who came soon after Verrazano explored the area in 1524. But as more Europeans arrived, the two cultures had small flare-ups. Delawares lived in peace for a little over 100 years with the white settlers because of their large number and strength, while small tribes were pushed out swiftly.

In the mid 1600's the Susquehanna conquered the Delawares, and the

Atlantic City, New Jersey Indian Monument. (left to right) Sculptor Peter Toth, Mayor Joseph Lazarow, Florence Miller, and Attilio Sinagra. Poplar. (photo by Press Bureau)

powerful Iroquois in turn conquered the Susquehanna in 1670, claiming sovereignty over the Delawares and freely sold their land to the proprietors of Pennsylvania. Now the principal avenue of expansion for settlement was through the Delaware Confederacy. This is not the first case, but one of the many cases where one tribe sold the land of others with no real authority.

The Wappinger group, relatives of the Delaware, participated in the famous sale of the land that is known as Manhattan Island, where modern New York is, for the much quoted price of $24. The educated guess of a modern economist is that the buying power of 60 gulden* worth of trinkets would have been more like several thousand dollars today, still a pittance of the land's real value.

The crimes of stealing the Indian's land or paying an unbelievable exchange for it, could almost be forgiven, but not so with the cruel inhumane sufferings practiced on them. Many atrocities were committed in the name of God. The Puritans proudly bragged and recorded their wholesale massacre of even women and children. Reverend Increase Mather rejoiced at the murders of the warriors, as well as innocent victims. The divine leaders of New England theocracies proved by Biblical interpretation that it was the sacred duty of all Christians to exterminate the Godless Indians.

In 1643 the raiding Mohawks drove the Wappinger Indians toward the Dutch settlement where they found protection. The refugees were attracted by friendly treatment. While they slept in a village on the Jersey side of the Hudson, the Dutch governor ordered their massacre. Eighty heads of men, women, and children were brought back to Manhattan, to Fort Amsterdam, where a New Amsterdam dowager played kickball with them in the street. At the same time an Indian prisoner was publicly tortured, castrated, skinned in strips—flayed from his fingers to his knees, and forced to eat his own flesh while all along he sang his death song. He was later dragged through the street. The Dutch governor was claimed to have laughed as the soldiers finally smashed his head on a mill stone.

It is only fair of me to mention that the Dutch had lost family members to warring Indian tribes. Their hatred for the Indian was great, but this could hardly justify their cruel actions. For the Indian, war, torture, and death was a normal way of life. So called civilized, God-fearing Christians should have known better and set a better example.

To rid the land of Indians, the Dutch adopted scalp bounty which in turn was adopted by most of the colonies at one time or another. Massachusetts paid £12 per scalp in 1703 (a lot of money at that time) and £100 by 1722. An enterprising killer could murder three old Indian men, two women, and a boy legally, whether they were friend or enemy, and collect $1500 in 1763. These were the unspoken atrocities committed against the Indians by our Christian Nation.

*As I was studying the now standing giant sculpture, a redheaded lady and her daughter walked up to me and demanded to know why on earth I

*gulden: Money unit of Netherlands, worth, at par, about 40 cents U.S.

would make a monument to the Indians. She informed me that last year when they were visiting a reservation out West, an Indian tried to rape her daughter. Her opinion was that they didn't deserve monuments. It seemed strange to me that the lady would hate all Indians because of the actions of a single one. There are bad people in every race.

The monument was now over halfway finished when reports that a potentially devastating hurricane was bearing down the East coast heading for Atlantic City. It rained all day long and the downpour hampered my work. On a moment's notice I decided to throw Smokey in the van and head for Peoria, Illinois—by way of Philadelphia, Pittsburgh, Columbus, and Indianapolis. The near 1,000 mile drive for a date would have been unthinkable to do for any other girl except Kathy. Was she ever surprised to see me!

Proudly she gave me a tour of her comfortable apartment and showed me her new furniture and car. She introduced me to her two dearest friends, Sharon and Stella, (both these girls lived in the same building). We had a great reunion. A week later I was back in Atlantic City to finish up the monument.

While in Atlantic City a 12-year old black neighbor boy often stopped by to watch the sculpture develop and was always eager to assist me in hauling my tools and feeding the dog. One day I had to leave suddenly on a short errand and upon my return, my friend was gone, as was $40 in cash, my rifle, and camera equipment valued at $400.

Several tall ships were tied up in the harbor for repair and show. Jeff Cleveland, an oceanographer friend, had a 40-foot sailboat with a dinghy. He allowed me to use the tiny 4-foot boat for fishing.

The August heat was too much for swinging a 5-lb. hammer, so with Smokey, I paddled the dinghy out to the harbor among the big ships. It was hard to navigate with a canoe paddle in the strong currents and wind, so I held the boat's rope in my teeth, jumped in the refreshing, cool water, and pulled the boat behind me as Smokey barked loudly. A large crowd gathered on shore watching me swim through the cluster of big boats.

"What the hell you doing here? You should be in the Olympics show off!" someone yelled. Some people just stared in disbelief. This feat wasn't new to me, I was a powerful swimmer and was able to swim long distances.

A quarter-of-a-mile down the bay, a small U.S. Coast Guard boat pulled alongside of me.

"The radio has been blaring for the past hour that some nut was swimming with a rope in his mouth pulling a boat. I didn't believe it—now I do!" the guard laughed. He was very cordial and offered to tow me back because swimming in the bay was against the law. It was only a short time ago a local shore patrolman chased me out, threatened to put me in jail, and fined me $17 just because I wasn't wearing a life jacket.

Before leaving Atlantic City I took the little dinghy out for the last time. It was now propelled by a small motor. With squid for bait I followed the fishing boats and caught several flounders. It was near dusk when I made my way back home from the open sea with a dozen good eating fish. At low tide the rushing water produced fearful large areas of turbulence across the mouth of the narrow bay. As the little boat hit the foaming water it was nearly torn apart. My fears of being capsized or of getting washed out to sea did not materialize. After what seemed like hours of navigating through the frenzied water, the little motor pushed the boat through the turbulence, but not before half of the back end was ripped off. Water was rushing in fast. One hand held the half-torn end in place while the other hand maneuvered the boat back to the harbor. The boat was almost lost, but the thing that worried me the most was losing the fish.

The evenings in Atlantic City were lonesome for me. Many thousands of people milled around on the boardwalk; even with the side shows, attractions, and beautiful beaches, I can scarcely remember making a friend. On some evenings, out of sheer loneliness, I was drawn outside the basin harbor gates and crossed the ghetto section of the city, defying the possibility of getting jumped just to mingle with the faceless crowds. Each excursion just left me more empty than before.

A tall ship with several young people docked at our harbor. Some of the sailors, who were pretty tough in their own right, walked through the same ghetto area on their way to the boardwalk. Coming back they got more excitement than they bargained for. Several blacks jumped and beat the hell out of them. They later surmised maybe the reason I wasn't jumped was because with my dark tan, the blacks assumed I was Puerto Rican. They didn't like to mess with Puerto Ricans, they said, because these people often carried knives.

The Indian was now finished and after applying many coats of wood preservative and varnish, we dedicated it with the Mayor and half-a-dozen other people in attendance. It was too bad for the Indian's cause and the people of New Jersey that the media's coordination was most ineffective. Aside from the local small newspaper reporting on it, no radio or TV people knew or bothered to come out to find out the meaning of my work. It was disappointing.

Florence Miller and Attilio Sinagra took me out to dinner and we quietly celebrated the finishing of the 20th Indian monument.

NO. 21 MONUMENT
OCEAN CITY, MARYLAND—SEPT. 1976

It was early September when the Ghost Ship pulled into Ocean City, Maryland, commonly referred to as the vacation capital of the East. People from Baltimore and Washington D.C. stream out here by the tens-of-thousands each summer to enjoy the beautiful beaches. The city's population swells from 1500 to over 100,000 during the tourist season.

The temperature was hovering well over 90 degrees. Smokey could hardly wait to get out of the hot Ghost Ship and go for a swim, but unfortunately dogs weren't allowed on the beach, so poor Smokey was left tied panting

*Ocean City, Maryland Indian Monument on the shores of the Atlantic.
Oak.*

under the van. The beach was crowded, but the cool ocean was refreshing. That evening I looked up Elizabeth Sanford, head of the city's Beautification Committee who corresponded with me and we set up a meeting with Mayor Harry Kelley. As the Parks Department prepared a place for my sculpture, the good news came that a log was found in Snow Hill. The next day after giving instructions to the Parks Department about the steel rods and cement needed for the foundation, I drove the approximately 17 miles to Paul M. Jones Lumber Co. in Snow Hill, Maryland.

The owner of the sawmill, Paul M. Jones, Jr., was a big man with a heart to match and we soon became good friends. He not only donated a big oak log, but also allowed me to stay and work on it in his sawmill yard until the base was prepared in Ocean City. The use of electricity and a chain saw for cutting the rough knots and squaring off the base of the log was also provided. For the next three or four weeks my stay was pleasant and I became acquainted with the townspeople.

All small towns have unique characters and Snow Hill with 2,200 people was no different. As soon as people found out about my sculpture they came to watch its progress. One girl was there nearly every day to see how the log was taking shape and even helped me by posing for some female figures. Before I left Snow Hill, this girl asked me to father her a child. Instead of a baby, I gave her a sculpture for her help and friendship.

We finally moved the half finished sculpture to Ocean City and raised it up on the finished cement base. My 21st Indian monument now proudly stood by the Atlantic Ocean overlooking his new domain in Inlet Park, by the southeastern corner of the city.

Though the weather was still very warm, most of the big summer crowds were now thinning out. Due to a city ordinance against sleeping in vehicles, arrangements were made for me to stay in the Oceanic Motel, adjacent to the monument. The woman in charge of the motel must have been annoyed with me because girls would call at all hours. On several occasions girls hung around my motel room at late hours and once two slept outside my door. Most of these girls were only friends of mine. It was flattering to have admirers, quite a change from humdrum and lonesome Atlantic City, New Jersey. My small carving that I left as a gift to the motel hopefully compensated for the inconvenience.

Mayor Harry Kelley dropped by often to see the progress on the sculpture and occasionally gave me complimentary dinner tickets to Phillip's Crab House, a fine local seafood restaurant.

Life was good in Maryland. My mind wandered to a harder time when the Nanticoke Confederacy ruled this part of the coast. Captain John Smith first explored Maryland in 1608, home of the Nanticoke Confederacy, Chapticon, Choptank, and Nacotchtank. Today there is not one official Indian group left in this state.

Through the process of bartering, a wet suit and surfboard were purchased and some evenings, with my surfboard, I swam across the inlet to Assateague, an island famous for wild ponies. The tranquility of the island was worth the long swim and the surf was bigger there. I became so involved in surfing that it was dusk before I started to paddle home against the strong ocean currents. A yacht came by and illuminated me with its floodlight and in the confusion I was taken off course by the currents. It was midnight before I found my way back to the fishing dock close to the motel. Some of the fishermen were startled at my presence in the black water and warned me of sharks that came in to feed at night.

It was October in Ocean City and the beaches were wide open as the wind tore at the Atlantic surf creating turbulence, as in the Pacific. This gave me a chance to use my surfboard and every day an hour or two was spent surfing. At certain times of the night, sea trout would make a run down by the fishing pier. I'd be fishing alongside others, and everyone was pulling them in but me.

My friend, Paul Jones, invited me deep sea fishing. At 5 a.m. we went out into the open sea and with much anticipation I tossed my line overboard, but before one fish was caught, the boat had to turn back to shore for fear of being capsized by an approaching storm.

All the work and fun was over as Maryland's 30-foot high, 4-foot wide, 100 year old oak Indian monument was finished. Mayor Harry Kelley, along with other dignitaries and spectators, came to the dedication.

NO. 22 MONUMENT
BETHANY BEACH, DELAWARE—DEC. 1976

It was late October and the weather was cool as Smokey and I drove into Delaware. The location for the Delaware Indian monument was originally planned to be in Rehoboth Beach, however it was a tossup between this city and Bethany Beach. The woman mayor of Rehoboth Beach was enthusiastic for this project, but the city council wouldn't give me the centrally located spot that I needed. They wanted it placed where few people would see it.

Paul Jones already promised to donate a log for the Delaware sculpture so I headed back to his Maryland sawmill. On my way I stopped in Bethany Beach and talked to Bayard Coulter, the town manager who was in favor of placing the Delaware monument in the center of town, however a vote of approval at the town meeting was needed.

Smokey liked the familiar surroundings of the lumber company in Snow Hill. A 27-foot long poplar log, 4 feet at the base, but narrowing down to 2½ feet at the top, was found. After studying the wood I saw an Indian protected by a giant eagle. Again the work continued at the sawmill and in November the roughed-out Indian and eagle were emerging from the log.

Kathy called and asked me to drive home to see her.

The log was ready to be moved, but at this time my mind was not yet made up as to where it would go. This extra time of indecision gave me a chance to see Kathy again.

After spending a few days in Illinois, I received word from Bethany Beach that the town vote was in my favor, should I decide to place the

Bethany Beach, Delaware Indian Monument. Poplar. (photo by Richard B. Kough)

monument in their town. Rehoboth Beach was given an ultimatum, either have the monument placed on the main drag or lose it. They lost it and I drove back to Delaware to oversee the moving of the sculpture from Paul Jones Lumber Company to the raising of it in Bethany Beach.

My work went along with extra speed and zest because December was almost upon us—the weather turned colder every day. Long johns, coats, and gloves helped against the cold. An electric space heater and electric blanket were my only sources of comfort in the cold Ghost Ship. There was no insulation in the van which made it difficult to retain any heat. After days of snow and sleet, the weather warmed up for a while which gave me a chance to brush on the several coats of needed preservative.

It hardly seemed that I left Maryland at all because it was only 10 or 20 miles from Bethany Beach, Delaware. Both are small states, sharing only a few miles of Atlantic seacoast. I loved the sea and decided that if ever there was a chance, my sculpture would be near the ocean.

Almost every evening Smokey would accompany me on a jog down to the ocean and enjoy the solitude. At times we were the only ones on the beach.

My faithful companion had an unpleasant experience once. One rainy day he was chained to the steel bumper of the Ghost Ship when all of a sudden he started howling and running around as if he were going mad. I rushed to see what the problem was and grabbed him by the collar. We were both bombarded by a high electrical charge! I thought of undoing Smokey's chain collar, but realized it would be too time consuming, so quickly yanked the cord. Poor wet Smokey received the shock of his life and me too. He was such a good dog. We often played frisbee. He captivated audiences and received applause as he caught the frisbee in the air and on warm days retrieved it from the ocean.

Mid December in Delaware was cold and the snow piled up. Luckily for me and my half frozen fingers the monument was nearly finished. There was just a little touch up work remaining before the dedication.

During a snowstorm a friend invited me to join him in a unique sport—pulling two tires behind a truck as sleds. The snow was packed hard on the pavement and we went flying down the highway. It was dangerous and illegal, but a lot of fun.

The acting chief, Kenneth Clark of the Nanticoke Council, was invited and spoke at the dedication. It was a real honor for me to meet him, his wife, and family.

The Conestoga and Delaware Confederacy, as well as other smaller tribes ruled supreme in Delaware. Now the Nanticoke and other remnants of the once powerful Indian nation still cling to their heritage in this state.

Charleston, South Carolina Indian Monument. Created from 500-year-old Darlington Oak at Historical Charlestown Landing. (photo by Thomas L. Tuten)

NO. 23 MONUMENT
CHARLESTON, SOUTH CAROLINA—FEB. 1977

Good news was received from South Carolina that a log was found so my departure was imminent.

Friends were never easy to leave behind, but the cold weather and icy streets of Delaware made it easier for Smokey and me to depart.

On our way south, we stopped off briefly in Snow Hill, Maryland to personally thank my friend, Paul Jones, Jr., for all the support he had given my Indian monuments for Delaware and Maryland. Earlier he bought a couple of my small carvings (one was a walnut eagle) and took me deep sea fishing. If not for generous people like him, it would be virtually impossible to accomplish my goal.

Our next stop was close to Virginia Beach, Virginia, where I promised the Jordan family a yard size sculpture. As the Ghost Ship was unpacked, Smokey took off to check out the neighborhood dogs. It was dusk when I started calling for him and with a flashlight in hand, searched the neighborhood. Suddenly there was a thud from the direction of a passing car. It couldn't be Smokey—but something told me it was. The bright beam of my flashlight pierced the darkness to reveal his shaggy lifeless form.

The next morning my friend, Mary, met me at the Indian monument at Mount Trashmore Park, Virginia Beach where I dug his grave. Misty eyed we covered him up remembering the happier days when we romped the surrounding hills and swam the lakes together. Mary promised to plant flowers on his grave the next spring. This was a sad occasion, putting to rest my faithful companion of over two years. Smokey's death brought back unhappy memories of Vancouver, Washington where a handsome little cocker spaniel was killed the same way as Smokey. I had buried him in front of the Vancouver monument.

With the yard sculpture finished, I was on the road again heading south, but this time it was more lonesome than before.

The big Darlington oak awaited me at the historical Charles Towne Landing in Charleston, South Carolina. After studying it, I envisioned the figure of a coastal Indian chief hidden in the wood. This 23rd monument was to be most unique because of its 20 feathered headdress. As the work progressed and the 500-year Darlington oak took shape, I took a little time out to look around the historical Charles Towne Landing.

A tour of the original settlement consisted of many attractions. My favorite was the animal park where all the wild animals indigenous to this part of the country were kept. Animals such as the giant buffalo, bear, elk, deer, mountain lion, alligator, turkey, grouse, and many more were exhibited.

Even though the weather was much warmer in Charleston, it did snow several times. The warm afternoon sun quickly melted it and frequently I had to take my coat off to keep from being too hot.

The Indian chief's features started taking on a realistic look and in early

February, with the cement base finished, the National Guard raised the Indian. My 23rd monument was now over halfway finished.

The next few weeks were hard times for me. It seemed like Kathy and I were drifting apart. Our lives seemed to take different paths and it had been many months since we had seen each other. Smokey's untimely death didn't help my sorrow. Past experience had taught me the best way to overcome the blues was to meet new people. The few friends that I made, though, didn't fill my emptiness.

Kathy was very pretty, but that was the least important reason I loved her. Even though she had plenty of faults, as we all do, I respected her as an individual. She was intelligent, sensitive, a warm vulnerable human being, but what captured my heart was her adventurous spirit (like mine). Though our paths seemed to be taking different directions at this time, my wish was to hold, protect, and love her.

So many men look for and expect physical perfection from women and yet they are anything but perfect themselves. Many men are shallow, they expect a woman to have a large bustline, slim waist, and pretty face. In reality, the physical character of a person should be of the least importance. What is really important is the heart; beauty is in the eyes of the beholder. If a man in this life is lucky enough to find a good woman who loves and respects him, he should cling to her because she is worth more than gold.

It was here in the historic southern city of Charleston that I started writing about the "Outsider", a story about a young man that didn't belong. He was an outcast that lived on the outer fringes of society, not accepted by either side. The young man was me.

The Indians too were outsiders, but unlike me they were an entity in themselves. Many refused to change their life style and were virtually exterminated.

The Catawba still live on the only Indian reservation in the state of South Carolina. After the Tuscarora were defeated in 1713, the Catawba were the largest and most powerful nation left in the coastal region. The Catawba declined with astounding rapidity due to the disuse of alcohol, disease, and attack by hostile roaming tribes. The Sewee and Yamasee, two coastal tribes, were small in number and when defeated by the Europeans they went into oblivion joining up with other neighboring powerful nations. My monument represents a composite of the coastal tribes, and the great Catawbas. I regret that much of the coastal tribe's history is lost forever. Many of these tribes were destroyed even before there was any written history of them.

A call from my friend, Fred Babcock, resulted in plans of driving down to his 100,000 acre ranch in Florida. My high hopes were to barter a 20-foot sculpture for a used motor home to make a favorable impression on Kathy.

A letter arrived from Kathy with the most sentimental poem ever. This poem and her very touching letter said in effect that she missed me and our love was the most important part of her life. To this day I carry that poem with me.

In late February the Indian sculpture was finished, but the dedication was planned for sometime in March. With eagerness to see Kathy, and not one for wasting time, my immediate departure was for Illinois.

NO. 24 MONUMENT
ST. LOUIS, MISSOURI—MAY, 1977

Slowly and cautiously I made my way up the still-snow-covered slopes of the Appalachian Mountains toward my 24th state. The treacherous road made it slow going, a detour to Illinois took me into Kathy's arms.

March was cool in E. Peoria, Illinois, but the sun warmed up our hearts and our days. A bright afternoon, on a pleasure drive in the E. Peoria countryside, we spotted a 24 foot Winnebago motor home for sale. It was old and worn, but with a lot of work it had real potential. With all my remaining cash and a small sculpture, I made a ridiculous low offer. The owner agreed to sell and we cautiously drove it down to the local garage (it had virtually no brakes).

While the Winnebago was parked by the side of the garage awaiting repair, we washed the grime off the exterior. Kathy measured the windows for new curtains as I sanded and painted the rusty bumpers, wheels, and door step. A little touch up paint and waxing made a tremendous difference. We stood back and admired the Winnebago and then began on the inside by stripping off the mixed colored adhesive wallpaper that covered the wood paneling. The ragged carpet was replaced by new shag. The Win-

Transition from Ghost Ship to 24-foot Winnebago motor home.

St. Louis, Missouri Indian Monument located in Forest Park. Oak. (photo by Parks Department)

nebago appeared almost new considering what it looked like before we bought it.

The brake shoes, as well as other parts, were replaced and the engine tuned. Thanks to Kathy loaning me money to help pay the huge bill, I was on my way to Missouri.

All my machine shop savings were gone, but I went to St. Louis in style. After living for over five years in my Ghost Ship van, the 24-foot Winnebago motor home was like a palace. The bathroom was located at the rear and was complete with toilet, bath/shower, sink, and closet. The living room consisted of two long parallel couches which turned into beds, and the kitchen, complete with table/booth, refrigerator, sink, oven, and cabinets, was in the front. The motor home slept six and my favorite bed became the rear couch.

The Lewis and Clark Sawmill in West Alton helped with this project. The owner kindly donated a large oak log and the work began on the 24th monument at the sawmill yard as the search continued around the St. Louis area for an appropriate site. It was decided Forest Park would be an ideal location, especially since Chief Pontiac was killed in a Cahokia village near here. Stories had it that he might be buried nearby.

The head of the Parks Department, Mrs. Georgia L. Buckowitz, was impressed with my work and cause, and decided that the monument would be an added attraction for the park.

In May we moved the partly finished sculpture to Forest Park. My happiness with the newly purchased motor home was dampened during this move. On the way, the rear tires came off. The sloppy mechanic in E. Peoria forgot to bend over the cotter pins. My slow drive through the city caused no accident, but had I been on the interstate, traveling at a high rate of speed (like on my initial drive to St. Louis), someone could have been killed. The E. Peoria mechanic didn't reimburse the money shelled out for a tow and repairs, so the $100 expense was my loss.

The work on the log continued and in no time at all the cement base was poured and we raised the sculpture on its pedestal.

The media throughout the country has always been either in my favor (not counting a couple of skeptic reporters) or indifferent as they were in Ft. Wayne, Indiana and Atlantic City, New Jersey. There was never a promoter for my work to inform the media about my arrival in a given area, or to tell about the meaning behind it. I assume it was because of this, that here in this sprawling city of over half-a-million people (2½ million metro), I was aware of only one major newspaper that took notice, one with a vengeful feud with the Parks Department. This paper used me as a patsy to get back at Mrs. Georgia Buckowitz. They made an issue of the fact that she gave me permission to locate the monument in Forest Park without consulting the board of directors, city, or anyone. The reporter tried to manipulate me against the Park's Administration which prompted my refusal to give any further interviews. It was my first taste of media exploitation.

The Indian now stood in the park looking toward I-40 where more than a million people drive through annually to enjoy the 1,326 acre park with all its attractions—a museum, outdoor theater, zoo, and more.

High from the scaffold I watched the procession of thousands of people—some stopped to talk to me and others just drove by staring. Sometimes as many as thirty people would congregate around the bottom of the scaffolds to watch me work.

Kathy drove the long distance from E. Peoria to visit me on the weekends. She would get nervous around the large crowds and stay inside the Winnebago parked under a tree thirty feet behind the monument. It was situated in a beautiful natural surrounding, one of the few places of tranquility left in this colossal city.

St. Louis has changed much since Chief Pontiac, an Ottawa, came here to visit his French friends. Pontiac's war held the British back for 3 years from the Great Lakes and the Illinois country and brought on one of the longest sieges on Fort Detroit in American military history.

The Missouri Indian tribe (probably of less than 1,000 in number) had the honor of this state being named after them. As if the white man's whiskey and disease wasn't enough devastation, they were almost destroyed by the Sauk and Foxes in 1798. They never fully recovered and in the early 1800's were annihilated by the Osage, ending their existence as an independent tribe. The few remaining survivors escaped to live among the Iowa and Oto Indians.

The Michagamea and Cohokia both lived in the present day Missouri and Illinois border area and many legends are associated with them. "Those who sleep," the Ioway, originally had their villages on the Des Moines River in Iowa, but moved to Missouri on the Mississippi River. By 1824 they, like most of Missouri's Indians, ceded their land to the U.S. Government and were moved to central Oklahoma meaning "Home of the Red Man."

*The nights were quiet in Forest Park. When people heard this was my home they gasped, "Aren't you afraid of someone attacking you? Not far from here is the bad section of town where you're liable to get mugged."

There was no need to fear anyone. Crime in St. Louis was rampant, but no major problems arose for me.

Rick Hampton was a local artist who showed me his method of drawing and painting. Throughout my travels many artists were met and each taught me something about art, always there's so much to learn.

My days were busy working on the Indian monument, now nearly finished and the evenings kept me occupied with small carvings, drawings, and writing. This didn't give me much time for TV which was all the same because my old beat up black and white 19-inch set hardly worked. The thought of watching my favorite animal shows in color was enticing, but a color TV was beyond my pocketbook.

One day my dream was almost realized. While chipping away, three men approached with a new portable color TV and wanted to sell it for $100. It seemed too good to be true! One thing that bothered me though, was these guys looked like crooks. Recently, the Rookies, a TV cop program, showed how crooks duped fools by selling them crated TVs which turned out to be nothing but old picture tubes. Ever so careful not to take a stolen TV, the names and addresses of the guys were recorded for future reference. The unwrapped TV was brought to me, but before the guys allowed me to check it out thoroughly, they insisted on seeing the money and became angered at my delay.

"Forget it!" they told me. "We don't want to play games!" and they started to leave.

My instinct told me to let them go, it was probably a hot TV, but greed took over. The color TV was the one thing I wished for and suddenly I was about to lose it. Against my best judgment, I gave them all my money (nearly $100).

The dream became a nightmare! The TV that looked spanking new didn't even work! Me! The worldly person, who's been around, turned out to be a sucker! A victim, not so much of the three crooks, but of my own greed. The police couldn't help me because the addresses I recorded were phony. An expensive lesson well learned through experience.

The dedication was held on the weekend and out of the 2½ million people in and around St. Louis, only three dozen showed up. Several Indians arrived for the ceremony, and we danced around the monument. Speeches fell on the deaf ears of a city, who unfortunately, was probably unaware of what was happening because of the lack of media coverage. Still I did meet many good people and it was with warm thoughts that my home in Forest Park, St. Louis, the Gateway to the West, was left behind.

NO. 25 MONUMENT
TWO HARBORS, MINNESOTA—JULY, 1977

Upon finishing the Missouri monument, I stopped in E. Peoria, Illinois to see Kathy who seemed distant to me of late. We discussed marriage, but my financial situation was near zero so it was still out of the question at this time. Kathy was disgusted with my situation and thought I was a dreamer. She would tell me. . .

"Grow up. Dreams are fine, but what about 'our' future? I can't live the way you do. Be more realistic with life, think of 'us' for a change."

It was hard to get Kathy to understand my dreams, but even harder not to try.

With a sad heart I said goodby and drove toward Minnesota. On my way north, I stopped in Davenport and Dubuque, Iowa. In Wisconsin stops were made at the Wisconsin Dells, La Crosse, Eau Claire, and Hayward. All of these cities were explored for possible future monuments. Hayward and the Dells area was a tossup for Wisconsin, but beause of the overcommercialism of the Dells, Hayward won out.

A short time was spent in Hayward taking care of preliminaries for the monument. The Hayward Chamber of Commerce searched for a log, while the road took me north toward Minnesota.

The scenic beauty of Lake Superior, with its rugged shoreline and blue

Two Harbors, Minnesota Indian Monument with artist's friend Medicine Man Jimmie Mustache, Chippewa. Pine. Located on Highway 61, Lake Superior scenic drive.

waters rivaled any ocean. This was definitely the place for one of my whispering giants. The next few days were spent traveling the shoreline (scenic Highway 61) from Duluth, Minnesota to Thunder Bay, Ontario. While walking in the stillness of the white birch forests (the tree's bark was used by the Indians to make canoes), my decision was made to place the monument in Two Harbors, a town of 4,400, twenty miles north of Duluth.

After searching far and wide, a 4-foot diameter, 25-foot long pine log was hauled in from Blackduck, a town near Bemidji. My hammer echoed over the cold and blue Lake Superior. The image of the Indian was already in the log, it just took a lot of work to chip away the wood that didn't look like an Indian.

June was warm and in Two Harbors the cold deep waters of Lake Superior (commonly referred to as "the sea" by locals) keeps the summer comfortable.

Many of the town people like Ralph Jacobson—the town's plumber; Melroy Peterson—the county auditor; and others too numerous to mention, helped acquire the needed materials. Some dug out and constructed the foundation, others helped to pour the cement, et cetera. My work progressed well and the area papers and the Associated Press carried articles about the "Sculptor and his crusade of honoring the Indians."

In each section of America one finds people with different racial backgrounds and Minnesota is a state with a large population of Swedish and Norwegians. I thought most of these people would be blonde, but to my surprise, many were redheads (like my Hungarian grandfather had been).

A redheaded Norwegian girl that I was seeing wanted to get seriously involved, but Kathy was still my love.

A month later a TV crew from Duluth came to do a news story on my work. This news coverage caught the interest of Raymond A. Murdock, an Ojibwa who hosted a talk show "Indian Viewpoint" and asked me to be a guest. After the half hour interview was over, Raymond spoke on the interesting subject of past and present day Indian problems.

Raymond Murdock will never forget his personal encounter with the humiliation of punishment for speaking his native Ojibwa language at boarding school. Such cruelties, he attested, were commonplace just a few years ago, with rumors of it still going on. What often happens to these Indian students is a loss of pride and respect for their culture. This is sometimes manifested by being caught in confusion between the two cultures and may ultimately lead to self-destruction; drugs, suicide, or alcohol. When a person has no pride, then he may not have a purpose to go on living. Contrary to many religious beliefs that pride will destroy you, the lack of it, often as not, is the real killer.

Raymond Murdock is a modern day educated Chippewa. (Chippewa is a corruption of their real name Ojibwa, which was hard for Europeans to pronounce and was garbled into Chippewa). His people came from the East, perhaps driven out by the powerful Iroquois, and by the mid-seventeenth century had settled the shores of Lake Superior. This move pushed the Fox south to live with the Sauks by 1670. Then many wars were fought between the Ojibwas and the native Cheyenne and Dakotas (Dakotas were later called Sioux). The Chippewas were the first regional Indians to receive firearms from the white traders and with this superior weapon they drove the Sioux from the woodlands.

At least four tribes of the Santee Sioux did stay in the vast Minnesota forests and thirty years after the American Revolution these Sioux still refused to acknowledge U.S. sovereignty. It was during 1815-1825 when they accepted the reality of the American power and Waneta, a powerful Sioux Chief, signed the Treaty of Prairie du Chien, accepting peace with the Chippewa and the United States. Now after nearly 200 years the Indians living in Minnesota invariably still cling to their traditional way of life on several small reservations. Many problems remain to be solved and I hope that my monument to these great people will help to alleviate at least some of them.

George Catlin was a great artist and a true friend of the Indians. In the 1830's he left an easy comfortable life behind in the East to document, through his art, the ways and life of the Plains Indians.

Catlin often spoke of the honesty and human worthiness of the Indians. None of his supplies were ever found missing throughout his travels.

One of the many tribes he painted was the Mandans, thereby perpetuating in pictures their culture forever. By 1837, only five years after his paintings, sadly the Mandans' numbers were decimated by smallpox from 1,600 to only 31 survivors.

When Catlin visited the pipestone quarries in 1836 (located in southern Minnesota) the Sioux mistrusted and seized him. This encounter nearly cost him his life. Later this same stone was named catlinite in his honor. The Sioux believed that the red stone was sacred because it was formed from the flesh of their ancestors.

The pipe was an integral part of Indian life. Over 1,000 years ago the Hopewell made some of the finest ceremonial pipes. Some tribes even developed pipes for pleasure smoking referred to as squaw pipes. The decoration of the pipe was important. The color of the feather meant war or peace.

No matter if the pipes were made from sacred pipestone, bone, slate, wood or clay, it was believed to be of divine inspiration.

The smoking of the Sioux calumet (grand pipe) meant the very presence of deities. All tribes adhered to this fact. To carry this sacred pipe ensured safety to the bearer and his party even from enemy tribes. It was a passport evident of peaceful purpose. "Peace pipes" were carried by early white explorers for protection from hostile Indians.

Tobacco became part of the Indian medicine, religion, and an indispensable symbol of their diplomacy. Medicine men used the pipe with different mixtures of tobacco, some with narcotic qualities in their ceremonies to heal sickness and to ward off danger and trouble. The pipe and tobacco was the center of the Indian's religious life.

*The Fourth of July in Two Harbors came with fireworks of all colors and the loud popping of firecrackers. Even the 60-degree, rainy weather didn't dampen the town's spirit.

During my two month stay, I learned how and when to swim in the chilly waters of Lake Superior. The trick is to swim on the days when the old northern wind blows in the warm surface water and even then to stay on the very surface, lest you freeze.

Being an avid swimmer I frequently went swimming. A wet suit was occasionally used to keep warm, and to prove my prowess, I would swim out a quarter-of-a-mile. People gasped and pointed because it was unusual to see anyone swim in the cold water. My only fear was the ever present lamprey (an eel-like creature that attaches itself and sucks the blood out of fish) which might attach itself on my soft defenseless stomach. It would be painful and difficult to remove, especially out in the deep lake.

One sunny afternoon I swam along the deserted shoreline of Superior, north of town, when a blonde girl came out of a secluded house to walk her dog. Upon swimming to shore, we began a friendly conversation. Her father came out cursing me and said unless I left, he was going to call the cops. I laughed and told him he doesn't own Lake Superior and slowly resumed my swim. True to his threat, a cop appeared. He told me that the man was paranoid and thought I was after his daughter. The poor girl's father was so overbearing that he seemed to have kept her a virtual prisoner in that secluded home.

Shortly before I left Minnesota, Calvin White Eagle of the Winnebagos, honored me with a gift of beads and a deer skin vest made by his lovely wife and invited me to be an honorary member of the Winnebago tribe.

A letter came from Hayward, Wisconsin that the log was ready and awaiting my arrival. With the finishing touches on my 25th monument done, and the last few coats of wood preservative on, I said goodby and headed toward Wisconsin.

Calvin White Eagle and family visits Peter.

Minnesota

Some of Peter's earliest sculptures.

Toth listens as Chippewa friend, Jimmie Mustache, speaks at dedication of Minnesota Monument.

*From Hayward, Wisconsin, Sheila Wise, friend Carol, Jimmie Mustache, and myself drove by car to Two Harbors, Minnesota to attend the dedication sponsored by the Chamber. The Information Center, next to the monument, was also dedicated. Jimmie Mustache was in full Ojibwa attire and gave a speech in his native tongue. We returned to Hayward that same afternoon.

NO. 26 MONUMENT
HAYWARD, WISCONSIN—SEPT., 1977

After the drive of around 100 miles it was good to be back in Hayward, Wisconsin. Awaiting me was a big oak log, 4 feet across and about 34 feet long. First I chiseled off the bark and studied it for the image of the Indian.

Hayward, Wisconsin Indian protected by giant eagle. Oak. (photo by Paul Riemer)

Creation from Douglas fir. (photo by Mike Sample, The Tribune)

The log was too long and narrow on one end, so the decision was made to cut off six feet of this end. After much mental measuring, I saw an Indian protected by a giant eagle. The eagle's wings enfolded the head of the Indian in a protective embrace. As the sculpture started showing some shape, the Hayward newspaper ran pictures of its progress.

Sheila Wise, library board member, was instrumental from start to finish in helping with the project. Our decision was to put the monument in the little park adjacent to the library. This is where my work continued. She allowed me to park the Winnebago next to the library and from them received electricity and water hookups. Fifty feet from the building was the log.

As the cement base was being poured, the principal from the Lac Courte Oreilles Chippewa Indian Reservation school, only 30 miles from Hayward, introduced himself and asked me to hold art classes and teach my method of sculpting to the young Indian students. We worked out a schedule where Mouse, a colorful Chippewa man, drove me to the reservation two to three times a week.

The reservation showed the existing poverty prevalent on most reservations, but the handsome Indian children appeared healthy, happy, and held great promise for the future. The school and community was situated among the peaceful lakes, tall pines, and white birch forests of northern Wisconsin. My art classes were held in an older church-like building with several classes coming and going all afternoon. Time was always too short, but I tried to teach the art of woodcarving to the talented and interested students.

Toth's art students from the Lac Courte Oreilles Reservation School, Hayward, Wisconsin.

Two young Ojibwas.

Some days my lunch was eaten in the cafeteria with my many Chippewa friends and students. It didn't take long for me to respect and love these fine people. I was honored for the giving of my time and talents at a Powwow where a pouch of tobacco, neck broach, eagle feather, and a beautiful ceremonial shirt made of blue velvet was awarded me. With the sound of drums beating and noise makers strapped to my legs, I was asked to lead the ceremony dances in a "Circle of Friendship." It was a great honor to be accepted by my adopted people, the Chippewa.

Ever since the Sioux were pushed out from the Great Lake's region, the Chippewas reigned supreme. There were other tribes living in Wisconsin in the early 1600 to 1700's; the Sauk and Fox, Winnebago, Menominee, Kickapoo, Munsee, as well as numerous other tribes.

*Though there was still a lot of fine work to do on the sculpture, it was nearly finished. On a clear morning while studying it from the library lawn a familiar figure came up.

"Looking very good, Peter," came the reassuring voice of my friend Jimmie Mustache, Running Elk, the local Ojibwa medicine man whom I had met several years ago at the Illinois dedication. He lived close by and came frequently to see me. Since my radio wasn't working, Jimmie Mustache gave me his; in return I made him a small sculpture. It was a great honor for me to talk to Running Elk who told me of the older days when things were so much different. He explained the Chippewa had large herds of ponies, and like their land, their ponies were usually stolen by the whites. Much of the early history was unfolded by Jimmie Mustache. He preached strenuously that the young Chippewa must use his language and keep his heritage alive. He was chosen to represent his people's culture at the Smithsonian in 1977.

One morning Bob Dose, Kathy's uncle from Illinois who was vacationing in the area, stopped to ask of my progress and was surprised to find that I had now finished over half my goal of sculpting one monument in each of the fifty states since last seeing him. As he left, he casually mentioned that Kathy was here in Wisconsin, just 30 miles north of Hayward, near Cable, where her parents owned a beautiful home on Lake Namekagon.

I had to see her! After a phone call to her mother, Rosemary, I received directions on how to get there. I packed up my tools and jumped on my motorcycle and headed toward the Jensen's house. On the drive out my mind was racing with thoughts of Kathy. Did she come up here with the hopes of patching up our relationship or were we really through? There was no doubt about the fact that I still loved her, more than ever, and was ready to resolve past differences and plan for our future. I wanted to marry her—the time was right.

We spent several days together trying to work things out and before we separated there was a promise of meeting again in Illinois. Kathy returned to her job in E. Peoria and my path led back to Hayward to finish the Wisconsin monument.

Jerry Holter, a local artist living at Clam Lake, stopped out to visit me. He is internationally famous for his woodcarvings. We became acquainted and he gave me some good advice and a couple of V-gouges which greatly enhanced my work. To this day we are good friends and I have learned much about our craft from him.

My work was finally finished and the dedication became a great celebration, thanks to the efforts of Sheila Wise and many others. Some of the Ojibwa children came in native attire and danced for the audience and the high school band played several numbers.

Chippewa Indian leader Rick Baker and other dignitaries attended. Jimmie Mustache couldn't be here on this day because he was still on the East coast at the Smithsonian Institution attending a cultural program. Representative Ken Schricker presented to me a citation from Acting Governor Martin Schreiber and the Wisconsin legislature thanking me for this gift and expressing their gratitude.

After the dedication ceremony the Chippewas invited me to come back the following year to attend the Harvest Festival where I was to be indoctrinated into the tribe. My parents were informed of this upcoming honor and my mother wrote back that Indian or not, I will always be her son. Unfortunately this honor, so far, has not yet materialized, due in part to Rick Baker stepping down from his position as LCO Tribal Chairman.

It was now October as my Winnebago headed south toward Illinois. With great anticipation and some hesitation, I drove into Toluca and met Kathy at her parent's house.

MARRIAGE—OCTOBER, 1977

There were no states lined up for the winter months. A serious decision was made on my immediate future. My plan was to make Kathy my own, if

Flying Feathers
Nearing completion. (photos by Morgan Parks)

Working on scaffolds 36 feet above the ground. (photo by Morgan Parks)

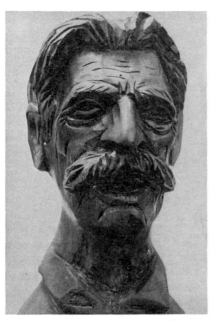

Mark Twain (walnut)

Indian maiden (pine)

Spruce eagle

Spruce bear

Kathy at the edge of the Grand Canyon.

Peter. . .Oops!. . .in the Grand Canyon!

she would be willing to risk the uncertainty of living with an artist. There was a backup plan. Should Kathy decide against marriage, time would be taken off from my goal of sculpting one monument in each of the 50 states. I would leave the big Winnebago in Illinois and drive the Ghost Ship (which was parked on the Jensen farm) down to Mexico and Central America to visit the Aztec and other Indian ruins, hopefully and finally to arrive at the Amazon River. I always dreamed of the great Amazon and wanted to navigate into the interior wilderness. Cost and danger would be astronomical, but my plans were to find two or three other adventurers to share the cost and danger.

My mood was ambivalent, happy but still worried about the financial responsibilities of married life. If a can of beans was all I could afford to eat, still the sacrifice for this cause would be made, but how could I expect Kathy to do likewise?

I arrived at the Jensens at 9 p.m. Kathy was happy to see me and with much pride told me of a great job offer. This was her chance to make a move up the ladder and increase her income by a substantial amount. Of course she would lose this chance if she married me. I could tell by her enthusiasm that she wanted to take the job.

The following day as I was checking out the Ghost Ship for my trip to Central America, Kathy came out with tears running down her pretty face and announced that she made up her mind to marry me. I hugged and kissed her.

We didn't want to make things hard on ourselves by wasting time, so plans were begun to get married as quickly as possible. It would be especially hard on Kathy to change her whole life style, but the sooner we would get married, the easier it would be on her.

On Friday I had arrived and by that following Monday Kathy was to start her new job, so she called in and apologized for inconveniencing them and explained why she had to refuse the new position.

Late that afternoon we drove to E. Peoria with her father's pickup and vacated her apartment. John from the downstairs apartment helped to carry out the heavy furniture and load it on the truck. Kathy lived upstairs, so carrying the big sofa down the narrow stairway was quite a chore. This was a sad day for her to leave friends (who were like family) and the home she had lived in for over a year behind. Marriage is such a major change in life, but to step off into uncertainty with me was even harder.

It was late that evening before the truck was tied down with its over-burdened load. Kathy followed me in her car, from a safe distance, and watched to make sure everything was securely in place. We stopped twice on Rt. 116 to tighten the ropes. The 40-mile drive went smoothly and safely except for the last mile—the rear tire blew out. We pulled to the side of the road, but found no spare tire in the truck. Kathy drove home to ask Lowell, her father, to help. In no time at all the truck proceeded to the Jensen home where we stored the furniture.

In the following busy days we went to the Streator hospital for blood tests, made appointments with Dr. Baz, the family doctor, and went to the

Lacon courthouse to pick up our marriage license.

The search began for someone to marry us. Kathy wanted to be married in a church, but the first minister we approached refused to perform the marriage. He said he didn't know us and couldn't possibly give us his blessings. It wasn't as if we were runaways—Kathy was 23 and I was 29. We were angry at the lack of responsibility shown by this religious leader. No wonder so many young people say "the hell with it" and live together. I suggested a justice of the peace, but Kathy wanted the former pastor of the Toluca Lutheran Church who confirmed her at age 13. He was unavailable though. The minister of the Toluca Lutheran Church agreed to perform the ceremony. First, we had to spend some time visiting and he inquired if Kathy was pregnant since we were in such a rush. We watched a filmstrip and were given manuals on married life.

As we prepared for our marriage and contemplated a honeymoon, good news came from California. Herb and Edna Miller, a California couple I met in Wisconsin, wanted me to come to southern California to make a monument in Desert Hot Springs. The Pueblo Indian Museum curator, Cole Eyraud, wanted me to make a sculpture there from a giant sequoia log. He even sent me money to meet some of our expenses on the long trip there. What a perfect honeymoon it would be in warm southern California and I would be able to use sequoia for the first time, something I had dreamed about for years. We were really blessed from above. The news was especially heavensent for Kathy, her fears were a little lessened at our future uncertainties.

One week from the day we decided to marry, we said our vows in the Toluca St. John's Lutheran Church with Pastor Hannemann performing a simple ceremony. Kathy wanted this to be a private and personal occasion, so only seven of the immediate family were present. We promised to take care of, love, respect, and be true to each other. At 4:30 p.m. on a cloudy October 23, 1977, we became man and wife.

We returned to the Jensen home for sandwiches, cake, and champagne. I was the main photographer with my 35 mm Cannon. My brother-in-law, Bruce, also took several pictures at the simple, but intimate reception.

Shortly afterwards we drove in a fine mist toward Ohio. We stayed in the Holiday Inn honeymoon suite in Logansport, Indiana. The following day we arrived in Akron, Ohio to see my family. Everyone was very surprised and happily that the perennial bachelor finally married. Our first days of married life was sunny, warm, and the fall colors were vibrant and alive. We drove around my home town and visited family and friends.

After a few days of pre-honeymooning, we went back to Illinois. Much of the following several days were unnervingly spent at the Streator hospital. Kathy had to have surgery to determine whether or not she had cancer. It was a trying and frightening way to start out a marriage, but I believe that Kathy drew courage from my presence. Fortunately, the tumor wasn't malignant and her recovery was quick.

We were soon packing the old Winnebago for the trip West. The Winnebago needed repairs, but unfortunately we were unable to accomplish

The Toths just after being married with Kathy's brother Bruce, and wife Linda.

Toasting to a new beginning at a small family reception on the Jensen farm.

this. Our rush for California was on before the bad weather set in.

It was late in the season (November), but fortunately we didn't run into any foul weather crossing the mountain passes. The California warm sunshine was a welcome change. It was like summer all over again. The temperature in the desert was over 80 degrees. What a perfect place for our honeymoon.

A 40,000 pound sequoia arrives in Desert Hot Springs, California.

NO. 27 MONUMENT
DESERT HOT SPRINGS, CALIFORNIA
NOVEMBER, 1977

We arrived at hot and arid Desert Hot Springs and pulled up to the four-story museum, fashioned after a southwestern Indian dwelling. This resort town was nestled at the base of the Little San Bernardino Mountains and the view from here was breathtaking. The desert valley was surrounded by a chain of mountains, some with snow covered peaks.

Kathy hugged me real tight.

"Well, Pete. We're really here. Aren't we the lucky ones to actually be able to live in this beautiful sunny valley? What a perfect honeymoon while you make your 27th whispering giant."

As I beamed with pride at having such a pretty, contented, and understanding bride, a man with white curly hair and a bright smile approached us.

"How do you do? I am the curator, Cole Eyraud, welcome to sunny California and Cabot's Old Indian Pueblo Museum."

Cole didn't waste much time pointing out the San Gorgonio Mountain with its white, 11,502-foot peak and the smaller, Mt. San Jacinto, with the world famous star-haven city of Palm Springs in its shadows. On that clear day this mountain seemed close enough to touch and it was hard to believe it was ten miles away. Cole explained to us from his firsthand experience that the desert floor could be 80 degrees, but by taking the Palm Springs tram to the top of Mt. San Jacinto, you would be in snow and 30-degree weather.

Cole was most proud of the museum as he ushered us into the cool, dark building. He told us about Cabot Yerxa, a lover of Indians, who built for himself this home fashioned after the Pueblo dwellings. He collected old timber, boards, nails—any odds and ends which he could use for construction. Over the years he kept adding rooms until now (still unfinished) it consists of 35 rooms, 150 windows, and 27 doors; no two windows or doors are the same size. He was the founder of Desert Hot Springs and lived as a hermit who traded with the local Indians. Every day he walked the near 10 miles across the hot valley floor to Palm Springs for water. Eventually he discovered hot mineral springs on his land, which the town is now famous for. The first resident may have been an eccentric, but he led a fascinating and unusual life. His home is now being preserved by Cole Eyraud as a museum and is open to the public. It was now also to become the home of one of my Indian monuments.

Our Winnebago was parked on the museum grounds with water and electric hookups.

As we waited for the arrival of the giant sequoia log, we acquainted ourselves with the museum animals. They consisted of two donkeys, a pony, a coati, raccoon, turtles, and a fox.

While the weather back in Illinois, according to Kathy's parents, turned bitterly cold, we had to run the air conditioner to keep cool. It made a racket, but worked a lot better than the stove and hot water heater which were both out of commission. The toilet smelled bad and Kathy was angry because my old Winnebago proved unfunctional and living conditions were difficult. Too many things didn't work and we lacked the funds to repair it. Before we bathed, water had to be heated in pans on the stove and poured into the tub. To make matters worse, the Winnebago was drafty and the winds blew sand through the window's loose fittings which covered everything with a thin blanket. Even our shag carpet was filled with sand and everything had to be continuously cleaned. This reminded Kathy of stories that she read about the Okies and the dust bowl days. Sand storms were frequent in this area. We could often see the sand whirling hundreds of feet in the air. On one occasion we drove through such a storm and had to turn on our lights for safety. You couldn't see two feet in front of your car.

Days became weeks, still the log didn't come—something about too much snow up in the mountains where the log was, which hampered the move.

Kathy found it difficult to adjust to married life and her new found freedom (she was used to working 8 hours a day in an office and now she had all this free time on her hands). The fact that she just gave up smoking three packs a day (even though she would occasionally sneak a cigarette or two) made her even more irritable. At times we argued a little, or a lot, but our love prevailed.

It was over a month and the log still had not come, so I kept myself busy with small carvings of elephants, bears, horses, and Indians, and even drew and painted a little.

Kathy desperately needed transportation so she could move freely to do the shopping and laundry. The Winnebago was left parked once we were at our destination because it was too time consuming and difficult to keep disconnecting our hookups, especially after we worked so hard to get it on level ground. She couldn't use the motorcycle either because it was too heavy for her.

We went to La Jolla to visit my family and with the money received from the sale of Kathy's Ford LTD, we bought a small Opel in Chula Vista. We then proceeded to drive it to Mexico and spent a day. Once we returned to my family, we went to the San Diego Humane Society and picked up a Dalmation puppy.

Kathy, like me, really loved the beach and the turbulent Pacific. Many evenings were spent there watching the sunset over the crashing surf. One morning my brother-in-law, Ron, and I went fishing. I got a little seasick, but caught a 3-foot blue shark.

From San Diego Kathy and I traveled north to Yosemite and the Sequoia National Park. The little Opel was cheap on gas and it was nice driving a car for a change. We enjoyed the enchanting sequoia forest where some of the trees grew unbelievably large. If ever God intended to have a church, it would have to be here among his giant majestic creations. The snowy winter mountain climate was getting to us, so we hurried back to the desert and summer weather.

Shortly after our return to Desert Hot Springs, we were fortunate enough to find a very nice furnished apartment for a reasonable monthly fee, which the Chamber of Commerce took care of (as well as our grocery bills). We moved into our first apartment and lived near the edge of the city. At night the eerie howls of coyotes could be heard.

After two months of waiting, the log finally arrived on a semi flatbed truck. Rain was falling as reporters and community spectators gathered to view this 40,000 pound mighty piece of redwood.

The heavy downpour and the ensuing darkness prevented me from working on the giant log, but the following morning no one could have pried me away from it. My sharp chisel sank deeply into the white sapwood and then the red heartwood. It was a great thrill for me to begin the liberation of my first "wooden" Indian for California from this magnificent sequoia.

Because of the huge size, it took a lot of chipping to get even an outline of the Indian. The work went along steadily in the following weeks.

A small problem arose in our need to obtain another huge log for the Indian's feather. A young logger, named Joe, assured us he could get a 4-foot wide, 15-foot long cedar from a mountain top near Idyllwild, not too far from Palm Springs.

Late the following day, Kathy, Joe, and I began the one-and-a-half-hour drive to the top of the mountain on a treacherous logging road up to where the cedar log laid in 3 feet of snow. The scenic view from this mountain was breathtaking. As we went higher, the snowdrifts kept getting deeper, even the jeep's 4-wheel drive could not get us through. By evening the jeep was so bogged down that the only alternative was to turn back.

As we began our descent, we were above the clouds and the sun was setting beneath them. It felt like we were in heaven, as if we could walk right out on the clouds that were lit up with a rose hue.

It took two more days and three attempts to bring down the log from the clutches of the snow. I'll never forget how cold I was on that mountain. My fingers were numb and my teeth chattered. So many times people assume that all one has to do is simply saw down a tree or log, haul it, and that's it. Well, I can personally attest to the fact that it's not always quite that simple.

About another month passed when cement for the base was poured. A time capsule was added.

Because many Indians have often expressed disgust at displays of skeletal remains of their ancestors, the skull of an Indian that was on display at the Pueblo Museum was placed in this time capsule as his final burial and resting place.

The Golden State, with its 22,294,000 people, is the most populated state in the Union (less than 4% are Indian). At the time of the first European explorer, Cabrillo, in 1542, this sunny, moderately temperatured country had an estimated 100,000 diversified native people living here. In 1859 their estimated number was less than 30,000. By the end of the century, they dwindled to roughly 15,000 souls.

The massacring of the California Indians was perhaps the worst destruction on human lives in this country's history. Prostitution and venereal disease ran rampant among the gold country Indians, and gang-rape of Indian women was commonplace. Their children were stolen and sold off as servants. It was a bad time to be a California Indian. The Mission Indians,

California monument in upright position on cement base. Separate feather, out of cedar, is now being anchored by Cole Eyraud and Sculptor Toth. (photo by Mrs. Jerry Skuse)

as many of the nearby desert dwelling Indians were referred to, were somewhat better off than their northern cousins. They were flogged, shackled, put in stocks, and imprisoned if caught trying to escape to freedom. Their labor and land was exploited, but at least they weren't killed. Open armed revolts against the Spanish tyrannical missionaries were few, though some Indian women aborted their unborn instead of subjecting them to near slavery, too.

Today there are over fifty tribes of Indians in California, not counting the many extinct tribes due to the overkill that was in full swing in 1848. Four main tribes are the Chumash, Yokuts, Wappo, and Yuki. The Indians closest to the Desert Hot Springs monument are the Agua Caliente. Much of Palm Springs lies on their reservation.

*When the cement was cured the monument was raised up on it with a huge crane and forty feet of scaffolds were put on both sides. Work began in earnest.

Kathy's excitement with this unusual land changed after our 4th month here. She tired of this desert and dreamed of the green fields and trees of her native Illinois. Hardly anyone had grass on their lawns in Desert Hot Springs. Most were sand and cactus. The only color was an occasional palm tree and a few lawns which were paved with green or rust asphalt. Kathy loved to go sightseeing in Palm Springs because the lawns and trees were so lush and beautiful there.

Kathy also missed her family and friends and felt like she was in another country out here on this arid land. In her distress she put on weight, from 106 to 130 pounds and for the first time in her life she had to diet.

Her father flew in from Las Vegas during our stay and spent two days with us enjoying the desert climate which helped Kathy's homesickness. It would take her years to adjust to the road and being away from home.

Money, like always, was tight while we lived in California and thanks to Cole Eyraud, the Chamber of Commerce, and the community, we pulled through just fine. At this time we were down to our last dollar.

During the rainy season, Desert Hot Springs experienced heavy rains and floods which washed away roads and cars. Debris littered lawns and property damage was extensive.

Soon after the rain, the desert came alive which brought on an amazing transition. Flowers of different colors covered the previously brown, parched desert. The desert in many places became a virtual blanket of flowers.

Plans were made for the dedication and invitations were sent out. The ceremony was to take place at 11:00 before the full heat of the day. A local club from Desert Hot Springs brought refreshments and we set up a display of sculptures in hopes to sell a few for our traveling expenses.

My family from San Diego arrived, as well as Dennis Banks, co-founder of the American Indian Movement, and now chancellor of D.Q. University. I was presented with a key to the city and a plaque of appreciation. May 20, 1978 was proclaimed Indian Appreciation Day. This was one day that we would not soon forget.

We sold a few sculptures that day and were pleased at the gala celebra-

At work on scaffolds 40 feet above the desert floor. Cole takes photograph from below. (photo by Walter Goad)

Toth and Eyraud pose with Native Americans at dedication. (photo by Jerry Skuse)

tion. The next week was spent preparing for our journey to our next state of Iowa.

NO. 28 MONUMENT
IOWA FALLS, IOWA—JUNE, 1978

The grueling drive to Iowa was made even more frustrating because the Winnebago broke down on our cross-country drive and left us stranded until help arrived.

As we entered the town of Iowa Falls, population 6,000, Kathy felt right at home. The grass was lush and green at this time of year and the crops were starting to come up in the fields. The rural farm surrounding was familiar to her and for the first time in a long while she was content.

We stopped at a phone booth and called Chamber member, Kraig Kasischke, our contact over the past few months. He met and drove us to the log as it lay on a cliff bank overlooking the Iowa River. It was a local cottonwood, small compared to the redwood I had just finished, but it would still make a nice monument. After cutting away a few chips, we left to get settled in for the night.

During our stay here we lived in an upstairs apartment at Kraig and Marcie Kasischke's house. We were happy with the cozy little place, but it would prove hot during the summer months.

Work began early the next morning, the rhythmic chock-chock of my hammer reverberated off of the Iowa River's high bluffs. This noise disturbed the famous cliff pigeons that were nesting a stone's throw from the landmark swinging bridge.

Verle Hunt came to say "hello" and check out the progress of my work. Just a little over a year ago he and his family visited me in Two Harbors, Minnesota. After finding out that I was making one monument for each of the 50 states, and the state of Iowa was not yet finished, enthusiastically he got my address and took several pictures of my work. He assured me that I'd be hearing from Iowa Falls soon.

Sure enough, several months back my first letter came from the Chamber of Commerce. Kraig Kasischke volunteered to work with me in finding a large log and make the other necessary arrangements.

Iowa Falls is a small close-knit and vibrant town with almost all the conveniences of a big city. With all it had to offer we were very proud to be part of this community.

The Iowa weather was hot and sticky and it rained often in the month of June, but this hardly slowed my progress.

As the log was taking shape, the couple living across the street from my project, Dennis and Jenenne White, became good friends of ours. Dennis and his friend Dan would take pictures of the different stages of the sculpture and at a latter time gave us a book comprised of these pictures.

Iowa Falls, Iowa Indian Monument above the cliffs of the Iowa River one block off Highway 20. Cottonwood. (photo by the Iowa Falls newspaper)

Dennis also helped square off the base with a saw and apply preservative which I sure appreciated.

By the time the cement base was put in, with the help of Kraig's father, Warren, and a half dozen other people, better than half the town's citizens stopped out to see what was going on.

So many people were good to us during our stay. We attended the block party of Ray and Mavis Day. Mavis is known around these parts as the "cookie lady" because of her delicious baked goods. She spent days collecting donations to pay for the spotlight on the Indian sculpture. Traudi Croot, our Austrian war bride friend, fixed us goulash the same way my mom made it. Verle Hunt and his family took us out to eat on several occasions and flew us over the community in his single engine plane. Dr. Paul Frandsen worked on our teeth and accepted a small sculpture as payment. We can't thank Kermit and Evelyn Neubauer, Francis and Rosemary McCord, the Kraig and Warren Kasischke families, the Brunkhorsts, the Whites, and countless other residents for the kindness and hospitality they showed us during our stay.

A crane was brought out and raised the now half-finished Indian onto the cement base as the Des Moines TV news interviewed me. The Des Moines Tribune ran a full page feature story on my work which headlined "A Sculptor's Magnificent Obsession." People sent us newspaper clippings from New York, Illinois, Georgia, Texas, Pennsylvania, California, and other states when the Associated Press nationally covered the Iowa Indian monument. It was exciting to see the news media take such a positive interest in my work for the American Indian.

As work continued during the hot month I often swam in the Iowa River to cool down. This same river was also used by the Indians for fishing, recreation, and transportation. Its water was the native people's highways.

Even though Iowa was sparsely populated by Indians, the name Iowa comes from the Dakota term "Ayuhwa" meaning "Sleepy People". The Dakota Sioux often came south into Iowa bringing fear to these "Sleepy People" (the Iowa) who numbered perhaps less than 1,000.

From the West, the Omaha often lived and hunted in the western Iowa border area. The state's Indians were removed to Oklahoma and other western states, but the Sauk and Fox found out they could buy their land back. With money pooled by the tribe, they bought acreages in Tama County and live there even to this day. The colorful Sauk and Fox (now called Mesquakie) often hold ceremonial dances which many tourists attend.

The dedication for the monument was held in the morning on the 4th of July. Kathy's parents drove from Illinois to attend this ceremony. We had such a fine dedication. Besides fireworks, one of the traditional celebrations of this town was an elaborate water-skiing show in which I was persuaded to join in. As the loudspeaker announced that the Indian's sculptor was coming around the bend, a cheer went up from the crowd. I tried to reciprocate by waving which turned out to be a grave mistake for a clumsy guy like me who hadn't been on skis in years. I went into a cartwheel, but luckily didn't get injured. Seconds later I got back on the skis to make an honorable exit.

With the celebration now over it was kind of sad because it meant that we would soon be moving on. During our two month stay in Iowa Falls we must have made friends with at least half the town. It seemed that people were trying to outdo each other with their kindness. Kathy often told me that we should settle down here because she fell in love with this town.

NO. 29 MONUMENT
TROY, KANSAS—SEPTEMBER, 1978

Several months back we received a most sought after letter from the little town of Troy, Kansas, 70 miles north of Kansas City. Thanks in part to Cindy Saltzgiver, our Illinois friend, who's family alerted the community about my work. This town already had a huge 5-foot diameter, 34-foot long, burr oak log available. They wanted to have my monument for the state of Kansas on the lawn of the Doniphan county courthouse in Troy.

My answer was "Yes" and at the same time rejected an offer from the Kansas City area. It's strange how some states offer me several spots to place my monument while others may not even answer my enquiries.

My next planned state was to be Nebraska. Two cities from this state asked me to make the Nebraska state monument in their communities. The Lincoln Indian Center in the capital city couldn't find a big enough log at this time. A month was spent waiting in Illinois for a promise of a 4½-foot diameter walnut log that a contact in Omaha said he could get, but this didn't materialize either.

During this wait we contemplated fixing up our somewhat dilapidated Winnebago, but repair cost was too high. Kathy was upset with the thought of leaving Illinois with this vehicle. Now was an opportune time to try and exchange our Winnebago motor home for a truck and camper trailer. After several ads in the local paper, a few people called, but only one man was serious and wanted our Winnebago. It was traded in exchange for his '74 Chevy truck plus some cash. We had hoped to get a better deal than this, but considering the sad shape the Winnebago was in, this deal was quickly accepted. The pickup had a topper on the back so it was convenient for me to pack all my tools, wood, and supplies. With the additional money we purchased a used 17-foot trailer. It was clean and had a complete bath and kitchen, all in good working order. We were very pleased about the exchange and our purchase.

Because of the long delays from Nebraska, we decided to go to Troy, Kansas. On our drive to this state the truck consumed a lot of oil and gas, but otherwise it ran real good. Despite the high winds we arrived safely in Kansas and settled on the courthouse lawn in Troy with the help of Mayor Blake. Electricity and water hookups were provided and our first night was spent in our little trailer which was to be our home for the next three months.

Early the next morning I started chiseling on the big log beside this historical courthouse where Abe Lincoln once gave a speech. Dean O'Ban-

Troy, Kansas Indian Monument, 70 miles north of Kansas City and 10 miles west of St. Joe, Missouri. Oak. (photo by St. Joseph News Press)

non came by and told me the history of this former tree and how big it was when he had cut it down. The tree had to be removed because of construction. Dean helped to square off the base with his saw and drilled a 4-inch diameter hole on the butt end of the log (this was to be the hole for a heavy steel pipe for wind resistance).

After two weeks the shape of an Indian slowly appeared. The sculpture was still in a horizontal position when a kickoff ceremony was scheduled for September 29th.

It was an exciting day. Governor Robert Bennett, area Indian spokesmen, and other dignitaries attended the celebration. The handsome Indian children mingled around the crowd in full attire. All went well and the day ended successfully.

Mayor Blake dug a 4-foot square hole for the monument's foundation (and later spent days on the base blocking it out with native stone). Jack Teegarden, who was the tireless coordinator of this project, gave a helping hand to brace up the forms as the truck poured the cement.

A week later the cement foundation was cured enough to raise the big Indian bust on top. As the crane arrived so did many of the townspeople. The elementary children were brought out to witness this event. The crane groaned under the terrific weight. The sculpture appeared bigger than the crane in an upright position. The crane had difficulty raising the sculpture. As its front wheels lifted up from the ground, several men jumped on the bumper in an effort to stabilize it. The kids were dangerously close; in their excitement, some of them shouted, "Hope it falls!"

I was uptight and a bit worried that the crane was too small. The operator wanted to give up, but I encouraged him to keep trying. Finally the pessimistic shouts of the children died down as the massive wooden Indian was lowered onto the steel rods protruding from the cement foundation.

The Kansas weather was exceptionally good that year and warm sunny days held out till November and my progress was steady.

It was virtually impossible for us not to intertwine our lives with the area's thoughtful people. Wolf River Bob, a colorful retired Hollywood actor, stopped several times with encouraging words.

"Someday they will make a movie of your monuments," he would say. "But as you're waiting in the wings, enjoy your life."

An elderly gentleman of 82 years, Mr. Goforth, stopped by nearly every day on his daily walks. He often spoke profoundly, drawing on his accumulated knowledge of life. He envied my youthful vigor, as I envied his wisdom of years. He often emphasized how we should love our parents while we have the chance. His one regret was not buying his mother a new dress. Over 80 years old and his zest for life hasn't slowed.

"Working with young people keeps me going. That's the secret to life, Pete," he would often say. "Do for others and God will bless you."

Garland and Cindy Blanton took us to an ancient Indian village campsite. It was now a farm pasture and cows grazed on the gentle slopes. This large area was covered with bits and pieces of pottery and other artifacts. Garland showed us a fire pit and we discovered a few charcoaled beans that

Troy, Kansas kickoff ceremony, September 29, 1978. Peter with Native American representative and Governor Robert Bennett.

Indian youth in native attire.

had been preserved over the years. We found broken arrowheads, flint chips, and scrapers. At one time this must have been a large camp. We were told the best time to go hunting arrowheads is right after a rain.

There were many historical places in this part of the state. A few miles west of town an early Indian Mission was preserved and turned into a museum. White settlers on their way West came down with smallpox in this area and those who died were left in an old forgotten cemetery near here.

We drove up to the high bluffs of Whitecloud (a town named after the famous Indian chief). The view from here was spectacular, four states could be seen. Below us was the meandering Missouri River with a small tugboat making its way up the strong current.

Many years back in history these high bluffs were probably used by the Indians to spot game and as a lookout point against enemy attacks. The scene probably hasn't changed that much except then a war canoe, not a tugboat, would have appeared. Though small in number the Kaw or Kansa Indians of this area were reported to be fierce fighters and originally came from Virginia and the Carolinas. The state of Kansas was named in their honor. The Kansa Indians gave the United States the only Indian Vice-President, Charles Curtis, of the Hoover administration.

Kansas was the home of many Indian tribes. Several were the Kiowa Apache, Omaha, Oto, Ottawa, Ponca, Quapaw, and Wichita. The Osage lived in the southeastern part of the state and were famous for their osage orange wood bows. Today the state's remaining vibrant tribes are the Kickapoo, Potawatomis, and Sauk and Fox.

Faithful companion watches Peter at work with mallet and gouge. (photo by Dave Johnson, Topeka Capital)

The area newspaper, TV, and radio followed my work closely. On the day of our first wedding anniversary we went to KKJO Radio Station in St. Joe, Missouri where I was a guest on a live radio talk show. It was very exciting because I had never appeared on a live show before. My favorite pastime was listening to talk shows with controversial subjects. They often stimulate me as I work into the wee hours of the morning.

Before the monument was finished cold weather set in. We encountered both snow and ice; our little trailer became very uncomfortable. Our heater didn't have a fan, so the warm air just rose to the top of the trailer and it was cold from the waist down. We had problems with our water hose and holding tank freezing up. By now Kathy was fed up with this small confined space. She was tired of breaking down the kitchen table and making a bed out of it in the evening and first thing in the morning reassembling it again for breakfast. She longed for the comforts of a house.

In early December the scaffolds around the Indian were taken down. We packed our belongings and left before the light of dawn. A dedication would be held, but not until the following year.

It was cloudy and cold as we made our way down Highway 36 and approached Hannibal, Missouri. After crossing the long bridge over the mighty Mississippi River, I pulled off on the shoulder. The Mississippi always had a magical quality to me. I remember reading how President Abraham Lincoln rode a raft down this river to contemplate the affairs of the Nation.

My mind goes back much farther in history, 3000 years back, to the days of the giant near-seven-foot tall Adina Indians with their advanced civilization. The wide-ranging sophisticated Hopewell culture (mound builders), also left their traces upon this land.

Now the Indian's culture is slowly being eroded, their language is being lost. I have encountered few young Indian people with a burning ambition to practice their native arts and crafts, language, and their true cultural beliefs. Even the bloodline is being threatened through marriages with non-Indians. Though there is promise of a renaissance, the uncertainty of the culture is still unclear, like the churning Mississippi River.

With a small sequoia carving of an Indian bust in my hand, I made my way onto the bridge and stared into the timeless waters of the Mississippi. My fingers caressed this rugged face in wood, his expression of sadness etched from my chisel, stared emptily at me. I held him over the water and my fingers loosened their grip and the lone sentry plummeted into the murky cold waters. The Mississippi's bosom carried him forward to a pressing journey on the currents of uncertainty.

In honor of a proud and noble people—Peter Toth's 37th whispering giant in Idaho Falls, Idaho. Native American, Herman Edwards, of the Fort Hall Indian Reservation, wears traditional northern plains ceremonial clothing as he gazes at the monument. (photo by Robert Bower, The Post-Register)

202

PREVIEWS OF BOOK II

Monument No. 30, finished May 1979
Oklahoma Indian Chief, stands at the Forest Heritage Center in Beavers
Bend State Park, Broken Bow, Oklahoma. Cypress. (photo by Ben Newby,
Tulsa Tribune)

Monument No. 31, finished August 1979.
Loveland, Colorado Indian Monument, located in South Shore Scenic Park in Loveland on Route 34. (Base of Rocky Mountain National Park, 50 miles north of Denver). Cottonwood. (photo by Karen Schulenburg, Reporter-Herald)

Monument No. 32, finished October 1979
Red Lodge, Montana Indian Chief, located at the northeastern entrance to
Yellowstone National Park, via Bear Tooth Pass. Ponderosa pine. (photo
by Peter Toth)

Winslow, Arizona Indian Monument. First to depict facial hair, commonly seen on Native Americans. Located I-40 Winslow. Ponderosa pine. (photo by Peter Toth)

207

Monument No. 34, finished May 1980
Texarkana, Texas Indian Monument, located at the Rest Area/Welcome
Center, I-30, Texarkana. Red Oak. (photo by Bob Burns, Texarkana
Gazette)

Texas

209

His Spirit

In a land of hills and quiet village
   which from here is an eternity far
Lived a quiet loving family fighting
   then fleeing the Cruel Red Star!
A lifetime's journey ahead of them
   sweat and toil all left behind.
Tearing their hearts and searing their minds
New places and people, hope and love every day
Helped a brave young boy to see
   that caring was the only true way!
The orchard and farm at Stone Mountain
That he would never see plowed
His family being in America and free again
   The young man called Peter vowed
I will build for the original people
   monuments from the valleys to the clouds
He with his wife, mallet and chisel would beg
   to right the wrongs, the pain
and the oppression of the American Indian
   From the heart and soul of this man
with the Earth mothers virtues
   He has left us a trail of Indian statues
By giving us these sacred tokens
   Our Love and Respect will be for him
As the Great Circle of Life forever unbroken
   Poem by Timber Lynx A. Fraser
                        writing by Gregory Fitzgerald

My Indian friend Timber Lynx (Wampanoag, Mic Mac) expressed his
feelings on my Trail of the Whispering Giants.

210

War dance performed by the Alabama-Coushatta Indians of Texas. (photo by Bob Burns, Texarkana Gazette)

Finished 10,000 pound bear on Highway 51, Lostant, Illinois. Contracted by Bob Dose; proceeds helped to pay for the publication of this book. Oak. (photos by Chris Kennell)

Monument No. 35, finished July 1980
Lincoln, Nebraska Indian Chief. NBC's Real People films Peter as he works in front of the Lincoln Indian Center. Cottonwood. (photo by Kathy Toth)

214

Monument No. 36, finished September 1980
Worland, Wyoming Indian Brave, located on the Washakie County Court-
house lawn. Douglas fir. (photo by Peter Toth)

Monument No. 37, finished November 1980
Idaho Falls, Idaho Indian monument. Dedication held on November 18.
Governor John Evans listens as Peter speaks out in behalf of the Native
Americans. (photo by Robert Bower, The Post Register) Douglas fir.

Monument No. 38, finished June 1981
Aberdeen, South Dakota Indian monument. Peter Toth and Mike
Nichols oversee the monument being lifted to its permanent base in
Nicollet Park on Sixth Avenue—Route 12. Peter poses with friends
in front of the finished sculpture. Cottonwood. (photos by Kathy
Toth and Dale Nally, Aberdeen American News)

Monument No. 39, finished August 1981
Mandan, North Dakota Indian monument, located at 6th Avenue
and 3rd Street, in front of the Stage Stop (4 miles from the Mandan
Indian Village and Fort Lincoln). Cottonwood. (photo by Kathy
Toth)

Monument No. 40, finished October 1981
Valdez, Alaska Indian monument, located at the Prince William
Sound Community College. Composite of the Alaskan Indians,
Eskimo, and Aleut. Sitka spruce. Bear also of spruce. (photo by
Peter Toth)

The first 2 months of work on the 40th monument in Alaska.

Monument No. 41, finished May 1982
Osceola, Iowa Indian Monument. Located on Route 34 (½ mile from I-35). This statue represents the Seminole War Chief Osceola. Cottonwood. (photo by Stan Samuelson, Osceola Tribune)

Among the many Narragansett Indians that came to the Rhode Island dedication, none were more distinguished than Princess Red Wing (bottom, center) and Ferris Dove (top photo, right) who is holding a huge war club. The late Mr. Dove was known as "Roaring Bull", the last traditional war chief of the Narragansett Tribe. (photos by Mrs. Edward McCabe, Jr.)

RIGHT: Monument No. 42, finished July 1982
Narragansett, Rhode Island, located on scenic Route A1A in Sprague Park. Stonework base constructed by the Narragansett Indians. Douglas Fir. (photo by Kathy Toth)

Rhode Island

223

Peter Wolf Toth's Indian friends at the Wampanaog/Mashpee Pow Wow, Cape Cod, Mass.—July 1983. Top Photo (left to right): Tony Pollard & friend, Peter Wolf, Drifting Goose. Bottom Photo: Peter Wolf with Tall Oak & family (Narragansett)

Monument No. 43, finished October 1982
Groton, Connecticut Indian Monument. Located on Route 117 at the
Groton Public Library (½ mile off I-95). Douglas Fir. (photo by Debbie
Beckwith)

THE FT. LAUDERDALE INDIAN STATUE NEARLY FINISHED.
Peter Toth uses a chisel on his 30-foot sculpture honoring Seminoles and
other Indian tribes. (photo by Deborah Meeks)

Monument No. 44, finished May 1983
Ft. Lauderdale, Florida Indian Monument, located on scenic Route A1A in
Alexander Park is dedicated with the Seminole Indians. Foreground is Joe
Dan Osceola, Peter Wolf Toth, and Fred Smith, Monument out of cypress.
(staff photo by Ft. Lauderdale News)

227

Dedication of the Plymouth, Massachusett's monument with the Wampanoag Indian Nation.

Monument No. 45, finished August 1983
Plymouth, Massachusetts Indian Monument located at the Information
Center/Rest Area, exit 5 south, Route 3. Red Oak from the Berkshires.
(photo by Dick Fallon, Enterprise)

229

Monument No. 46, finished October 1983
Bar Harbor, Maine Indian Monument located on Route 3, one half mile
from the head of Mt. Desert Island. Elm. (photo by Jim Frick, the
Ellsworth American)

230

Monument No. 47, finished July 1984
Burlington, Vermont Indian Monument located in Battery Park
overlooking Lake Champlain. Red Oak. (Photo by Kathy Toth)

Monument No. 48, finished September 1984
Laconia, New Hampshire Indian Monument located in Opechee
Park. The dedication ceremony drew a crowd of over 3,000 people.
Red Oak. (Photo by The Evening Citizen)

Monument No. 49, finished November 1984
Springfield, Massachusetts Indian Monument located at the Route 5
entrance to Forest Park. Pine. (Photo by John Suchocki, Morning
Union)

233

Over 2,000 people came to dedicate the Springfield, Massachusetts Indian Statue. Indian dignitaries attending were Chief Red Blanket, Chief Matachaman, Chief Drifting Goose, and Great Oak. (Photos by John Suchocki and Tom Lawor)

234

Monument No. 50, finished May 1985
Paducah, Kentucky Indian Monument located in Noble Park. Red Oak.
(photo by Peter Wolf Toth)

Monument No. 51, finished August 1985
Akron, Ohio Indian Monument located at the Fairlawn Elementary School
on West Market Street (Route 18). White Oak. (photo by Kathy Toth)

Kathy Toth warms up with a cup of coffee beside a giant cottonwood eagle created by Peter in Murray City Park, Murray, Utah. This eagle stands 12 feet high and weighs 10,000 pounds. Finished in November, 1985. (photo by Peter Wolf Toth)

Monument No. 52, finished November 1985
Murray, Utah Indian Monument located in Murray City Park on State
Street (south of Salt Lake City). Cottonwood. (photo by Richard M. Prehn)

Monument No. 53, finished June 1986
Reno, Nevada Indian Monument located in Idlewild Park. Douglas fir. Log donated by George Coulter, Sierra Pacific Industries. Stonework by Tony and Jeff Groux. (photo by Jack C. Beaman)

239

Monument No. 54, finished September 1986
Las Cruces, New Mexico Indian Monument located in Apodaca Park.
Monument "Dina" meaning "people" in both the Navaho and Apache
tongues is created from pine, shipped in from California's Sierra Nevada
Mountain Range. Log donated by George Coulter, Sierra Pacific In-
dustries. (photo by James A. Wagner)

Monument No. 55, finished November 1986
Johnson City, Tennessee Indian Monument located at Guaranda
Gardens/Metro Kiwanis Park on Knob Creek Road. Monument
"Junaluska" was created from oak. Mr. Robert S. Youngdeer, Principal
Chief of the Eastern Band of Cherokees and Peter Wolf Toth pause to
speak after the formal dedication ceremony. (photo by the Johnson City
Press-Chronicle)

Monument No. 56, finished September 1987
Hillsboro, Oregon Indian Monument located in Shute Park on Route 8.
Monument "Kno-Tah" is created out of Douglas fir. (photo by Michal
Thompson, Hillsboro Argus)

242

Monument No. 57, finished December 1987
Astoria, Oregon Indian Monument located at the west entrance to the city
on Coastal Highway 101. A traditional Northwest Coastal Indian hat,
woven from the inner bark of the cedar tree is depicted. Monument "Ikala
Nawan" or "Man Who Fishes" is created out of cedar and honors the Clat-
sop and Chinook Indians. Stonework by Joseph Herman. (photo by Kathy
Toth)

"THE COMPLETION OF A DREAM"
— HAWAII, THE 50th STATE —

With the completion of a giant Polynesian statue in Hawaii on May 22, 1988, Sculptor and Author Peter Wolf Toth has now successfully fulfilled his dream to honor the Native People in all 50 states.

Monument No. 58, finished May 1988
Haleiwa, Hawaii Polynesian Monument located on Kamehameha Highway at Sunset Beach on Oahu's North Shore. Monument "Maui Pohaku Loa" was created from a seven-foot-wide Douglas fir that was donated by Weyerhaeuser, coordinated by Robert W. Laderoute. The rock on top of this monument's head ties in with ancient Hawaiian legend. (photo by Kathy Toth)

245

Monument No. 59, finished October 1988
Wakefield, Michigan Indian Monument located on Sunday Lake, Highway
28 (upper peninsula). Monument "Nee-Gaw-Nee-Gaw-Bow" honors the
Chippewa Indians and was created from a pine donated by the Ottawa Na-
tional Forest. "Ish-kway-gaw-bow," a brother statue, stands atop In-
dianhead Mountain at the Wildernest Lodge. (photo by Andy Hill)

246

Chief Phil Goulais   Sculptor Peter Wolf Toth

CANADA
THE FIRST INTERNATIONAL WHISPERING GIANT
THE DREAM CONTINUES

Monument No. 60, finished September 1988
North Bay, Ontario Indian Monument located at the Information Center
on the Route 17-11 bypass. Monument "Nibiising" in honor of the Ojibwa
and all Canadian Indians is created from pine. (photo on this page and page
247 by Drew McAnulty, The Nugget)

Peter and Kathy Toth working on book. Awards shown in the background are a few that were accumulated during the over 18 years of ongoing work to sculpt one whispering giant in each of the 50 states. (photo by Chris Kennell)

(This article appeared in the State Journal, Lansing, Michigan, Feb. 15, 1981)

Peter Toth: man to remember

By Mike Hughes

He drifted into town back in '75, a stranger who had the audacity to be different from the rest of us.

Everything about Peter Toth seemed different. He had a Hungarian accent. He had little visible means of support. He spent his days chipping away at huge hunks of wood, and he wanted to give us something for nothing.

Peter Toth

No one really trusted him, of course. But Toth persisted and we got the gift despite ourselves.

Today, Toth's creation—a giant Indianhead sculpture—reigns majestically over Potter Park. Memories of Toth returned recently, when he was featured on the TV show "Real People." That gave the rest of the world a chance to look at a rare modern hero.

Toth, you see, is a sort of noveau Johnny Appleseed. He wanders across the continent, leaving a trail of statues.

When he came here, his story seemed unlikely: He wanted to create an Indian sculpture in each of the 50 states. It would be a -gift to Americans and a tribute to Indians.

There was a lot of bureaucratic reluctance at first. Then the Parks Department started to give him some help.

And the result was worth it. Toth's statute is immensely popular with the kids and adults, a genuine local landmark.

Nowadays—according to "Real People"—there are 34 other states with Toth creations. The guy has a young bride and a small trailer, but his lifestyle remains otherwise unchanged.

There's something more about Toth, incidentally: He has the good sense to create works that relate to people.

Some of the other local 'landmarks' reflect a curious arrogance. Those works—the Heizer discs and the De Rivera swirl—are cold and distant and obscure and hands off. They virtually demand that the man-on-the-street dislike them.

That's not true of Toth's piece (or for that matter, of Marty Eichinger's fine "Windlord"). People are drawn to it instantly. Kids love it. Until a chain went around it, they would come up and touch it.

The Heizer and the De Rivera widen the gap between art and the people. The Toth and the Eichinger help close that gap.

Toth's sculpture brings us quiet moments of majesty. And it's nice to turn on the TV set and find that one of the world's good guys is still on the move.

Mike Hughes, is an assistant metro editor for the State Journal, Lansing, Michigan, Feb. 15, 1981.